CITIZENS, PARTIES AND THE STATE

CITIZENS, PARTIES
AND THE STATE
A REAPPRAISAL

Alan Ware

Princeton University Press
Princeton, New Jersey

Published 1988 by Princeton University Press, 41 William Street,
Princeton, New Jersey 08540

Library of Congress Cataloging-in-Publication Data

Ware, Alan.
  Citizens, parties, and the state: a reappraisal/Alan Ware.
    p. cm.
  Bibliography: p. 261
  Includes index.
  ISBN 0–691–07763–0
  1. Political parties. 2. Democracy. I. Title.
JF20501.W37 1988   87–30281
324.2′04—dc19   CIP

Printed in Great Britain

For my Mother and Jane

CONTENTS

LIST OF TABLES AND FIGURES

PREFACE

When David Held first approached me in 1985 about the possibility of writing a book to reassess the contribution made by parties to the advancement of democracy I was rather unsure about the project. I had been working on theories of parties, and on change in American party organizations, for over a decade, and there were now other issues in political science on which I wanted to conduct research. However, I was also aware that there was a rather large number of important arguments which I had not really explored in my earlier work, and other aspects of parties that had not been fully developed there. In the event I was very glad that David's enthusiasm for the project persuaded me to take it on, and I am grateful for the support I have received from him, Polity Press and Princeton University Press.

Perhaps my greatest debt is to my colleagues in the Politics Department at the University of Warwick. One of the advantages in being a member of a large department, where there are several scholars with interests in comparative politics and political theory, is that it is always possible to 'wander down the corridor' to seek advice and information from others. Nearly all my colleagues were pestered by me at some stage during the writing of this book, and they never failed to be helpful in discussing aspects of party politics and of democratic theory with me. I am most grateful too for the insightful written comments I received from both Peter Ferdinand and Richard Gillespie, and, most especially, from Willie Paterson and Derek Urwin, who read the entire first draft of the manuscript. I am also indebted to Desmond King, of Edinburgh University, and Albert Weale, of the University of East Anglia, for their perceptive criticisms of that first draft. Obviously, though, full responsibility for any errors and any inadequacies in the arguments presented here is mine alone.

Finally, I would like to thank Mrs Dorothy Foster for typing so efficiently the final draft of the book.

Alan Ware
Warwick, March 1987

1

PARTIES AND DEMOCRATIC THEORY

This book is about the contribution made by political parties to the advancement of democracy in the modern state. Although it is an issue which would seem to lie at the very heart of the work of both political theorists and political scientists, it is not a subject about which much has been written during the last twenty to thirty years. The reason for this curious lack of attention to the problem that exercised the minds of many of the founding fathers of the modern study of politics, including Ostrogorski and Michels, lies in the development of theoretical and empirical research in politics during this period.[1] To put the matter briefly, there was a fragmenting of research from about the 1950s onwards, so that those scholars who were concerned with the nature of the concept of democracy, and its relation to other concepts such as liberty and equality, were no longer the same people who had great expertise in the working of political institutions. Moreover, interest in the empirical study of politics moved sharply away from institutions like parties to focus on other aspects of the political process. The causes of this stark separation of democratic theorists from specialists in political parties and of much less interest being shown in political parties, are too complex to analyse in detail here, but a short account can be presented.

The collapse of some liberal democracies in the inter-war years was instrumental in creating a revival of interest in the 1940s and 1950s in the nature of democracy, and of the means of maintaining democratic governments. One of the best known analyses was Joseph Schumpeter's *Capitalism, Socialism and Democracy*, which was published in 1943, though Schumpeter was an economist and not a political scientist.[2] Yet at the same time, and in the years following, there were also many important books by students of politics that focused on both normative and empirical aspects of democracy. E. E. Schattschneider's *Party Government*, published in 1942, was an outstanding early example of an attempt to relate party practice to democratic theory.[3] Parties were not the only institutions that were examined, however, and Dahl and Lindblom's classic study, *Politics, Economics and Welfare*, was concerned with institutional arrangements of a very wide-ranging kind.[4] Indeed, Dahl's work in the 1950s and early 1960s represents, perhaps, the high-point of this inter-relation between theoretical and empirical studies.[5] While there is much with which to disagree in his interpretations of liberal democracy and markets and in the conclusions he reached, there can be no doubt that Dahl provided a synthesis of political theory and political science that has scarcely been equalled since. However, even by the late 1950s this approach was in danger, and while in Britain empirically informed works of democratic theory, such as A. H. Birch's *Representative and Responsible Government*, appeared as late as 1964, in the United States a revolution in political science was radically undermining it.[6]

There were two, related, stages to this revolution. In the 1940s a few American political scientists had realized the potential that analyses using social surveys might have for the study of politics. In the 1950s this was to lead to the growing influence of sociology, and of sociological techniques, on political science. In particular, it was to facilitate the application of systems analysis (that is, of Parsonian sociology) in the discipline. For nearly two decades, David Easton's *The Political System*, published in 1953, was a book with which most American political scientists believed they had to come to grips.[7] In some cases, the sociological influence was to produce a kind of sociological determinism in the study of politics – politics, it was believed, could be largely understood by examining the *social bases* of institutions like parties, and there was a tendency to diminish the significance of institutional explanations of political phenomena.

By no means all of the effects of this behavioural movement – the movement to create a political *science* through the study of political *behaviour* – were undesirable. Nor were all those who supported it second-rate scholars. Dahl himself had heralded its achievements, and it certainly did have the effect of ridding American political science of the unfruitful dominance of a legalistic tradition.[8] But, as with many intellectual revolutions, behaviouralism and systems theory attracted 'those of lesser ability' who could understand the methodologies it had generated but who could not appreciate the methodologies' limitations.

Within the American political science community the result was three-fold. Research came to be dominated in many areas by the gathering of quantifiable data, even when this data was of little use for dealing with the major issues facing political science. More significantly for our purposes, a wedge was driven between political science and traditional and analytic political theory. For many of the crude behaviouralists, the latter was a peripheral area of study which could at best hold back proper political science. It was seen as peripheral both because it was concerned with 'normative' issues, of how polities should be organized rather than with how they actually were organized, and, because like the great political theories of the past, modern political theorists took little interest in producing survey (or similar) data with which to substantiate their arguments. Finally, after the initial concern to apply behavioural techniques to the study of institutions like parties, the main thrust of the behavioural movement was to deflect attention away from institutions *per se*.

Consequently, even with subjects where there had earlier been a fairly close interaction between empirical studies and non-empirical political theory, such as in the analysis of parties as mechanisms for advancing democracy, a split developed between those who studied parties (often their social bases) and democratic theorists. The worst excesses of the behavioural movement lasted no more than ten to fifteen years, and it did have much less impact on political science outside America, although there were notable exceptions, including the Scandinavian countries.[9] Moreover, there were areas of empirical study that were so unpromising for behaviouralism that it made few inroads there. Nevertheless, not only has it had a lasting effect on some research areas, including parties, but the very size of the political science profession in America has meant that this 'domestic revolution' has produced some curiously large gaps in the study of parties both in that country and elsewhere. Thirty years ago this book would have been merely one of a number of similar studies; today it is rather unusual.

In continental Europe, and especially in Germany, there was a later development which was also to have an adverse effect on the study of parties. The revival of interest in Marxism, and especially of Marxist theories of the state, in the 1960s drew attention away from parties as actors in the political system. Further impetus to this tendency was provided by the student revolt in France in 1968 which, by destabilizing the regime, exposed the weakness of parties either as agents of social change or as instruments for preserving a regime. The influence of neo-Marxism was to wane in the later 1970s, but it had left its impact on the subjects which had dominated research at German universities during that decade. More generally, there were developments in the 1970s in political science that were to continue the peripheralization of parties in the discipline. In particular, researchers became concerned with policies – with *outputs* from the political system, rather than *inputs* to it. Because of this, less attention was paid to parties, and the most significant debate about parties in the last decade or so has concerned whether parties matter – that is, whether the policy outputs of a government are influenced by the kind of party (or parties) which forms it.

Nevertheless, of course, we have not so far explained why empirical and theoretical studies have not 'come together' in the years since the heyday of behaviouralism. To account for this we must examine developments within democratic theory and the study of comparative politics, for since the 1960s there have been changes which make it far more difficult for political scientists to write the kinds of books their predecessors had written a decade or so earlier. Within democratic theory there was now far more interest in, and research based on, economic theory; in brief, democratic theory now required far greater knowledge of developments in welfare economics than it had previously and, later, far greater competence in mathematics. The starting point for this had been the publication, in 1951, of Arrow's *Social Choice and Individual Values*, in which the author had demonstrated that it was impossible for all of four seemingly innocuous conditions to be maintained in the process of making a collective choice based on the preferences of individuals.[10] At least one condition would have to be violated. Arrow made two assumptions in what is usually referred to as his 'Impossibility Theorem' – all individuals can express a preference between alternative policies, such as x and y (or can express indifference between them), and the preferences of each individual are transitive, so that if she prefers x to y, and y to z, she must thereby prefer x to z. The four conditions which he argued seem essential if collective choice is to be a coherent notion are:

1 Non-dictatorship: there must be no individual whose preferences determine the nature of the collective choice, regardless of the preferences of anyone else.
2 The Pareto principle; if everybody prefers x to y, then the collective choice must rank x ahead of y.

3 Independence of irrelevant alternatives: the collective decision in relation to x and y must be based only on how individuals rank x in relation to y, and must not involve comparisons between these alternatives and any others, such as z.
4 Unrestricted domain: any possible ordering of the alternatives, x and y, by individuals is admissible in generating the collective choice.

Arrow then demonstrated that at least one of these conditions would have to be violated in generating a collective choice, and subsequent proofs have shown that the same is true even if only three of Arrow's four conditions are employed.

Arrow's highly influential book and most of the subsequent comments on it could be easily understood even by the most innumerate political theorist, but by the 1970s a far more technical literature on this and related subjects in the now-new field of 'public choice' had appeared. Mastering this required skills not previously demanded of political theorists and in accommodating itself to mathematical analyses there has been an inevitable weakening of links with those who study political institutions. However, we must also not exaggerate its effect so far on political science. In some areas of study the work being done by economists and mathematicians is simply not understood, or is ignored, by political scientists. This point has been made forcefully by McLean in relation to theories of voting:

> The most recent writer (Michael Dummett) to present the theory of voting to a lay audience complains justly that much of the work that has gone into it is 'like water gushing from a disconnected pipe' because no politicians and almost no political scientists show any awareness of it . . . Comparing the bibliographies of recent works on electoral reform (by a political scientist) and the theory of voting (by a mathematical economist), Dummett found that J. S. Mill was the only author they both mentioned.[11]

Yet anyone who doubts the effect that public choice theories are having, and will continue to have, on how we examine issues in democratic theory has only to glance at the presentation outlined in Riker's *Liberalism Against Populism*.[12] One of the ironies of this book is that the author was actually an expert in American political institutions before he turned to the mathematical study of politics, but this is highly unusual among specialists in public choice theory.

Not only have the problems which concern democratic theorists 'moved away' from those directly related to institutions, but there have been developments in the study of comparative politics which have accentuated this split. Here, though, the change is not so much that political scientists have had to acquire new skills but that the sheer amount of material published on political systems is now enormous. It is for this reason that there have been few detailed comparative analyses of parties, and von Beyme's recent book can be counted as a *tour de force* just because of his ability to come to grips with a huge literature in several languages.[13] The importance of expertise in the *comparative* study of parties, for anyone examining the role of parties in the advancement of democracy, is that knowledge of a single political system is inadequate in developing general hypotheses. Even among the liberal democracies, there is sufficient diversity in the parties' roles for a concentration on any one system to be of limited value. Indeed, the main criticism that can be advanced of the books in the 1940s and 1950s that were concerned with this subject is that most concentrated far too much on British and American parties. Nor was this surprising; remarkably little had been published in English on parties elsewhere. Duverger's *Political Parties*, which was first published in French in 1951 and in English in 1954, was the first truly comparative work on parties to appear, and it was not until the late 1960s that articles and books in English began to appear regularly on 'smaller European democracies', such as the Netherlands and Austria.[14]

Whilst emphasizing the split between democratic theory and the study of political institutions, we must, nevertheless, be careful not to overstate the tendency. In the 1960s and 1970s there were studies that examined certain aspects of democracy and attempted to relate theoretical arguments to particular institutions. Perhaps the most important were those which focused on the value and role of participation in the political process, and which examined this in the context of institutions where cross-national comparisons were less relevant. Of special significance here were the analyses of democracy in industry, of which Pateman's *Participation and Democratic Theory*, which appeared in 1970s, was one of the most influential studies.[15] Nevertheless, the main argument, that a split did develop, stands, and this book is an attempt to return to an older tradition of examining the contribution institutions can make to the advancement of democracy. It is a very general survey of parties that is presented here; while, undoubtedly, there is need for a more detailed study, this would require collaboration between experts on many different regimes and probably would take years to complete. This book is intended as a kind of 'stop-gap', drawing attention to the issues which will be worth examining until such a study is completed.

In establishing the framework for the rest of the book in this introductory chapter, we will examine three issues. First, what are the different elements of democracy? Second, what are political parties? And, third, how have political theorists seen parties as capable of promoting, or hindering, democracy within a society?

THE NATURE OF DEMOCRACY

At the risk of possible over-simplification, it is useful to identify three main elements in the concept of democracy. Not every democratic theorist accepts that all three elements are part of the concept, and democratic theorists disagree both about the relation between elements and the means by which each might be promoted, but there can be little doubt that it is on these elements that most debate has occurred. For brevity, these elements are called here *interest optimalization, the exercise of control* and *civic orientation*, and we examine each in turn.

INTEREST OPTIMALIZATION

One argument accepted by many democratic theorists is that, for a decision to be democratic, it must produce certain kinds of results for those within the relevant 'arena'. Before saying more about this argument, though, we should first notice an area of controversy which largely falls outside our discussion here – how do we define the 'relevant "arena" '? On the one hand, it might be argued that anyone who is affected by a decision should be included in the making of it, and a failure to include him or her makes that decision at least somewhat undemocratic. Britain in the nineteenth century, say, cannot be counted as very democratic because most of the population did not even have the vote. But, on the other hand, it is far from clear that a failure to consult *all* affected persons does detract from the democratic character of a decision. For example, would we say that a decision taken by a cycling club to go on a tour was not democratic because they did not consult the motorists who were slowed down by their presence on particular roads? What seems to be at issue here is how *directly* people are affected by a decision, but specifying the conditions that must be satisfied for the inclusion of all directly affected persons is actually rather difficult. For the most part, political theorists have assumed that the boundaries formed by nation-states are especially important arenas when discussing democracy; others, though, have denied that it is justifiable to consider the extent of democracy by focusing on the nation-state and its citizens.[16]

The idea that democracy entails particular sorts of results was referred to by Thompson as the 'democratic objective', and he argues that it is widely accepted by democratic theorists:

> Of the objectives or functions towards which the conditions [of democracy] are directed one which appears in some form in all democratic theory is the democratic objective. The democratic objective stipulates that a political system produce rules and decision which, of all practical alternatives, are those which will satisfy the interests of the greatest possible number of citizens.[17]

For a process or system to be democratic, then, the rules and procedures employed must bring about results that optimally promote or defend the interests of the largest number of people in the relevant arena.

There are several points which should be made about this first element of democracy. One is that, even among those who accept the democratic objective, there is considerable disagreement as to what is meant by (in Thompson's words) satisfying 'the interests of the greatest possible number of citizens'. Leaving aside the point we just alluded to, as to whether citizens (or in the case of smaller bodies, members) are the only people whose interests we should consider, there is a serious problem about what is meant by the notion of *satisfying interests*. In the early 1970s one fashionable approach among liberal political scientists in America was to interpret this in terms of the distribution of resources in society and to equate democracy with the promotion of equality in society.[18] For them, America was not very democratic because the political system permitted a high degree of social and economic inequality. Alternatively, like Arrow, welfare economists have usually conceived the democratic objective in terms of a social welfare function and have argued that a system is more democratic the more closely are each person's preferences reflected equally in the policies and decisions produced by that system. The democratic objective is thereby seen in terms similar to that of 'clearing the market', in an economic market, and for many economic theorists this is the only element of democracy. However, specifying democracy in this way still leaves room for profound disagreement on the question of the distribution of resources which can be used to express preferences. For some economists, democracy merely consists in clearing the market optimally, and the distribution of resources which are used to express preferences has no bearing on whether the process is democratic; democracy simply consists in the imposition of market-clearing mechanisms on societies, in which the distributions of resources which have occurred historically are accepted as given. Citizens are politically equal, therefore, in that no one unit of resource is weighted more heavily than any other. However, other democratic theorists who have also employed a 'social welfare function' notion of democracy have argued that how any politically relevant resources are distributed does bear on the democratic character of a regime and that certain levels of inequality are incompatible with democracy, irrespective of whether the results directly reflect the balance of expressed preferences. Nor are these the only ways of conceiving the democratic objective.

Another point we should note is that not all democratic theorists do accept the democratic objective. For them, democracy must be understood solely in terms of the 'inputs', rather than the 'outputs' of a system. In a rather similar way to Rawls' theory of social justice, democracy is seen in procedural terms.[19] Providing the procedures meet the requirements of democracy, the results they produce are irrelevant. Even if we could show that another set of procedures produced superior results, in terms of the results better reflecting each person's preferences, this would be irrelevant in discussing the democratic status of the procedures actually used. One of the clearest expressions of this approach is Barry's:

> I reject the notion that one should build into 'democracy' any constraints on the content of the outcomes produced, such as substantive equality, respect for human rights, concern for the general welfare, personal liberty or the rule of law. The only exceptions (and these are significant) are those required by democracy itself as procedure. Thus, some degree of freedom of communication and organization is a necessary condition for the formation, expression and aggregation of political preferences.[20]

Barry does require that there must be a formal connection in a democratic system between the preferences expressed and the policy results, but he does not require that policies, in any way, *reflect* preferences.

A final point is that some democratic theorists have argued that Arrow's 'impossibility theorem', together with the many proofs and theorems that have been developed subsequently, has demonstrated that the objective, in a democracy, of optimally satisfying people's wants is unattainable. This, indeed, is the main thrust of Riker's book.[21] But it is important to be clear what these theories rule out. The problem is not that preferences can *never* be aggregated optimally, but that, given certain distributions of preferences, this may be impossible. (There may be cyclical majorities,[22] or the opportunity for some people to express 'strategic' preferences rather than 'sincere' preferences, and thereby gain an advantage in the aggregation process over those who express 'sincere' preferences.)[23] This has two important implications for democratic theory. Whether preferences can be aggregated optimally depends on the structure of opinions in the society. In homogeneous communities, where there is an ethos favouring the development of consensus, the problems of interest aggregation are likely to be much less than in large pluralistic societies where an equilibrium of policy views is likely to be exceptionally fragile. It is for this reason that those who claim that democracy cannot be established in nation-states, but only in much smaller arenas, have tended to pay relatively little attention to the public choice literature. But there is another, and for our purpose more significant, implication for democratic theory. Even if we accept Riker's point – that it is unlikely interests can be aggregated successfully in large societies – this does not mean that the only control citizens could possibly exercise is the right to 'throw out' their rulers in periodic elections. This brings us to the idea of the exercise of control.

THE EXERCISE OF CONTROL

A second element of democracy is the notion that, irrespective of whether preferences or interests can or should be aggregated optimally, democracy provides the opportunity for people to exercise control over certain aspects of a regime or organization. The argument is that, even if particular distributions of preference lead to non-optimal results, acts of voting and other methods of decision-making at least provide for some kind of connection between people and the content of social decisions. But exactly what is it that people have control over? Here democratic theorists vary widely. At one extreme there are those like Schumpeter, Sartori and (in his most recent work) Riker, who emphasize that only a very restricted form of control is available.[24] Democracies are those regimes where there is the possibility of people voting to remove those who govern them. Indeed, as we shall see, in Sartori's version it is the mere possibility that leaders could be removed, and not actual competition, that provides the crucial element of control. Others, though, have argued that this limited form of popular input scarcely constitutes democracy, and that democracy only exists where there are mechanisms for other forms of popular input into the state. This is the argument that elections and other devices must provide choices for citizens, and ways of controlling those who take decisions on behalf of citizens when decision-making by the people directly is impossible or inappropriate. But what sort of choices and control may be possible? One of the most important arguments is that the formulation of policy proposals, and close scrutiny of those responsible for developing and subsequently implementing them, enables choices to be placed before citizens. That all decision-making arrangements may involve cycles and voting paradoxes is not as devastating an argument, for two reasons, as it is in the case of interest optimalization. One is that, in the real world, policy results are usually not unrelated to the wants people have: decision-making mechanisms rarely allow policies which hardly anyone wants to be agreed on finally. Certainly, we can find instances of this, but it does not seem to be that common. More significantly, many democrats who argue in favour of citizen control (and extensive citizen choice) reject the assumption underlying the debate about interest optimalization, that, initially, citizens have *preferences* in relation to most public policies. Rather, they argue that citizens only come to acquire views that can properly be counted as preferences once they have been involved in the process of formulating collective choices. Even if a voting paradox or a cycle should be evident in the decision-making process, the very act of being part of the policy-making enables citizens to exercise control over their lives and that (in itself) is a central value for the democrat. In other words, on this view the value of democracy is not that everybody gets their preferences counted and hence can partly obtain what they want, but that the people come to develop wants which can then be expressed through the mechanisms of collective decision-making.

One of the most obvious problems in a modern state in giving citizens control over decisions affecting their lives is that of size. In anything other than the smallest arenas of decision-making, it is not possible for every member of a group to participate fully in the decisional process: there is simply not the time available for this. There are two main solutions to this problem available to the democrat. One is to decentralize decisions, whenever possible, to the smallest arenas that can be devised, but this solution has its limitations. In some circumstances decentralizing decisions can have adverse consequences for all the participants, either because these 'low-level' arenas lack the resources and skills necessary for the participants to take informed decisions, or because such arenas encourage participants to place local interests ahead of more general interests in the society. The other limitation is that, for some kinds of decisions, decentralization is just not possible. National defence policies, for example, cannot be formulated by a large number of independent neighbourhood committees or shop-floor committees in a factory. The other solution, then, is representative institutions – bodies which have members who, between them, can represent the interests or views of a much wider group of people. Representative government, of course, has been seen by many as the key to establishing democracy in a modern state. The issue over which there has been widespread disagreement, though, is the extent to which representation is a complete substitute for democratic control or a device which must be used in combination with others, to facilitate control by a large number of people. Conservative democrats, like Schumpeter, Sartori and others, have taken the first view. For them, the ability to remove representatives is the distinguishing feature of modern democracy. During the 1960s many of the writers who took this sort of view were called 'democratic elitists' by their critics, because they conceived democracy solely in terms of elites competing for political power. Other democrats, however, have argued that representative institutions are only part of the constituting features of a democratic polity. They argue that, while such institutions are essential for checking leaders and for offering policy choices to the electorate, they do not provide very much control for citizens. Consequently these democrats stress the need for other kinds of mechanisms in a polity for increasing the control which individuals can have over decisions affecting their lives; there is, nevertheless, considerable disagreement as to what the most appropriate mechanisms are for facilitating this control. In part, these differences also reflect disagreements in relation to their third element of democracy – civic orientation.

CIVIC ORIENTATION

A third element of democracy concerns the kinds of objectives that people are supposed to be pursuing in their interactions in the polity. On the one side are those who argue that democracy fully exists only when those who are involved in its processes are oriented towards the shared interests of the members of the polity, and not their own individual interests. This tradition, which can be traced back to Rousseau, views participation as the principal way by which people will come to place shared interests ahead of particular interests. For them, participation has a *developmental* function – through their interactions with others in decision-making processes, people come to appreciate the value of widely shared interests and accept the need for all to exercise restraint in the promotion of special interests. Those who reject this third element argue that, when examining whether a regime or a process is democratic or not, it is irrelevant whether people are community, or publicly, oriented in the objectives they pursue or whether they are merely out to promote their own self-interest.

But what mechanisms will promote a civic orientation? Generally, it has been argued that institutions facilitating direct human interaction in the decision-making process are more favourable to this. Neighbourhood government and decentralized systems of worker self-management have been the kinds of arenas usually seen as supportive of the developmental aspects of democracy. On the other hand, devices which may provide for direct democracy, but which do not encourage direct contact between all participants (such as referendums), have often been regarded as not compatible with citizen development.

As has been suggested already, democratic theorists not only disagree as to whether all three of these elements do constitute part of the concept of democracy, but they also disagree as to how these elements are related to each other (if at all) and as to the precise nature of particular components. Important debates emerge as to whether certain kinds of processes are democratic (for example, can one-party states be democratic?), but there can also be disagreements as to *how* democratic a certain process is. Consider the granting of manhood suffrage, a reform which was introduced in most western European countries at about the end of the nineteenth century. Obviously, having the opportunity to participate in the election of representatives to national assemblies increased (if only slightly) the amount of control those who had been previously disenfranchised had over the state. But how much more democratic did this make these states? In part, disagreements will centre on differing views about how people's lives were affected, but there will also be disagreements as to how much value we should place on any increase in control compared with, say, processes that develop a civic orientation. Again, some democrats have argued that the granting of universal suffrage in the twentieth century has completed the process of democratization, while others have argued that the enfranchisement of women only slightly increased popular control and that there are still few mechanisms in western society through which people can participate with others in those activities which affect the conduct of their lives. Radical democrats, as they are sometimes referred to, are critical to the absence of participatory devices in the workplace and in local communities. For them, western democracies are no more than partially democratized states. This idea that there can be *more* and *less* democracy in a process, an institution, or a regime is important, and it is misleading to believe that a process must either be democratic or undemocratic. Moreover, reforms which make a process more democratic in one respect may make it less democratic in another. Consider the following example of an institution which appears to have become more democratic.

During the 1960s the elected women members of the party committee which effectively controlled the Democratic party in the American city of Denver ceased to be mere 'co-captains' of their precincts – that is, functionaries who were supposed to assist in party organization but who had no real say in the decisions made by the committee. They were then given full rights of participation and voting at all meetings of the committee, and the system of male captains and female co-captains was abandoned. There is an obvious sense in which this change made the organization more democratic. Yet, at the same time, the increased size of the committee meant that individual members had less opportunity to express and develop points of view at meetings; the control any one individual could exercise declined. Equally, unlike a body of fifty people, one of a hundred is less likely to have a strong sense of corporate identity, and the committee was certainly a much less cohesive body than it was in earlier years. Participation in it was not as effective in directing its members to the pursuit of shared goals. On both of these grounds, then, we might want to argue that the organization also became less democratic because of the reforms. Evaluating how democratic we think it is now depends on what value we place on each of the elements of democracy, as well as on our judgements as to what exactly has changed.

Given these areas of disagreement about the nature of democracy, it is only to be expected that there would be widespread controversy between democratic theorists as to the kinds of social arrangements which are compatible with democracy. This can be illustrated by outlining some of the views which those who would regard themselves as democrats have taken about the relation of a market economy to democracy. One view commonly held by conservatives is that democracy is possible only with an extensive market economy. The argument is that, by decentralizing to a market decisions about the goods people want, control by the individual over his own affairs is being maximized. A political system that allows people to vote in national elections provides a safeguard against the undermining of this decentralized system: the state has to ensure that economic actors keep to the rules of the competitive game, because elections provide a check on those who control the state. Another view, and one which has been advanced by Dahl, at least in his early writing, is that democracy is compatible with both market and non-market economies.[25] For him, the expression and aggregation of preferences which is the hallmark of democracy can exist alongside both a capitalist and socialist mode of economic production. To the extent that both are aimed towards responding to people's wants, neither has any inherent disadvantages as a complement to a political process in which sensitive responses to preferences are crucial. Then, again, there are those democrats who argue that, at the very least, unregulated capitalism is incompatible with democracy. In relation to the three constituent elements of democracy we identified, they find three objections to markets. First, a market system is incapable of operating to provide for the equality of resources which they say is an integral part of the expression of preferences under democracy. Although each unit of preference is counted equally in a market, different people are very likely to acquire vastly different holdings of resources, so that each person 'does not count for one' in the aggregation of preferences. Second, they argue that, while perfect economic markets disperse power, such markets are an idealization and in the real world markets produce various patterns of concentrated power. In many markets it is the producers who acquire this power, leaving consumers, as a group, with relatively little: the distribution of control is likely to be unequal. Finally, these more radical democrats contend that markets provide only for control over people's individual affairs: they accentuate the pursuit of self-interest. A market-dominated polity is likely to be one in which polity-wide interests are not much valued or pursued, because there are no forums in which these values can be fostered.

Even at the most general level of social institutions, then, considerable divergence of opinion among democratic theorists has developed. The kinds of institutional structures supportive of the democratic theory of Robert Dahl are different from those which are compatible with the democratic theory of, say Sartori, on the one hand, and C. B. Macpherson, on the other.[26] Naturally, this leads to very different views being developed as to how political parties might advance democracy, and what kinds of internal structures and activities parties should develop if they are to further democratization. Before we can turn to discuss this, though, we must first ask the question – what exactly are political parties?

WHAT ARE PARTIES?

Similarly to trying to define and describe the proverbial elephant, this question is not quite so easy to answer as might be imagined. The boundary between parties and other kinds of political organization is not always clear. This problem is recognized by the American Political Science Association which has a subsection for those who study parties but which is called 'Political Organizations and Parties'. The firm distinction between parties and pressure groups, which traditionally used to be emphasized in first year undergraduate lectures on British politics, is not very helpful in other contexts. Another problem is that any definition of a party which is sufficiently broad to embrace those organizations which style themselves as parties may not yield a very useful analytic construct, because some of the organizations it embraces have remarkably little in common.

We might begin, however, by saying that parties are bodies that intend to exercise some control over a state, and that its members are not simply the representatives of a single interest in society. What is distinctive about this definition? We can best see this by comparing it with the definition offered by Janda, whose study of parties covered most types found in the modern world. Janda is very much in the mainstream of the behavioural approach to parties and his definition is similar to many others. While recognizing that it would not cover all institutions that call themselves parties, he says that 'In studying political parties, we are interested in the set of *organizations that pursue a goal of placing their avowed representatives in government positions.*'[27]

Obviously, there are two main differences between our definition and his. Janda requires that for something to be a party it must intend to put its (avowed) representatives in government, while we merely require that the party seeks to exercise some control over government. The reason for not following Janda here is that at times some parties (the Conservatives in Finland, for example) have known that they will not be allowed to enter a government coalition, while there are others whose aim is the destruction of an existing state or regime. (On independence in India, Gandhi wanted the Congress party to dissolve.) Janda's definition is simply not general enough. But in saying that parties seek to exercise some control over the state, we are not providing a means of distinguishing parties from, say, pressure groups. This is why we require, at least initially, that for a body to be a party it must be the representative of more than a single interest, a restriction not required by Janda's definition. We can now try to 'unpack the boundary problems' our definition poses.

The first problem is that not all multiple-interest bodies seeking to exercise control over a state are necessarily parties. The Christian militias in the Lebanon are an example. In the era of parliamentary democracy in the Lebanon the bodies from which the militias sprang did have parliamentary wings that most assuredly were parties. But under certain conditions of civil strife, a party as such may have no role to play. Certainly, even when there is such a role, the relationship between a party and a militia, and the relative importance of their respective operations will vary depending on their fortunes in both the political and military arenas. For example, in the 1980s Sinn Fein (the political party wing of the Irish nationalist movement) became more prominent in Northern Ireland, as the British army was having more success in containing the military wing, the IRA. But we cannot dispose of the problem of the boundary between parties and other organizations, as some political scientists have done, by altering the definition of party to include only those bodies which pursue control of the state by legitimate means. There are many examples of organizations which are recognizably parties that have chosen to, or been forced to, pursue power outside the recognized legitimate means of influence. The Chinese Communist party did not cease to be a party during its years of armed conflict, in the 1930s and 1940s, with the Kuomintang. Nevertheless, there clearly is a point at which a body is so preoccupied with its military organization and so little concerned with the non-military mobilization of civilians that it ceases to be useful to describe it as a party. Nor are military organizations the only problem in this respect. There is the issue of organizations which have many of the characteristics of parties but which have to remain dormant. Political repression may force them to restrict membership to those who can be trusted, so that they act more like a sect than the 'broad church' which is the more usual approach of parties today. They intend to exercise influence over the state, but their means may have to be indirect and disguise the party origins of a particular activity. In many cases, the party may continue to have its formal existence in exile – as did the Spanish Communists after the Civil War. When repression becomes less extensive, the party may then be able to come out of 'hiding' and in some respects act more like a party. But taking account of these sorts of proto-parties in a definition is rather difficult.

Another problem is that, while control of a state may have become the immediate goal for a party, this may not be its long-term objective. Many European socialist parties had internationalist aims in their early years, aims which were finally marginalized by the First World War. But an even clearer instance of parties where the internationalist objectives dominated ambitions to control the nation-state were Communist parties, for whom control of particular states was merely instrumental in the promotion of the international revolution of the proletariat. A modern example of an 'internationalist' party is the Green Party in West Germany, which conceives of itself as the German wing of a wider movement. The exercise of control in the West German state is simply a means of achieving this. This having been said, parties, other than very small sect-like groups, normally find that the very existence of the state forces them to apply most of their resources to exerting influence within national boundaries. A further difficulty is that interest aggregation which, as von Beyme notes, modern systems analyses regard as the function of parties, has not been practised by all parties.[28] As he notes in discussing the German Refugees Party: 'Sometimes the leadership of a party has become so integrated with that of an interest association that it has become hard to see which function was the most important to the political protagonists.'[29] Of course, in recognizing these 'boundary problems', we must not forget that most parties do attempt to bring together (at least) several distinct interests in a society, are primarily concerned with controlling the state and use recognizably legitimate means to do so, although they may use other means as well. (The National Socialists in Weimar Germany are an example of a party using both legal and extra-legal methods of influence simultaneously, at least in the last few years of the Weimar republic, and a modern example is Sinn Fein/IRA.)

But, even if we consider only those parties which fall clearly within our general definition, there is the further question of whether these bodies have sufficient in common to be analysed together. One of the hopes in the early days of the 'behavioural revolution' was that it would now be possible and useful for empirical studies to compare a wide range of parties. In fact, the few truly comparative studies that there have been have yielded remarkably few hypotheses of any interest. Little that the Democratic Party in America does in aggregating interests bears much resemblance to what the Bulgarian Communist party has to do in aggregating interests, and it probably has even less in common with most parties in sub-Saharan Africa. One of the most extreme sceptics of the potential for wide-ranging comparative studies is MacIntyre. In relation to mass-parties in Africa, of the kind which developed in Ghana under Nkrumah, he asks:

'Why do we think of these parties, rather than as, say churches?' The answer that they have some of the marks of American political parties, and that they call themselves parties does nothing to show that in fact the meaning of 'party' is not radically changed when the cultural context is radically changed, or that even if it is not changed the description has not become inapplicable. The intentions, the beliefs, the concepts which inform the practices of African mass parties provide so different a context that there can be no question of transporting the phenomena of party to this context . . .[30]

In expressing scepticism about what we might expect to find from world-wide comparative studies of parties, we do not wish to rule out altogether the possibility that there might be something that we could learn. After all, they are all organizations that are seeking to control the state. However, this book rejects the sociological approach, which was inspired by the structural functionalism of Talcott Parsons, that assumed there were certain functions which had to be performed in any society and that we could compare parties with respect to how they so performed them. Nor do we accept the other extreme position which claims that a party can be understood solely in terms of the particular society in which it operates. With states in the same geographical region, or when there is a shared cultural heritage, it is likely that there may be important features which the parties share – and, in fact, two well-established traditions of studying parties have been analyses of parties in particular geographical areas (such as western Europe), and analyses of parties which must operate in similar ways in order to control the state (such as parties in liberal democracies).

Liberal democracy, then, has been one of the principal units around which studies of parties have been based; there is good reason for this, given that the need to mobilize mass electorates is a major influence on how parties in these states can operate and this is a feature common to all liberal democracies. But it must be recognized, too, that for some purposes of comparison it may be useful to widen the scope of analysis to include parties in other kinds of political systems. Two examples may be cited here. The Communist parties in western democracies obtain their organizational forms from that developed in the Soviet Union. We might be able to increase our understanding of the peculiar pressures liberal democracy imposes on party structure and practice by comparing certain aspects of democratic centralism as it operates in western Communist parties with the East European experience. Again, not all parties facing competition for the vote of a large electorate are found in liberal democracies. Some states, including South Africa and Rhodesia after UDI, have had ruling parties whose tenure in office has depended on mobilizing a mass electorate, and they might yield useful comparisons with parties in liberal democracies. Many of the organizational constraints parties face are the same whether all adults are enfranchised, or some large social groups are explicitly excluded. This is a conclusion with which some democrats feel uncomfortable, because the objectives and values of regimes like South Africa are far less defensible than those of most one-party states. But this should not blind us to some important similarities between white-ruled South Africa and the liberal democracies at least until the mid-1980s.[31] However much the policies pursued by the South African government are anathema to us, and however much the malapportionment of electoral districts enabled the Nationalists to take power in 1948, the fact remains that there are a number of important parallels between South Africa and the western democracies in relation to electoral and party management. In that respect, but in that respect only, the South African regime has far more in common with the liberal democracies than do, say, most other regimes in Africa or those in East Europe.

The main focus of this book, however, is parties in liberal democracies. Before discussing the reasons for this, it is important to explain what is *not* entailed by this choice of subject matter. We do not assume that liberal democracy, as it is currently practised, is

either an especially democratic system of rule or that, as some
optimistic writers assumed in the 1950s, liberal democracies
progress to more democratic forms of rule. Rather, one reason for
focusing on them is that, in the absence of competitive parties, it is
difficult, though as we see in chapter 3 perhaps not impossible, to
demonstrate how interest optimilization or the making of
collective choices could be approximated. Of course, not all
democratic theorists accept these as elements of democracy, but
they are sufficiently widely held for us to begin by examining
regimes which may have devices for realizing them. A second
reason is that some of the parties in these regimes are the major,
though not the only, instances of parties which encourage
widespread participation in their own internal affairs and, through
that, in the wider polity. Only occasionally, as in Yugoslavia, do
we find in other kinds of regime widespread participation in
political parties which is directed towards the formulation of civic-
oriented objectives.

Even in liberal democracies, however, the concept of a party is a
broad one. The term was used, and still is used, to refer to those
elite groupings which emerged in legislatures before the
enfranchisement of a mass electorate, a process which did not
begin in most regimes that were to develop into liberal democracies
until the late nineteenth century. Well-defined elite groupings
emerged and disappeared in the British parliament at various times
from the late seventeenth century until the mid-nineteenth century,
when the parliamentary parties were transformed into parties with
mass electoral bases. In the United States, too, recognizable
parties, centred on the Congress, developed in the 1790s, although
as in Britain there was a period when these groupings dissolved but
they re-emerged and were transformed into recognizably modern
parties at the time of mass enfranchisement in the 1820s. With the
exception of Belgium, where parliamentary parties centred on a
clerical–anti-clerical cleavage developed in the 1830s soon after
independence, parliamentary parties were somewhat slower to
develop on a permanent basis elsewhere simply because sovereign
parliaments developed rather later. In France, where there was a
parliament relatively early in the nineteenth century and manhood
suffrage as early as 1848, even parties centred on parliamentary
elites did not become a major political force until well into the
twentieth century. (In many respects, indeed, French parties
remained rather unusual among European parties until the
establishment of the Fifth Republic in 1958.) One of the few
states where elite, parliamentary, parties did exist at the same

time, or before, those in Britain and the United States was Sweden, where:

> As early as the eighteenth century, during the so-called Era of Liberty, Sweden had a highly developed parliamentary system with two parties, the Hats and the Caps. They were mainly organized inside Parliament, which at the time consisted of the Four Estates. This old parliamentary system was abolished by a coup d'etat by the king in 1772.[32]

The main feature of the eighteenth- and early nineteenth-century groupings was that a relatively high degree of cohesion might be achieved in parliamentary affairs, while at the same time there was little formal organization supporting the activities of the individuals who were acting together. Certainly whatever organization was required for the purposes of mobilizing a rather small electorate was supplied by individual members of the elites for their own purposes and, in conjunction with those in the social elite in their own locales, through social networks of deference and dependence.

However, the term 'party' is also used to refer to large and highly integrated organizations – organizations that resulted either from franchise expansion or came into being to promote interests that were not represented in legislatures. The late nineteenth century was a crucial period in this respect, because in the first half of the century mass-party organizations had existed only in the United States. Although, for example, a party-oriented electorate was emerging in England in the years 1857–68, the organizational structures which could exploit this electorate did not develop for another decade.[33] It was only in 1877–8 that the debate about the merits of the organizational form associated with the Birmingham Caucus became a major issue among the Liberal party's elite. Within twenty years, though, both Liberals and Conservatives had produced mass-level organizations that could mobilize electorates, which, because of the franchise extensions in 1867 and 1885, were now huge compared with electorates of the pre-1867 era. By 1902 the organizational form was sufficiently established for Ostrogorski to publish a well-known critique of British parties.[34] In terms of influencing future party developments, the German experience, however, was at least as important as the British. A highly integrated party, based on a mass membership, was already established among German Catholics in the 1870s, but it was the use made of this type of organization by the German Social

Democrats that was to become a model for many other socialist parties.[35] The very scale of political activities made possible by this organizational form eventually forced most elite-based parties to find ways of combating the advantages mass organization seemed to offer.

Clearly, then, the elite-based parties of America in the 1790s, or Britain in the 1690s or the early 1830s, are very different kinds of institutions from the later organizations that we call parties. For this reason we find a different approach adopted in histories of the British and American parties from that employed in comparative studies of modern parties. The former stress the *continuity* between the earlier, parliamentary, parties and the twentieth-century parties: the emphasis is very much on the elites grafting on mass organization bases so as to be able to mobilize much larger electorates. When comparing modern parties, though, it is more usual to begin with the periods in which there were pressures for large organizations to be created; for these purposes, the development and, for the most part, subsequent replacement of the elite, parliamentary-based, parties is peripheral. Even an ardent behaviouralist would see little point in comparing a modern party with the Whigs or Tories during the period 1690–1714, which was, in fact, a highly partisan period in the British parliament. There is simply insufficient in common between the two sorts of bodies. Obviously, this book is concerned with parties in a modern state.

HOW DO PARTIES ADVANCE DEMOCRACY?

We must now turn to examine how parties might be thought to advance democracy, and this is best done by looking at each of the three elements of democracy identified earlier. We begin by considering interest optimalization.

Among those who have argued that aggregating interests optimally is an important, or perhaps the only, democratic value, there have been broadly three approaches to the role of parties. The first, often adopted by those who advocate a minimal state in which organization does not get in the way of 'market clearing', is hostile to parties. In some versions, even representative democracy may pose a threat, but among those who accept the need for a state, it should be a state in which organized power that might interfere with market activity is minimized. A very different view is that parties do have a role in helping to structure the vote, but they are seen as only one form of political organization and the main forum for articulating preferences in the political system should be interest groups. This view is most closely associated with the analytic pluralism of American political science in the 1950s. In the versions of both Truman and Dahl, parties merely faciliated the working of political institutions through which preferences were expressed.[36] Different again is the approach of those who argued that the electoral process itself was a major mechanism for aggregating preferences. However, a major problem for its proponents is one we have noted already: that the act of voting can create paradoxes and cycles, so that not only are parties needed to simplify the choices for the voters, but a particular kind of party system is required to prevent 'cycling'. This was a major theme in the early writing of Riker, a period in which he took a radically different view of democracy-as-preference-aggregation than he was to later. Riker advocated a two-party system because, as Weale has argued:

> The effect of a two-party system is to force voters to think of issues in the same way, namely in terms of a choice between party A and party B. In short [for Riker] the role of political parties is so to define issues and clarify choices that voters have to decide between them, with no room for the subtler qualifications of their position that might lead voters to favour some third alternative.[37]

In this book we do not discuss *directly* the role of parties in advancing this element of democracy. There are two reasons for this. The first is that some of the arguments about the effects of party competition parallel arguments that we do discuss in connection with the idea of parties allowing voters to exercise control, especially by facilitating choice. The second is that, for those who believe that parties are important in the optimal aggregation of interests, it is *party systems* as much as parties which are the crucial variables. In particular, as for Riker (in his early works), it is the number of parties which is crucial. Now, while one of the central arguments in this book is that parties are not merely epiphenomena which are sociologically determined, it is certainly the case that many aspects of a state's party system are affected greatly by socio-economic factors. We cannot, for example, necessarily alter a party system simply by changing the electoral system, as some earlier political scientists thought. Consequently, to the extent that this book is concerned with the issue of how parties can be used as instruments of democratization in the future, it is most appropriate to focus mainly on aspects of parties which may lend themselves to manipulation.

Among those who accept that parties should be instruments of popular control, there are two very different traditions. On the one hand, there is the idea that parties should offer people choices and that these choices should be implemented as public policy – irrespective of whether the decisional procedures actually produce cycles or paradoxes. Behind this lies the idea that by offering policy alternatives, parties enable citizens to develop ideas about the sort of political future they want and to express their opinions about this in the decision-making process. On the other hand, there are those who have argued that popular control should be limited to acting as a kind of safety value – giving the electorate the chance to remove political leaders when the latter implement a series of wholly unwanted policies. Not surprisingly, these two traditions have given rise to two very different views of the role of parties in a democracy.

Those, such as the American E. E. Schattschneider, who emphasize *choice* by the people as being a principal feature of democracy, have focused on three requirements of parties for choice to be effected. One is that there must be some connection between the alternative sets of goals and objectives presented to voters by parties and what a government can try to implement. Because none of the electoral systems actually used in liberal democracies guarantee that one party will always have a majority in the legislature, and thereby ensure that *one* of the packages of policies presented to the voters will be implemented, these democrats favour a two-party system, and political institutions that encourage two-partism.[38] Their reason for advocating this is rather different, however, from the reason just discussed in connection with Riker. The point is not so much that voting cycles might be possible under multi-partism but that, unless there are two parties, there is no guarantee that a single party will have a legislative majority, and if it does not, the important decisions about policies will not be taken by the voters but by party elites in post-electoral bargaining. The policies of coalition governments, it is argued, may bear little relation to the policies presented by individual parties to the electorate. Another requirement is that there should be a high degree of control of party policy programmes by a party's supporters. There are two reasons why democrats who advocate the notion of popular choice might favour internally democratic parties. Such parties would extend the arenas within the state in which citizens could be involved in making choices relating to the state's objectives; and, involving such people in the process of constructing policy programmes will make it less likely that unspecific and ambiguous statements will take the place of actual policies in the programmes presented to the voters. That is, democratic control of a party makes for both more democracy and acts as a mechanism to prevent distortions in the process of electoral choice. (However, decentralizing decisions about policies might pose problems for voter voice if, for some reason, the party members making the relevant decisions are little interested in trying to win votes for the party.) The final requirement is that parties should be able to implement their policies once in power: they must have sufficient control of the state that the choices made are not rendered meaningless. It is because of this last requirement that those who have propounded the view that parties are central in affecting electoral choice are often referred to as advocates of *party government*. But, while they favour extensive party penetration of the state, there has been much less agreement as to how much it is desirable for parties to penetrate society. Nevertheless, as we shall see, extensive party penetration in both arenas would also provide a basis for reduced mass control of parties. The question of how parties can best promote voter choice, therefore, is an extremely complex one.

We must now turn more briefly to the role accorded to parties by those who conceive popular control not in terms of voter choice, but as the ability to remove a set of leaders. For most of these democratic theorists the fear is that parties in government will try to do too much, and that in their endeavours they will be 'pushed' by their activists, members or associated interest groups. Nevertheless, there is a problem which was recognized by the first of these 'modern' democrats, Joseph Schumpeter. If elected leaders are to be allowed to get on with governing relatively undisturbed by voters or organized interests, they must be backed up by party organizations that can 'deliver the vote'. Schumpeter very much favoured old-fashioned political bosses who could organize the vote for those who would actually govern. The trouble with this solution, for those who accept this limited view of democracy, is that highly organized parties might be taken over by other kinds of activists and by interest groups, and bureaucratized parties may contain employees who have a stake in extensive party penetration of the state. Consequently, in its more modern version, as in the work of Samuel Brittan, this kind of democratic theory has been more critical of parties.[39] This has meant that, since the 1970s, there has been a coming together of two rather separate strands of democratic theory: the post-Schumpeterians who had always placed parties at the centre of their arguments, and the American pluralist tradition (Truman, Dahl and their followers) which has emphasized weak and decentralized parties. For both, parties should act as a safeguard against tyranny, but they must act in such a way as to be relatively weak forces themselves within the state.

Finally, we must consider how parties have been treated in relation to the third element of democracy – civic orientation. Once again, we find radically different traditions. One of the main strands of participatory democratic theory has been much opposed to parties and party activity. This is the strand which can be traced back to Rousseau, and which values individual participation in small social units and sees parties as sources of division which can only weaken the developmental aspects of participation. On this view, parties lead to the hardening of support for group and individual interests, at the expense of more general interests. Far from complementing participation in industry and in communities, participation in parties develops attitudes and values which are hostile to public-regardingness. (Of course, this is not the only source of anti-partism. Some conservatives have seen in parties the instruments for socio-economic change, while, for example, the Progressive reformers in the United States were also antagonistic to parties because of the venality of nineteenth-century American parties.) Against this, there is the view of those who see parties operating in ways compatible with the development of public-regardingness. Parties educate the public about issues and objectives for that society, and, it is argued, participation in parties is also a way by which particular interests come to be reconciled with more general interests. In other words, participation in parties does not undermine participation in other arenas, but may actually be superior to it because the interests of individual firms and communities must be accommodated to other interests. Clearly, if parties were to operate in this way, they would have to be very extensive organizations, penetrating society deeply. This, of course, is the opposite of the Rousseauan tradition.

We have outlined a general framework with which we can begin to understand how parties can help to advance democracy. We have identified three elements of democracy – interest optimalization, the exercise of control, and civic orientation. We have also seen that a broad range of organizations call themselves political parties, and that it may be useful for purposes of political analysis to confine attention to parties operating in generally similar conditions and facing similar sorts of constraints in their attempts to exercise power. Now, of the three elements of democracy, arguments about the role and activities of parties have been most prominent in debates about how citizens can exercise control, and the remainder of this book reflects this emphasis. However, disputes about how, if at all, parties can enable interest aggregation to occur in large societies are still current in political theory, and part of the discussion in chapter 3 bears on this issue. Similarly, there have been debates about the ability of parties and party activity to create a civic orientation among citizens, and aspects of these issues form part of the discussion in chapters 3, 4, 5 and 6. This brings us to the subject of the organization of the arguments in this book.

We begin, in chapters 2 and 3, by considering a controversy of central importance to debates about interest optimilization and the exercise of control by citizens. This is the role of party competition. In chapter 2 we address the question of whether democracy is possible in a one-party state. This is a crucial issue, because supporters of liberal democracy have always maintained that in the absence of competition there is no means for ensuring that voters either come to develop preferences, or that leaders have any incentive to attempt to aggregate these preferences. We shall see that the case for one-party democracy remains unproved. But what exactly does political competition contribute to the advancement of any of the elements of democracy? This is the subject of chapter 3, where we see that competition does provide for the possibility of citizens exercising choice, but that not all elections necessarily do so. The main thrust of chapters 2 and 3 is that the kind of electoral competition provided in liberal democracies does seem to be necessary for democratization; consequently, the remainder of the book focuses on parties in these regimes, although, where appropriate, examples from other regimes where there is electoral competition are introduced. Chapter 4 presents an analysis of parties as organizations in liberal democracies, and does so in terms of four dimensions of the dichotomy between 'public' and 'private' bodies. One of the major disputes between democrats has been about how, indeed if at all, citizens should participate in parties. Participation has been valued both because it facilitates citizen choice and because some forms of participation encourage public-regarding attitudes among citizens. Chapter 5 concerns the ways in which citizens have participated in parties, and the potential for more extensive, and different forms of, participation in these partially public and partially private organizations. But participation is not the same as control, and chapter 6 examines whether parties can be controlled by their members or whether some form of elite domination is inevitable. But what of the power parties themselves can exercise? Leaving aside the problem of whether interests can be aggregated optimally, this poses a difficulty for the democrat. The ability of a ruling party (or parties) to get its policies implemented is surely a requirement of democracy – if they cannot do so, then the exercising of citizen choice is rendered unimportant. Yet parties that penetrate both state and society extensively may provide resources for political elites which render them less responsive to control from below. Chapter 7 examines the experience of parties in liberal democracies in penetrating state and society, and the effects on the advancement of democracy. Finally, in chapter 8, we draw together much of the preceding discussion and examine how some possible future trends in party politics might affect the role of parties as agents of democracy.

2

DEMOCRACY IN A ONE-PARTY SYSTEM

Perhaps the most controversial argument in the twentieth century regarding the role of parties in the advancement of democracy has concerned competition between parties. In relation to this the most important, but not the only, disagreement has been that between liberal democrats and orthodox Marxist theorists. In essence, the argument of those who can be described as liberal democrats has been either that democracy can be sustained only when there are parties competing against each other, or (in the case of some of the most conservative liberal-democrats) that, for democracy to be sustained, there must at least be the possibility of more than one party contesting elections. In response, orthodox Marxists have argued that the form of democracy found in the western states is a sham. According to Marxists, the class structure of these western societies prevents the party of the proletariat from competing on fair terms with the bourgeois parties, and competition between bourgeois parties cannot generate political control for the proletariat. Instead, Marxists have argued in favour of the one-party state, with democracy being practised through the principle of democratic centralism within a party of the proletariat. We examine the concept of democratic centralism shortly, but it is first necessary to point out that, on the one hand, some of the orthodox Marxist arguments about western-style democracy can be embraced within an essentially liberal theory of democracy while, on the other hand, some Marxists have departed from the orthodox view of the role of the proletarian party.

Within a basically liberal view of democracy, it is possible to accept that social and economic arrangements in the western states prevent democracy in these regimes from being very extensive. Some radical democrats have argued that market economies, which give little influence in the productive processes to either workers in the industries themselves or to consumer groups, distribute power very unevenly in these societies. Equally, they contend, in these societies social mobility is extremely limited, so that the opportunities for most individuals to *increase* the control they have over decisions which affect them are also restricted. On this view, liberal democracy may not provide for that much democracy within the state. Nevertheless, such theories of democracy remain *liberal* theories providing the proponents accept that without electoral competition there are no mechanisms for sustaining democracy in the long-term. In other words, liberal theories of democracy are ones which assume that electoral competition is a necessary condition for democracy to be practised within a state. Of course, liberal theories constitute a broad spectrum of theories of democracy. They range from the most conservative theories, which argue for a minimum amount of state activity and the widest possible scope for market activity, to theories arguing for a wide range of services to be provided by the state agencies and for either community or worker involvement in decision-making in economic enterprises. In the Marxist tradition one of the most important developments in the past twenty to thirty years has been the proliferation of different strands of Marxism. Of particular relevance here is the growth of ideas associated with 'Eurocommunism'. In some Communist parties in western states, and especially in Italy, Marxist ideas about the inevitable consequences of class conflict were greatly modified, and the right of the non-Communist parties not just to exist in a socialist state but to compete for power with Communists was accepted. As a result, the distinctively Marxist approach to democracy (at least, as it had been outlined by Lenin) was effectively abandoned, if only for the time being, by some Communist parties.

In this chapter and the next we examine the idea of party competition. For the moment our focus is on the claim that democracy can be practised in a nation-state when only one party is permitted to field candidates in elections for positions in government. We begin by considering the Leninist notion of democratic centralism, but then widen the discussion to embrace also a rather different strand of argument – the claim that single-party regimes provide the greatest potential for democracy in contemporary Africa.

DEMOCRATIC CENTRALISM

Leninists argue that in a socialist state there can be only one political party, or rather there can be only one party that is allowed to control the state. (The state, as in Poland, may allow other parties to exist and to play some part in the political system, but they are not permitted to compete for power with the Communist party.) But, according to Leninists, the Communist party is itself organized democratically, on the lines of democratic centralism and this means that there is no need for other parties. The principle of democratic centralism was first outlined by the Bolsheviks at a conference at Tammerfors in 1905, and it was incorporated into the Soviet party's statutes in 1917. It provides for the democratic election of party officials, and for the periodic accountability of all party organs. However, while party members participate in the making of decisions, they must accept decisions once they have been made: factionalism and disagreement on party policy is not allowed. Moreover, decisions of higher party organs must be accepted by those lower down. But is this a democratic theory at all, or is it, as many liberal writers have argued, a sham? As might be expected the answer to this is actually rather complex, but we can briefly examine some of the more important arguments.

Our starting point is that there is nothing inherently undemocratic in an organization requiring disciplined acceptance of a policy once it has been made. It is the same principle which is embodied in the idea of collective responsibility by the Cabinet in Britain, as well as in the belief that parliamentary representatives should not vote against the decisions of their own party in the legislature. Just as Hobbes opined we would be forced to live in a dangerous state of nature if we did not all agree to accept the rule of a sovereign, so any organization would find it difficult to act effectively if its members did not freely accept the need for compliance with constitutionally agreed decisions. Again, democratic bodies can require lower-level units to comply with the decisions of higher-level units without ceasing to be democratic. Indeed, the democrat who values people making choices in matters that affect their lives is committed to the view that decisions which have been agreed should be implemented: disobedience by lower-level units may prevent the choice from being effected properly, and this is anti-democratic in nature. Civil disobedience has been an important issue for democratic theorists precisely because two important elements of democracy seem to be in conflict. On the one hand, disobedience can constitute 'free-riding' and can undermine the whole basis of collective decision-making, while, on the other, disobedience may be the only effective means open to an individual or a group to draw attention to how a particular decision (or decisions) actually subvert democratic procedures.[1] The enforcement of discipline within a party, then, would seem to be a requirement of an internally democratic party and, more generally, consistent with the practice of democracy within a state. The problem for any democratic theory is specifying when, and by what means, individuals may properly refuse to comply with a decision, and this brings us to several difficulties with democratic centralism as a form of democracy.

One problem is that, in the context of a one-party state, democratic centralism provides no check on anti-democratic tendencies in the party. Those who oppose decisions which they believe undermine the party's democratic character are effectively denied both 'exit' (because no other parties are permitted) and 'voice' (at least after the relevant decisions have been made).[2]

Another consideration, which we examine more fully later in this chapter, is that the demand that there be only one party which can ever control the state deprives the system of a means of checking bad decisions. Party members who disagree funda-mentally with a decision cannot oppose it within the party, nor is there any other forum through which they can continue to press their point of view once they leave the Communist party. Now the point is neither that this is liberty-reducing (it is, although this is a separate issue), nor that in some cases democracy might be undermined, but rather that there is no way of redressing an *incorrect* decision. As a result the connection between the intentions and wants of those participating in the party and policy outcomes can remain broken indefinitely. As we see shortly, this problem might be resolvable without having to abandon either the idea of one-partism or the prohibition on factionalism in the Communist party, but even this solution would fall outside the Leninist notion of democratic centralism. Yet another problem is that the Communist party in the Soviet Union, and in the eastern European countries which have adopted this party model, is not open to all. To become a member of the party is a privilege not a right – would-be members must serve something resembling apprenticeships before they may become full members of the party. (An important exception to this was in East Germany between 1946 and 1948 when, in order to bolster the legitimacy of the regime, the Communist party merged with the Social Democrats to form the Socialist Unity Party. By admitting Social Democrats directly as members, the Communists modified the strict Leninist practice on party membership.) This means that the democratic requirement, that all citizens should have the opportunity to participate in the making of choices for that society, is not fulfilled.

It is also important to dispose of an argument which is sometimes put forward to try to save the claim that democratic centralism is compatible with democracy. This is the view that we cannot simply look at procedures when assessing the democratic character of a regime. After all, rulers may fully understand the 'law of anticipated reactions' and be supplying the people with what they want. Moreover, in any advanced industrial state they will have to do this to a considerable extent; only in very poor states, like Duvalier's Haiti, can rulers get away with doing what they like to the vast majority of people. There are two objections to this argument. The first is that, although it has had a number of defenders, the idea that democracy consists solely of optimally aggregating interests (giving the people what they want) is unsatisfactory. Procedures do matter in assessing whether a system is democratic.

Consider the following example: Suppose someone were to say that Liverpool Football Club was a highly democratic organization and he was asked to justify this claim. He then justifies it by pointing to the fact that between 1965 and 1985 its supporters had seen their team become the most successful ever in British football history; during these years the supporters had been able to watch highly entertaining teams, containing some of the best players of their generation; again, the players earned high wages; and the club earned a lot of money through their successes in British and European competitions. While we may well agree that being a Liverpool shareholder, player or supporter would be very satisfying, we would surely wonder what this had to do with the claim that the club was a highly democratic one. At least in part, we should require some indication of how decisions were taken in Liverpool F.C. before agreeing with the claim. The point is that in highly undemocratic organizations people could quite properly be very contented with their lot; *if aggregating wants or interests optimally is a condition for democracy, then it is not a sufficient condition*. Now, of course, it is not being suggested that we should always prefer democracy to other forms of rule: if democracy entails civil strife or a much lower standard of living, then quite rationally we might prefer some other form of government. But this does not make it a democratic form.

The second objection to the argument for 'saving' democratic centralism as a democratic principle is that, even in advanced industrial societies, there is still considerable scope for governors to repress the governed. There are not constraints inherent in such societies which prevent the collapse of previously democratic regimes into regimes which practise mass repression. The relatively high level of economic development in the Weimar Republic was not a barrier which prevented its collapse and the rise of the Third Reich, so equally is there no reason to believe that democratic centralism could not also be the basis of repression in an advanced economy. (Of course, the level of economic development does influence how repression can be introduced, and against whom it can be directed; in that sense Hitler's Germany was more difficult to govern than Duvalier's Haiti.) However, having made this argument, we must be careful not to accept the similarly fallacious argument that democracy is the natural enemy of repression. It is not, and there are many instances of dominant ethnic and religious groups which have been relatively democratic in relation to members of their own group but which have adopted repressive policies against minority groups which also inhabit the state which they control. The democratic impulses of the Jacksonian movement in the 1820s and 1830s were the impulses of those who wanted to 'open up the west' – policies which destroyed the rights and ways of life of the American Indians of the Great Plains. The strongly democratic ethos in Israel in the late 1940s and 1950s did not prevent Palestinians from being driven from land they had occupied before the creation of the state of Israel.

The argument so far in this chapter has been about the long-term stability of democratic centralism as a democratic device. But, it might be argued, why do we not look instead at those parties which practise democratic centralism to see to what extent decisions are controlled from beneath. The simple answer to this is that those one-party regimes which practise this principle have not permitted political scientists to study intra-party relations. It is possible, of course, that in some instances and in some parties, members have exercised a high degree of control, but we have no evidence for this. What indirect evidence there is suggests that, in the Soviet Union and in the eastern European countries which follow the Leninist model, democratic centralism has tended to produce far more centralism than democracy. In part, this is the result of the small memberships of Communist parties in eastern Europe, but it also stems from the absence of alternative checks to those internal to the party. In theory, leaders in the Communist parties are elected but in practice higher echelon officials seem to be able to control the votes of lower echelon ones. This is not too surprising since it has also been a common feature of non-Communist parties in liberal democracies. Nor does the experience of Communist parties in western states tell us very much about the democratic potential of democratic centralism in one-party regimes, because both the political culture and political 'market' they face may require the parties to organize themselves differently. As Hine has said of the Italian Communist party:

> One and a half million members do not stay inside a party like the PCI, operating in a pluralist society with strong democratic traditions and several leftist party alternatives, by bureaucratic manipulation and coercion alone. In fact the party leadership has to remain extremely sensitive to grass-roots and trade-union opinion, and it is clear that its behaviour since the late 1970s has been strongly conditioned by such considerations.[3]

The main problem, then, with democratic centralism as a theory of democracy in a one-party state is that, even if widespread participation in the party were permitted, it lacks the mechanisms to check decisions and leaders, if the 'wrong' decision happens to be passed or leaders come to accumulate excessive power in their own hands. It does not provide the means for a return to democracy when anti-democratic tendencies set in. However, while the dispute between liberal democrats and orthodox Marxists has been at the centre of ideological conflict since the founding of the Soviet state in 1917, arguments about democratic centralism have had remarkably little influence on liberal democratic theory. It has been all too easy to dismiss the claims made for democratic centralism. Nevertheless, in recent years liberals have had to take account of rather different claims about the practice of democracy in one-party regimes, and it is to these that we now turn.

TOWARDS A THEORY OF THE DEMOCRATIC ONE-PARTY STATE?

Because of the apparent limitations of the principle of democratic centralism, the argument that democracy could be practised in one-party states was one that was little discussed until, perhaps, the late 1950s and early 1960s. The emergence of this issue was the product of two separate developments. On the one hand, there were changes affecting Communist regimes in the years after the Second World War. Before the war western Communists and neo-Marxists had been concerned primarily with the establishment of socialism; capitalism was seen as a discredited force because of its failure to provide economic prosperity and employment. The war changed this. While, in general, it helped to legitimize the left and to increase support for left-of-centre parties in the elections immediately afterwards, it also helped to legitimize western-style democracy. This had been a 'people's war', or so it had been portrayed, against fascism, and political elites in the capitalist democracies claimed for this form of government a share of the credit – perhaps more than its fair share – in that success. Democracy was now a far more important political value with which both socialists and Marxists of all hues had to contend. However, the realization that the regime under Stalin was far from being the 'future which worked' (as it had been portrayed in the 1930s), precluded the Soviet Union from being used as a model for an alternative democratic method to that found in the western systems. Stalin's death in 1953, and the subsequent efforts at de-Stalinization, provided the background against which neo-Marxist theories of democracy could be developed. The culmination of these intellectual currents was the publication in 1966 of a series of lectures by the eminent Canadian political philosopher, C. B. Macpherson – lectures in which the author attempted to show how democracy was possible in one-party states, both in Communist regimes and regimes in the Third-World.[4] The main thrust of Macpherson's argument was that the formal conditions necessary for one-party democracy could be specified, and that some regimes in the 'real world' might be able to meet these conditions in the future and would become practitioners of one-party democracy. These conditions are: full democracy within the party; party membership being open to all; and membership not entailing activities which are beyond the capacity of the average person.[5]

The other development was the writing of African nationalists who wished to construct African politics on very different lines from those of the European colonial powers:

> Ultimately the project was to replace the value-structure of the European with one more directly linked to the aspirations of the African people. Césaire, Damas and Senghor began to publish in the 1930s, and by the 1940s and 1950s their work had found echoes in Anglophone Africa, especially in the theories of Kwame Nkrumah and his ideas on African personality.[6]

However, the person who did most to extend these ideas and to popularize them, certainly in the English-speaking world, was the Tanzanian political leader Julius Nyerere. Nyerere wished to reconcile two objectives. He believed that a potential for direct democracy lay in the traditions of consensus and community which underlay African village life. Nevertheless, this form of democracy had to be realized in the context of nation-states which were multi-ethnic groupings that owed their existence to the accidents of European colonial expansion. The danger was that multi-partism might lead to irreconcilable strife between different tribes, so that he argued in favour of the single-party state as the framework within which democracy could be practised. For Nyerere, the one-party state was not a convenience but a necessity for democracy in Africa. As Nursey-Bray argues,

> the maintenance or creation of a unified society is crucial to Nyerere's theory of democracy, which is why it is linked to his proposals for the development of *ujamaa* socialism, a socialist experiment founded on *ujamaa* villages, the aim of which is to maintain or, where necessary, recreate the virtues and values of traditional society.[7]

For the most part, the supporters of one-party democracy in both its neo-Marxist and its African nationalist forms have failed to convince mainstream democrats in the west. Some conservative democrats have simply dismissed the whole notion, sometimes on remarkably peculiar grounds – Sartori, for example, seems to believe that one-party democrats must presume human beings are altruists and that their arguments must fail because of the implausibility of this presumption.[8] A more general problem has been that the regimes which have sometimes been canvassed as potential exemplars of one-party democracy have proved to be relatively undemocratic and yield few signs of democratizing. For example, de-Stalinization in the Soviet Union did not lead to the growth of intra-party democracy in that country, even though the worst manifestations of that regime were removed; China's Cultural Revolution was not a democratizing force; and, while Tanzania has shown that genuinely competitive elections can be held in one-party regimes, the effort at creating political input to the regime from below has proved far less successful.[9] The aim of this section is to examine whether this lack of attention to one-party democracy is justified. In considering the issue it is important to distinguish three rather separate points: What formal conditions would a one-party regime have to meet for it to be a democracy? In theory, what institutions, mechanisms and procedures might be predicted to bring about, and sustain, one-party democracy? And what evidence, if any, is available in evaluating the potential for the emergence of one-party democratic regimes? The most useful starting point in this exercise is with the conditions specified by Macpherson.

We have seen that Macpherson identified three conditions which had to be met for a one-party state to be democratic: full democracy within the party; party membership open to all; and membership involving only those sorts of activities which are within the capacity of the average citizen. Macpherson's critics have argued that these conditions are too weak and that regimes which met them might still not be democratic regimes. In particular, Lively has criticized two aspects of Macpherson's formulation of the conditions necessary for one-party democracy.[10] He contends that 'full democracy' is an inadequate condition, if this is taken to mean that only individuals, and not factions, may participate in party affairs. Again Lively argues that the requirement that everyone be *eligible* for party membership is too weak; democracy requires that all members of the electorate be members of the party. But, Lively suggests, if these revisions to the Macpherson conditions are accepted, one-party democracy becomes virtually indistinguishable from two-party democracy.[11] Such a state would be a one-party state in name only, the party factions would be the counterparts of parties in liberal democracies and the party members would simply be the equivalent of the voters in those regimes.

Before considering whether Lively's objections to Macpherson's conditions are valid, we must consider whether, if they were, it would follow that a one-party system could simply be treated as a two-party or a multi-party system. Certainly, if different factions regularly put forward their own slates of candidates and if most citizens usually voted in these intra-party elections, it would seem we might have a system which was scarcely distinguishable from other kinds of party systems. However, the argument really hinges on what we mean by 'factionalism'. It is a term to which a number of different meanings have been applied – ranging from pre-party formations based on shared interests to sub-units of parties. Usually, factions are taken to be long-term groupings, but in some usages of the term (for example, Huntington's) this assumption of permanence has been modified.[13] If we accept, and this is the most reasonable assumption, that Lively is referring to party sub-units having some permanence, then his argument about the indistinguishability of one-party democracy from other forms does seem to follow.

However, we can then see a possible objection to accepting Lively's argument that one condition of one-party democracy must be the possibility of factions forming within the party. Why, it might be asked, should we demand of one-party states that permanent groupings within the party be permitted if such a regime is to be counted as democratic? After all, for a writer like Nyerere it is the very selfishness of factions which poses the major threat to attempts to maintain democracy in the multi-tribal states created by the European powers in Africa. The answer to this lies in a long-standing liberal argument that an important feature of democracy is *responsible* government; by simplifying the alternative choices voters must make, parties are seen as a major element in making political elites responsible to the electorate. Without competing parties, or without organized factions in a party competing against each other, there is no means of ensuring that elites can be held accountable to an electorate. But, irrespective of the arguments that can be put in support of the idea of government responsibility (and the present author has himself made such a case) [14], we must be alert to the possibility that some device other than competition between 'organized teams' might be capable of realizing it. For example, it might be argued that competition between 'tendencies', or non-permanent groupings, would provide some element of responsibility but that, in addition to intra-party elections for individual leaders, regular referendums on whether the entire elected government remain in office would ensure responsibility. This latter requirement would be needed to overcome the objection that the election of individual politicians, as in Tanzania, gives little scope to the citizens to hold the *government* responsible to them. While such a condition would fall outside the Nyerere framework, it might seem to provide similar safeguards to his against the dangers of permanent factions, while meeting the need for government responsibility to the electorate.

It might be tempting to conclude that we have found a way to overcome Lively's point that, if factions are not permitted in a one-party state, there is no means of making elites responsible to the masses. Nevertheless, while a combination of individual competition for public offices and periodic referendums on the entire government might provide for control of the highest levels of leadership in the state, it is less clear that this would provide for control over middle-level functionaries. These are officials at a level too high to be controlled by individuals mobilizing directly against them (as in the neighbourhood, or in a medium-sized firm or institution), but who would not be 'caught' by the referendum proposal we have just discussed. Controlling these kinds of functionaries is difficult in any kind of political system, but the advantage of party or factional competition is that it increases the likelihood that such officials will believe themselves tied to the electoral fortunes of their higher-level masters. In the absence of 'team competition' it is less clear how such ties would develop. This is not to say that it is *impossible* to find mechanisms for controlling such officials, but for the moment it is not obvious that relatively simple mechanisms could be devised.

But what of Lively's other criticism of Macpherson's three conditions for one-party democracy – that all citizens should participate in the party, and not just be eligible to do so? Macpherson requires merely that the party be open to all citizens: providing they have the right to join the party one of the conditions of democracy would be satisfied. This places him in rather odd company as a democratic theorist. For one of the arguments directed against the so-called 'democratic elitists' in the 1960s was that they were concerned with eligibility to participate rather than with actual participation. Critics rightly pointed out that non-participation may not be a sign of satisfaction with the political process and that the extent of democracy was related to participatory practices and not just to rights. Nevertheless, Lively's requirement that, whether leadership accountability could count 'as democratic would depend on the extent of party membership',[15] seems to be too strong a condition. Just as the radical democrats overstated their case against 'democratic elitists', by rejecting eligibility to participate as at least being *some* indicator of the scope of democracy, so too it might be argued that if membership of a party in a one-party state is easily attained then, providing the other conditions were also met, that state is democratic *to some extent*. Obviously, we could then relate *how* democratic it is to the amount of actual participation – and a fully democratic one-party state would involve extensive participation in party structures.

The main thrust of our argument so far is that the notion of one-party democracy does not seem completely absurd, but that there does seem to be a major problem for anyone espousing such a theory as to how middle-level elites are to be controlled. This brings us directly to the second issue outlined earlier: the mechanisms required to sustain one-party democracy.

Certainly, any proponent of one-party democracy would have to explain how intra-party relations could be organized to provide influence for ordinary party members, and some of Macpherson's critics have taken him to task for not addressing the issue. In part, this criticism is unfair. As we shall see in chapter 6, devising procedures for competitive party systems which give party members control over both their leaders and over party policy has proved elusive, so that is not a problem unique to the one-party democrat. Of course, the critic might retort that internal democracy would be crucial for democracy in a one-party state, while it is less important where there is also inter-party competition. But, again, the supporter of one-party democracy might claim that this assumes that competition constrains parties, and the discussion in chapter 3 does suggest that the electoral mechanism can be a highly imperfect device for controlling parties. However, the problem of middle-level elites is one that cannot be dismissed so easily, and it is an issue to which we must now return.

Let us suppose that an advocate of one-party democracy has suggested, as we discussed earlier, that the problem of responsibility to the electorate can be effected in a one-party state by allowing individuals to challenge incumbent public officials in elections and by periodic referendums on whether all public officials should be retained in office. How would the possibility of electoral defeat for senior party officials in either of these two electoral forums affect the behaviour of, say, the following two kinds of party functionary. *A* is a relatively long-serving party member who has been appointed, because of his background in the party, to a policy-making position in the civil service; he is not, of course, a career civil servant. *B* is a political organizer at the regional level for the party; because of his faithful service to the party, he has also been appointed to the board of directors of a number of semi-autonomous state agencies, such as the one responsible for running the nation's airports. Now, at least in theory, the liberal democrat can explain how party competition can constrain the behaviour of these kinds of functionaries. If there were party competition, *A* would have a stake in implementing as effectively as possible the government's policies, because a failure to do so may increase the possibility of his party losing office, an event which would presumably lead to his removal from office as well. Equally, *B* has an incentive not to use his roles as party organizer or bureaucratic overseer for personal gain, because activities which discredit the party may reduce its popularity at the next election; he may take part of the blame for electoral defeat as a party official and also may not be re-appointed by the new governing party to his various directorships. Of course, in practice, these constraints may be rather weak, especially when a party is so dominant in a political system that it is nearly always in government. But in the one-party state these constraints do not exist at all. Even if the entire government is voted out in a referendum, there is no reason to believe that the incoming government (members of the same party as the outgoing one) would purge A and his fellow political appointees. A's career will not depend on the electoral fortunes of *particular* senior members of his party. Indeed, in the case of unpopular or failing policies, distancing himself from these policies when that is possible may well be a better long-term strategy for his career than being faithful to his political masters. In a one-party state B's role must necessarily be rather different than under party competition. While he will help to mobilize support for the party, he cannot (if intra-party elections are to be fair ones) help to organize the election of particular party members or be involved in defending an entire government's record in a referendum.[16] Like A, B would not be tied into the electoral system. But, if he is not, then one of the major constraints on him using his position for personal gain, or for the benefit of the party organization more generally, would seem to be absent. If, say, he sells licenses, or is simply incompetent in overseeing the administration of the nation's airports, there is no electoral incentive for his political masters to remove him, or even to concern themselves with what he is doing.

Obviously, in any organization there are constraints on how officials behave. But the point about one-party states is that a vital source of leverage over middle-level functionaries is missing. They cannot be controlled from beneath by vigilant participation in institutions, nor are they linked to the political fortunes of the high levels of party leadership. As was suggested earlier, though, it might be possible to devise other means of checking the power of these officials, and it is to one potential source for this that we now turn.

The fears that party leaders may actually dominate members, even in a formally democratic party, that middle-level elites may have autonomous bases of power, and that majority interests in the party may systematically exclude minorities, have led many liberal democrats to dismiss the possibility of one-party democracy. The belief that one-party democracy cannot deal with these circumstances seems to lie behind Sartori's claim that its advocates presume altruism on the part of political actors. Now, certainly liberal democrats would be correct in rejecting one-party theories if there were no means of protecting members against the use of party power; but writers like Sartori have not really considered the possibility that the means for this might be found in wider social structures, rather than in narrowly defined political ones. Institutions like the family, churches, occupational groups and so on might be a check against party power at a variety of levels.

When discussing what he calls 'one-party pluralism', Sartori, for example, fails to mention theories like Nyerere's in which the 'balance' to one-partism is provided by participation through traditional social structures. Structures such as villages in Nyerere's theory, would serve as arenas for other forms of political participation and their vitality would provide the means for checking the abuse of power by party leaders.

Far from being an obscure 'escape route' for the theory of one-party democracy, social structures would seem to be one of the main elements of constraint in any political system if the abuse of power is to be checked. Certainly, the existence of competing parties is insufficient to prevent regime collapse, as is evident in the cases of Weimar Germany or the French Fourth Republic. But, once we have admitted this point, a number of very serious objections to a possible 'checking' role for social structures in one-party states become apparent. One problem is that the social structures which can prevent the 'hi-jacking' of the state by a party cannot be created anew. Unless there are long-standing loyalties to such institutions they will never have the strength to be centres of resistance when party leaders abandon their democratic commitments. This is likely to restrict the number of regimes in which one-party democracy would be possible. Moreover, at the outset of one-party rule the party must not be seeking to encapsulate all social life, for in doing so it is likely to undermine many of the institutions which might otherwise check it. But extensive penetration of society is precisely what many advocates of one-party democracy believe is desirable. In the case of neo-Marxists it is necessary to rectify imbalances of power in market societies, while, for its advocates in Africa, the party is a unifying force, so that *the less the party penetrates society the less able it is to be this*. Again, to be effective, these non-party institutions must not be rigidly hierarchical, and must involve some degree of participation by the masses, for elite-controlled social institutions may simply find it easier to work in conjunction with the political elite than oppose it. This was the case with the Catholic Church in the Hitler, Mussolini and Franco regimes. (It may also be doubted whether the village traditions on which Nyerere sought to draw in promoting *ujamaa* socialism were ever quite as compatible with political input from beneath, as contrasted with elite-encouraged consensus formation, as he himself believed.) Finally, it is far from clear that, even in a polity with strongly established villages, churches and other intermediate organizations, such institutions could act to check directly the activities of the middle-level party functionaries, such as *A* and *B*, whom we discussed earlier. As with the Catholic Church in Poland, we might expect that their areas of greatest influence would be either at the national or at the most local levels, rather than at the level of middle elites. Once more, we return to an issue that seems to pose an intractable problem for the one-party democrat.

In view of the difficulties we have outlined in devising a theory of one-party democracy and in constructing possible institutions through which it could be practised, it would be surprising if in the real world (the world with which Macpherson claimed to be dealing) we were to find any such democracies. It would even be surprising if we were to find any that seemed to be potential exemplars of this. Many one-party states have been formed so that the self-interest of a particular elite or ethnic group can be pursued. Whatever their political rhetoric, regimes such as that in Tunisia or in many of the sub-Saharan African states, are not committed to internal democracy within the ruling party. The Soviet version of one-partism is equally unpromising for the democrat. Despite the commitment, in theory, to widespread participation at the policy-formation stage, through the doctrine of democratic centralism, Soviet decision-making does not seem to involve this; or rather, because scholars have no access to the internal politics of the CPSU (or other Leninist parties in eastern Europe), we have no evidence that democracy is being practised.

The very different developments in the Communist party in China also fail to provide sustenance for one-party democracy. Nathan's recent study of 'Chinese democracy', in the immediate post-Mao years, demonstrates that the participation found in that system is designed to make the state function better in responding to needs, rather than to serve as a channel for demands. The author relates this to traditional Chinese views about the relation between the individual and the state which is based on the idea of harmony. As Nathan says:

> The reforms have made the Chinese political system more pluralist only in a special narrow sense – the same sense in which the post-Stalin Soviet and Eastern European regimes are pluralist, because they invite bureaucratic interest groups and specialists to contribute

to the making of complex decisions. And the system has become more participatory in a special sense – it cultivates a greater flow of information and sentiment between citizens and the state. As a consequence the present regime seems better able to manage social conflict, gather information from the people, gain their support, and combat bureaucratic abuse than was the regime of the later years of Mao's rule.[17]

While Western observers are generally now more sympathetic to the internal policies of this regime than those of the Soviet Union, there is no evidence that the ruling Communist party has been any more democratic than its Russian counterpart. Whether moves in late 1986 to permit competition between candidates in local elections in China signals a major shift in policy remains to be seen.

We are left, then, with one or two regimes which might provide instances of one-party democracy. One is Tanzania which Nursey-Bray describes as the 'success story of African politics'.[18] Regularly contested elections in the party have been maintained for over twenty years, and government ministers have been thrown out of office by the ballot box. But the regime has failed in two respects. On the one hand, critics have argued that the *ujamaa* villages have become mechanisms 'for increasing the production level of cash crops'[19] and have not become the egalitarian, socialist institutions on which direct democracy could be founded. While Nursey-Bray himself is sceptical about such claims, he does admit that the state has not been able to deal with the increasing dominance of bureaucracy. This suggests a further important point about the 'checking role' of non-party institutions, and one that is not confined to one-party states. The institutions must be capable of checking not just the excesses of party elites but also of bureaucracies, and it is clear that non-party groups are likely to be crucial in effecting this. Not the least of the problems of establishing one-party democracy in an economically poor country like Tanzania is that it lacks the kinds of social elites that might be able to play such a role.

There remains the case of the relatively little-studied Communist party in Yugoslavia.[20] Unlike Poland, where other parties have been permitted to exist but not to challenge seriously for power, Yugoslavia has not opted for what Wiatr described as a 'hegemonic party' but has maintained a one-party system.[21] However, while the party still commits itself formally to democratic centralism, it does not practise it in the Leninist way. While the parties in each of the six republics are supposedly bound to implement policies agreed upon by the national party leadership, in fact, since the late 1970s, they have implemented what they have chosen to implement. The potential fragility of the state, because it is composed of six nations with very different traditions, is one of the factors which serves to provide a checking mechanism to the excesses of one-party rule. In addition, of course, Yugoslavia is well known for the ethic of worker self-management, and it is this ethic which has become the central element of the Yugoslav road to socialism and it is around this that policies and institutions have to be arranged. Indeed, survey data is available to show that, especially among younger party members, worker self-management is regarded as the basic principle of party organization.[22] The principle of self-management places restrictions on the centralizing tendencies of democratic centralism in two ways. It limits the influence of party leadership in institutions like economic enterprises; and it provides an alternative to the Leninist model in the conduct of intra-party relations themselves. The Yugoslav party also seems to have gone further than most other ruling Communist parties in opening up the party to citizens. In Yugoslavia the would-be party member does not have to endure a qualifying period as a 'candidate' member of the party before becoming a full member. Membership is available to any citizen and, from what limited comparative data are available, it would seem that membership is relatively high compared with most other Communist regimes. Thirteen per cent of Yugoslav adults are members – a membership density that is exceeded only by the party in North Korea. (However, the extent of democracy in the party is constrained by the fact that the party membership comes predominantly from white-collar workers and from the intelligentsia.[23]) Furthermore, since 1952 the party has had a policy of reducing the influence of party officials, and bureaucratization in the party, by reducing their numbers. Today the party apparatus constitutes only about 0.3 per cent of party members, which is perhaps one-fifth the size of the party bureaucracy in the Soviet Union.

There is evidence too of democracy actually being practised by the Yugoslav party. In 1966 the government in Slovenia resigned after it was defeated in the republic's parliament, although this resignation was subsequently rescinded.[24] Indeed, in the 1960s a spirit of democratic participation did begin to infuse the party, and Morača et al. have argued that: 'The League of Yugoslav Communists in the process of the so-called re-organization (at the end of the 1960s) had already changed so much that it had become a quite free political forum, and within it almost all political currents of opinion in the country struggled among themselves.'[25] In the 1970s the rotation of party and state posts was introduced, with individuals being restricted to two terms of office – that is, they could be re-elected to a position only once. However, this has not served to decentralize power in the party that much. Far from dropping out of politics once they have served in a major office, members of the political elite tend to move on to other high-level offices. (This problem of rotation not opening up access to the higher echelons of the party has also affected the attempts of the Greens in West Germany to prevent the growth of entrenched elites.) Rotation also has the consequence of reducing responsibility within the system – by the time difficulties and errors in decision-making become apparent, it is quite possible that the relevant officials have moved on to other posts and can no longer be held responsible for what has happened. Finally, the party organizations in some of the Yugoslav republics have introduced competitive elections for party offices at the highest levels and some officials have been turned out of office. This does not extend to the national level though and, for example, the person nominated for the presidency of a republic's party might well not be that republic's nominee for the national presidency.

Nevertheless, the evidence that one-party democracy is emerging in Yugoslavia is far from conclusive. The Yugoslav party is an extremely complex one and, for example, one of the main institutions providing popular input into the political system, the Socialist Alliance, is not formally part of the party though there are overlapping memberships at the leadership levels. Again, when the longer-term future of the state was discussed by Yugoslav political elites in the late 1960s, the emphasis seems to have been more on the growth of a no-party state, rather than on democratizing the party. Although in the 1980s there is more discussion of party democratization, it is not clear that this will be the direction of any future reforms. It can also be argued that the need for the party to accommodate itself to its citizenry has been occasioned by two obvious features of the state, which are highly unusual: On the one hand, there is a widespread commitment by political elites to the preservation of the state while at the same time there are strong nationalist tendencies within the constituent republics towards semi-autonomy. On the other hand, the foreign policies pursued by Yugoslavia since the late 1940s have made it peculiarly sensitive to threats to the survival of the state; in some ways, therefore, it can be seen as the converse of Finland, a country where the political elite has been free to order its domestic priorities, but not its foreign policies, because of the Russian presence.

CONCLUDING REMARKS

In assessing the possibility of democracy emerging and being practised in a one-party state, the best verdict we can reach is one available under the Scottish legal system – not proven. Those who have rejected the idea that one-party democracy is possible at all have probably overstated the case against it. Nevertheless, it is far from obvious that a theory can be developed to explain how abuses of power, especially by middle-level party elites, can be corrected in a one-party state. Moreover, when we examine the most likely exemplar of one-party democracy in the real world, Yugoslavia, conclusive evidence that extensive democratization is emerging there is lacking, although unquestionably procedures seem to be more democratic there than in virtually any other one-party state. There is also the problem that the peculiar history of the country and its multi-ethnic social base, do not really allow us to draw parallels with other countries as to the pressures on a party to abandon democratic centralism. In Yugoslavia the practice of democratic centralism in the Leninist mould might well have made the state ungovernable, and some form of decentralized rule was essential if tensions between the different groups were to be contained. It is for these reasons that the primary focus in this book is on the relation between parties and democracy in states in which party competition is permitted. Nevertheless, the discussion in this chapter has enabled us to see that when discussing the extent of democratization a *rigid* distinction between one-party states and states which permit party competition may be difficult to sustain.

3

THE IMPACT OF PARTY COMPETITION

One of the central elements in democratic theory in the twentieth century has been competition between organized political parties. For some writers, such as Schumpeter, this element is by far the most important. But even those who have rejected the Schumpeterian model have often argued that the availability of alternative parties competing for power is a distinguishing feature of democracy. This is not surprising, for, as was argued in chapter 2, while the idea of one-party democracy *might* be a coherent one, the conditions necessary for the emergence of one-party democratic states seem to be rare in the real world; thus, it is to states with competitive parties that we must turn when examining the contribution of parties to democracy. Nevertheless, the idea of competition itself is one which often generates much confusion in discussions of democracy, so that the first part of this chapter will involve 'unpacking' the concept of competition. Then we can turn to examine the impact of party competition on regimes.

Competition is relevant to all three elements of democracy. It has been seen as a mechanism by which interests can be aggregated optimally. However, some of those who have accepted that interest aggregation may be impossible (because of voting cycles and so on) have still seen it as promoting democracy. One view is that it enables citizens to constrain governments because they can dismiss a government. Another view is that competition provides for citizen control, in the sense that, because of competition, citizens can develop preferences about social objectives and then express these preferences through devices (like voting) which provide some kind of connection between preferences and outcomes. Then there is the argument that competition can provide a political education for citizens; on some versions of the argument, this can help to produce a more civic-oriented electorate.

COMPETITION IN ECONOMIC AND POLITICAL ANALYSIS

Perhaps the most useful starting point is to consider how economic theory has treated competition in the market, given economists have devoted far more attention to the concept than political theorists. In some varieties of liberal economic theory emphasis is placed on the incentive competition provides for innovation by firms, and this is a theme to which we return later. In neo-classical economic theory, though, competition has two important and related consequences for an economic system: it provides choices for the purchasers of goods (or services), who are assumed to have preferences already; and it restricts the behaviour of suppliers of the goods in the market. But what choices are provided, and how is behaviour restricted? The answers to these questions depends on the extent of the competition in the system, and this can range from perfect competition through various forms of imperfect competition to duopoly. In a world of perfectly competitive markets the purchaser/consumer is faced by an unlimited number of suppliers for each of the products he wants. He can choose from whom to purchase, but perfect competition also restricts each supplier to offering for sale identical products to those of his competitors and at identical prices. The supplier is constrained in this way because lower-quality products or higher prices will prevent him or her from making any sales; conversely, higher quality goods or lower prices will prevent a normal return on capital from being realized – either way the supplier will go out of business. Under perfect competition it does not matter from which supplier the consumer chooses to buy, the result will be the same in terms of quality and price. Where choice does become important for the consumer is through his ability to choose which products to buy: he can choose to buy, say, either grade one or grade two Cox's apples, and with perfect competition these would be two different products.

Of course, perfect competition, represents an 'ideal' construction – a model with which to compare the real world. Rarely, even with agricultural and other primary products, have markets corresponded to this ideal but this does not undermine the value of the concept in helping us to understand the logic of competition. Traditionally, economists have commenced their analyses with assumptions of perfect competition and then relaxed this assumption as necessary when building models of particular markets. However, one of the difficulties in attempting to generalize about the relationship between the degree of competition, on the one hand, and 'choice' and 'restriction', on the other, is that there is no single dimension along which we can measure degrees of competitiveness. What we can do is specify some typical cases of competition. In many instances of imperfect competition both the choice available to the consumer and the constraints placed on the supplier are different from those under perfect competition. There is often some difference between the products of different suppliers, so that the distinction between the choice available within one market and choice within the market system as a whole becomes blurred. Cadbury's chocolate is not the same as Nestlés. At the same time, where there are a limited number of suppliers, the individual supplier is more able to control the quality of the product or its price to his or her advantage. Where there are a very small number of suppliers, and at the extreme only two, the opportunities for high profits *may* be great. However, this will depend on the relationship between the suppliers. Some duopolies are highly unstable with regular price-cutting wars which diminish profits; others involve a much cosier relation between the supposedly competing firms. With some products, duopolistic competition can stimulate extensive innovations in product design; while with others, duopoly can encourage the firms to be content with retaining their share of the market by producing their current goods. (An interesting example of the former is the market for babies' nappies (diapers) in the United States, which is dominated by two large conglomerates, and in which competition for market share has centred on major improvements in product design.)[1] Again some firms under duopoly offer very different products from those of their competitor so that the consumer has a choice as to what sort of product he wants, but here the constraints on price will be less. (The more distinct the products, of course, the more each resembles a product of a monopoly.) But, in other cases, as with the British detergent industry in the 1950s, the choice facing the consumer may be one between almost identical products which are marketed as being radically different from each other. Indeed, the British soap manufacturers even produced goods which they promoted as competitors to their own very similar products.[2]

What becomes apparent with economic competition is the connection between the provision of choice to the consumer and the restraints placed on the supplier. Under duopoly, for example, the consumer may be faced with genuinely alternative products or by similar ones which the suppliers are seeking to differentiate from each other, but the very availability of this choice is a factor which weakens the restraints on individual suppliers. Under perfect competition, however, the choice a consumer exercises between individual suppliers is a meaningless one for him or her because identical products are being sold at the same price, but the restraint imposed on these suppliers is absolute. In analysing particular markets in an economy, then, we would not separate the 'choice' element from the 'restraint' element. Yet this separation has been a major theme in a number of accounts of political competition. Before we consider whether such a separation is of value, we must first outline an example of this separation in democratic theory.

This example concerns the arguments of Giovanni Sartori. The main thrust of this account of electoral competition is that in the political arena it is not actual competition which is the most important feature but the existence of potential competition. Sartori draws a fundamental distinction in relation to the holding of elections; he distinguishes states where only one party is permitted to contest elections from those states where opposition parties may form. Consequently, for Sartori, the one-party regimes in the USSR and Yugoslavia were not comparable with the one-partyism of Mexico or the southern states of the USA.[3] The choices actually offered in a political 'market' are only a secondary concern for Sartori, and it is the restrictions which potential competition impose which are crucial. As he argues, 'in the arena of politics, the essential protective benefits of a competitive structure stem, primarily, from the principle of "anticipated reactions", from the anticipation that the consumer will or might react.'[4] In other words, in politics monopoly itself can yield the desired restrictions on the behaviour of a monopolist, providing it is not a legally enforced monopoly.

Now an economist would find this sort of account of competition puzzling. After all, monopolies are sustained by barriers to the entry of new suppliers, and while state enforcement of a monopoly is one such barrier, it is only one of a number of factors which can protect a monopoly. Moreover, the point about an absolute monopoly is that there are no possible substitutes for the product, just as there are no alternative suppliers for the product itself. The only choices facing the consumer in deciding what to purchase is whether he can do without the product, or whether he can accept buying less of the product than he would if the price did not include provision for the excess profits of the monopolist. Under absolute monopoly the absence of choice goes hand in hand with the absence of constraint on the suppliers. Once we move away from a situation of absolute monopoly in an economy, more options become available to the purchaser. As we have noted, though, there is not a simple relationship between an increase in the number of competitors and actual choice available to the consumers. Oligopolistic markets vary with regard to the opportunities they actually present to the consumers, because of the varying connections between suppliers. It is for this reason that decisions about the desirable limits of market concentration in particular industries are complex. There is no simple formula which a body like the Monopoly Commission can apply. But the point is that, for such agencies, the undesirable elements of monopoly they seek to control relate both to the absence of restrictions on the suppliers and to the reduced choice for the consumer. It is precisely this link that conservative democrats like Sartori deny; for them it is the availability of a device restricting the behaviour of even a monopoly supplier which is paramount. But if some writers have treated political competition in a different way from economic competition, are they justified in doing so?

Sartori himself recognizes that his analysis of political competition departs from economic analysis and he mentions a number of respects in which competition in the two arenas differs. The problem is that while these differences surely exist, they scarcely justify the emphasis on the role of *potential* competition which is characteristic of Sartori's argument. One of his points is that monopoly control of the state entails a market relationship between buyers and seller.[5] This is true but trivial. In both cases the breaking up of the monopoly will involve action outside the market arena – there are no internal regulatory mechanisms in an economic market which survive to undermine the establishment of monopoly. In both cases recourse to political protest will be necessary. Again, Sartori argues that the economic market is a 'more sensitive' mechanism and the 'economic consumer is in a far better position to appraise his utility and to defend himself'.[6] In making these points Sartori does direct our attention to some obvious differences between markets and elections. Most citizens do not have preferences about policies and objectives for their society, in the way that they have preferences for goods and services they can purchase, because they are so rarely active in the 'political market'. Elections are held infrequently. This means the 'consumer' simply cannot develop the sort of expertise he does in economic markets. Furthermore, because he has so little impact individually in determining whether he gets what he wants in politics, the 'consumer' has little incentive to acquire the information and skills necessary to defend his interests. But these arguments suggest the very opposite conclusion to the one Sartori wishes to draw. Infrequent elections and a 'rationally ignorant' electorate would mean that *potential competition* is likely to be a much weaker threat to the *de facto* monopolist in the political market than in the economic market. 'The mere possibility that another party could arise'[7] is not the weapon Sartori takes it to be, given what he says about those who would have to be instrumental in effecting it. Indeed, the very conditions in which political markets operate suggest that Sartori's distinction between *de jure* monopolistic parties and others is of little importance. Rather, if competition were to be a significant device in restraining parties, it would surely be actual competition that would do so rather than the mere threat of opposition.

Why, then, do we find in theories like those of Sartori an attempt to separate the 'constraint' and 'choice' elements in relation to party competition, and to emphasize the former when explaining the importance of party competition to democracy? Sartori is not a highly eccentric writer – to the contrary he falls very much in a tradition of democratic theorizing which originates with James Mill and Bentham. It is in Mill's work that we can see how the debate about political competition was conducted very differently from arguments about markets. Writing in an era before the rise of mass political parties, Mill's concern was with how representative institutions could provide checks on the activities of government. Therefore, while his 'Essay on Government' is obviously not about parties, the kinds of arguments about representation which were laid out there came to be embraced in many twentieth-century theories, when parties were key actors in elections. For Mill the problem of government was to prevent the abuse of power. This necessitated a body which could check the acts of government, so that the collective interests of citizens were not harmed. This body had to 'have an identity of interest with the community; otherwise it will make a mischievous use of its power'.[8] To ensure that such a representative body did have this identity of interest a much greater electorate was required than the actual British electorate at the time Mill was writing, 1820. In some obvious respects there are parallels between Mill's view of representation through an electoral system and the utilitarian view of the market he defended. In both arenas people are expected to be concerned with *interests* and in both there is a mechanism which enables that concern to be realized. But the differences between political representation and markets are more important; elections are seen by Mill as an essentially defensive mechanism – they are not instruments for determining *what* governments will do but for ensuring that they will *not* do certain things. Here, as with Sartori's arguments, an election is a device affecting the reactions of government – under a representative system a government would not act against the interests of the community because this would trigger opposition from elected representatives. Unlike the market, therefore, elections have been seen by many utilitarians and those influenced by utilitarianism not as instruments for effecting choice but as instruments for constraining government.

One challenge to the orthodoxy that political competition was merely a device for limiting what government could do emerged during the twentieth century following the domination of national elections by political parties. This was the attempt to connect elections to the notion of voter *choice*. There were two sources of this challenge. The first came from social democratic parties which started to put forward, far more formally than had other parties, programmes of legislation and executive action they intended to introduce once in power. In Britain this led to the popularization of the so-called mandate theory of representation. Competition between parties was competition over which programmes would be chosen by the electorate, and which would then be enacted by the winning party. Birch has summarized this theory in terms of four propositions:

1. that mass democracy will give a meaningful influence to the electors only if they are presented with two or more alternative programmes of action between which they can choose, knowing that the party which wins will do its best to put its programme into effect . . .
2. that a party winning a parliamentary majority . . . is not only entitled but obliged to pursue its stated aims, having a mandate from the people to this effect . . .
3. that this will not put too much power into the hands of party managers and leaders if each party is internally democratic . . .
4. that individual MPs are therefore obliged to support their party in Parliament, since they were elected on a party platform . . . [9]

Although Birch argues that this theory, which lies behind the doctrine of responsible party government, is justified by only the left in British politics, it is more correct to argue that all British parties conduct themselves at elections and in office as if they accept mandate theory and the responsible party government model. Indeed, in the period since Birch made this point (1972) the British Conservative party has increasingly acted in conformity with the model. Only with regard to *formal* democratic procedures within the party have they not moved in this direction, and even here it should be pointed out that the Conservative party in the 1980s gives more weight to rank-and-file opinion than hitherto.

A second view that political competition involves *choices* originates in liberal economic theory itself. From the mid-twentieth century onwards both economic and political mechanisms for allocating values came to be seen as alike in being instruments for effecting social choice. On this view economic and political competition are similar devices for translating consumer/citizen preferences into optimal public policies, and in some cases there have been attempts to analyse political competition in terms of economic theory. The most influential early works in popularizing this view of elections were Dahl and Lindblom's *Politics, Economics and Welfare* and Downs' *An Economic Theory of Democracy*, although Arrow's earlier *Social Choice and Individual Values* was a major catalyst in focusing the attention of economists on issues which would draw that discipline closer to the concerns of democratic theory. Within twenty years a new branch of economics – public choice – was fully developed. Writing in 1979, Mueller defined this new topic as follows:

> Public choice can be defined as the economic study of nonmarket decision making, or simply the application of economics to political science. The subject matter of public choice is the same as that of political science; the theory of the state, voting rules, voter behavior, party politics, the bureaucracy, and so on. The methodology of public choice is that of economics, however.[10]

Political competition has been one of the main subjects studied by public-choice theorists, and it was competition between parties that was studied by Downs in the first explicitly economic approach to the study of democracy. For Downs, voters were like consumers and parties were like firms, and as in economic theory he sought to explain both the constraints the political market placed on the suppliers and also the types of choices that would be made available to the consumers.

There is, however, a crucial difference between the 'social democratic' and the 'liberal economic' view of voter choice. The former have tended to see citizens as not necessarily having the information or the opportunities to make frequent decisions in political arenas, so that in many cases they do not really have preferences. Like the non-American who knows nothing about the United States or American football, but is asked whether, say, she prefers to see the Los Angeles Raiders or the Detroit Lions win the Super Bowl, the citizen is not in a position on many issues to express either a preference or indifference. The point about elections and other devices is that, by involving people, they enable citizens to develop preferences and, possibly, to exercise some control over their lives. On the 'liberal economic' view citizens are assumed to already have preferences (or to be indifferent) between any possible alternatives, and the point of political competition is simply to aggregate these preferences so as to create an optimal set of public policies. Consequently, while the 'social democratic' and 'liberal economic' views are alike in rejecting the older tradition that elections merely provide constraints on rulers, they differ radically about the nature of voter choice.

Another challenge to the view that political competition is only a mechanism for constraining government has emanated both from the 'social democratic' view of citizen control and from democratic traditions which emphasize civic orientation. Electoral competition could provide a political education for the citizens, and not just about the immediate choices available to citizens; in competing for votes parties would necessarily be drawing attention to conflicts within society and of alternative means for ameliorating or removing them. Electoral activity, thus, defines and shapes political reality for the citizens. The idea that parties could play this role emerged only during this century and is compatible with, and often linked to, mandate theory. It is an idea which requires there to be parties as electoral intermediaries, because in a world of competition between individual candidates the voter would have little chance of sorting out the multitude of proposals being advanced. Parties would be needed, therefore, so that political reality could not only be identified for the electorate but also simplified for them. The nineteenth-century writers, who had argued for the 'developmental' advantages of political participation, had not seen electoral competition as something which would provide for this. Instead, it was to participation in local government (for John Stuart Mill) or to single-issue groups (for Ostrogorski) that attention had to be given if the public were to receive a political education. By itself, electoral politics did not demand activity on the part of the voter so that its educative value was suspect. Moreover, the experience of electoral competition in America indicated that parties would compete in ways that did not provide such an education. Writing in 1902, Ostrogorski was highly critical, too, of the failure of the extra-parliamentary caucuses in Britain to engage in political education. Instead, he argued, they had developed merely as 'electioneering machines'.[11] The subsequent growth of programmatic parties of the British type in the twentieth century produced a rather different attitude to the potential of political competition as an educative experience. However, exponents of this view often tended to understate it. For example, in the much-debated report of the Committee on Political Parties of the American Political Science Association, the emphasis is placed primarily on the need for clearly defined party programmes, so that the electorate would be more able to effect a choice in voting. But there are passages in this report which suggest that a failure to 'educate' through programmatic politics will leave democracy unprotected from demagogues; for example, 'When there is no clear basis for rating party performance, when party policies cannot be defined in terms of a concrete program, party debate tears itself loose from the facts. Then wild fictions are used to excite the imagination of the public.'[12]

We have argued, then, that competition through elections has been seen as having three possible advantages for a political system: restricting the objectives and policies a government can pursue; allowing the electorate to effect some form of choice as to how they are governed (although there is disagreement as to what choice involves); and providing a political education for the citizenry. In the remaining sections of this chapter we discuss the evidence as to whether competition between parties is able to produce these advantages. Since the subject of the book is parties, we do not consider most other aspects of competitive politics. For example, we do not examine the effects of electoral constraints on the behaviour of individual politicians; a number of important studies utilizing 'ambition theory' have explored the relationships between the career ambitions of elected politicians in America, their behaviour in office and their election strategies.[13] However, there is one important exception to this. Before turning to examine party competition, it is useful to consider briefly how competition might work in the absence of parties. This can best be done by looking at the most comprehensive effort to abolish party politics in a liberal democracy – the introduction of the nonpartisan ballot in the United States.

NONPARTISAN ELECTIONS

Attempts were made in the United States earlier this century to exclude parties as electoral intermediaries. This took the form of removing the names of parties from ballot papers, to create so-called nonpartisan elections. Between about 1900 and 1920 reformers associated with the Progressive movement succeeded in introducing nonpartisan ballots in more than sixty per cent of cities with populations of more than 5,000, and, in addition, elections to two state legislatures (Nebraska and Minnesota) were made nonpartisan. The movement had its main strength in the west and mid-west, so that it is here that the nonpartisan ballot is most commonly found – in California, for example, every city employs such a ballot. Nonpartisanship, of course, was only one of a number of reforms – including primary elections, initiative referendums and recall elections – which were designed to weaken party organizations. It involved direct legislation against parties but, because of the constraints of the American Constitution, reformers could not go so far as to prohibit party *activity* in the legally nonpartisan elections. In fact, the legal status of parties under nonpartisanship was often little different from that of British parties before 1970 – they were merely unable to 'advertize' themselves on ballot forms; in reality, though, nonpartisanship had a far greater effect than this comparison might suggest.

Partisan elections continued to exist alongside nonpartisan ones. Even in Minnesota and Nebraska, contests for the American Congress and, of course, those for the presidency were fought by parties. Not only did party organizations remain in existence but the availability of partisan offices towards the top of the political 'career ladder' inevitably affected attitudes to parties among lesser office-holders. Indeed, because the congressional committee system was organized entirely around party, the ambitious lesser-office holder could never have been either indifferent or hostile to parties. But, if the coexistence of partisan and nonpartisan elections means that we do not have here clear-cut examples of the abolition of parties, neither is it plausible to argue that parties *would* disappear if they were all made illegal. The nineteenth-century ideal of the independent minded representative, who weighs up the arguments and reaches a considered judgement, is a chimera. Studies of appointive judiciaries reveal that it is scarcely applicable there, and the logic of electoral competition provides incentives for those with shared interests to collaborate and organize. Even more than in a developing society, attempts to remove parties completely in advanced industrial societies would be, to use Sartori's expression, a 'fragile' solution.[14] Consequently, the American experience in abolishing parties is perhaps best regarded not as a limited case but rather as major an effort at removing parties as is possible.

The aim of the early twentieth-century reformers was to divorce elections for nonpartisan offices from the influence of parties. In this their success was incomplete. Nearly thirty years ago Adrian produced a typology of nonpartisan elections; he argued that there were five main types of nonpartisan system, ranging from examples like Chicago where party control of these elections was complete, to cities where there was neither party activity nor slates of candidates who campaigned as a 'team'.[15] However, Adrian concluded that extensive activity by parties was rather uncommon and that the most widespread type of system in the larger cities was one in which slates of candidates were supported by various interest groups, but with the party organizations being only sporadically involved in the campaigns. In smaller cities – those with a population of under 5,000 – the reformers seemed to have achieved their aims: the most common system here was one in which neither slates nor parties were active. Since then major changes in American political parties seem to have modified, though not radically transformed, this situation. One of the most important changes was the increasing competitiveness of party politics in the states, a development with origins in the New Deal electoral realignment but which took decades to work through the political system. Because, in particular, Democrats were now active in previously Republican areas, there was a 'spillover' from this activity into increased party involvement in nonpartisan contests in a number of larger cities. This process was incomplete at the time Adrian published his typology. However, within a few years American party organizations, and especially the Democratic organizations, were declining as electoral intermediaries, as the candidate's own organizations became the predominant ones. This meant that where the party organizations had been formally involved in non-partisan elections there was a tendency for this to be replaced by more informal involvement by party activists and by elites associated with politicians who held partisan public offices. In summary, then, partisan involvement may have become more widespread in nonpartisan elections, but the role of party organizations has generally declined. However, the basic typology identified by Adrian remains relevant; nonpartisan elections in America still vary enormously with regard to party input.

In the absence of parties, the electoral mechanism did not work well in constraining elected politicians in America. One of the flaws in a view of democracy which values individual, rather than party, representation is that it assumes that voters will have sufficient information on which to base their decisions. Studies of public opinion and voting behaviour from the 1950s onwards demonstrated that in all liberal democracies this assumption was not valid; voter information about electoral politics was rather limited, for the obvious reason that it only touched upon their lives peripherally. Voters did acquire some information about parties and their programmes, but very few ever acquired knowledge about individual politicians, except in the case of national elections. Not surprisingly, therefore, knowledge about individual candidates in nonpartisan elections has always tended to be very low, and the result has been that the best-known candidates, the incumbents, would usually win. Indeed, the impact of incumbency was so strong in Oakland that a self-perpetuating elite emerged with incumbents resigning in the middle of their terms; they would be replaced by appointees, who would then use the advantages of incumbency to win the next election.[16] Oakland was a city where the Democratic party had been weak until the 1950s, so that there were few partisan influences to offset the effects of incumbency in city elections. Where there was a much greater party presence, as in Milwaukee, there was little difference between the electoral vulnerability of partisan officials and nonpartisan ones.[17] Only when nonpartisan elections were highly partisan in character, therefore, was the electoral mechanism a source of voter control.

If American nonpartisan elections tend to produce officials who are less constrained by electoral competition, then they also produce officials who are more likely to be both Republican and of higher socio-economic status than partisan elections.[18] Nor is this surprising. The absence of party organizations from election campaigns means that candidates themselves have to find funds for campaigning, either from their own resources, by fund-raising, or from interest groups. More conservative candidates, especially those with business connections, have a clear advantage in this respect, as, of course, do those with higher incomes. Whatever its deficiencies, party competition tends to produce public officials who, as a group, more closely resemble the socio-economic profile of the whole population and who are more representative of the views of that population, than does individualistic electoral competition. But the extent of this bias must not be exaggerated: in the Ohio cities surveyed by Rogers and Arman 53 per cent of partisan offices were filled by Democrats as against 39 per cent of nonpartisan offices. The greater bias seemed to be with respect to personal income – while 53 per cent of all nonpartisan officials were in the highest income category (in 1967 more than $15,000), only 19 per cent of partisan officials earned this much.[19] However, the general point stands, nonpartisan politics favours socio-economic elites.

Another significant feature of nonpartisan politics is that the absence of parties in legislative chambers can lead to incoherence in policy-making. Rather than being an asset, the lack of linkage between one legislator and another can produce policy packages which, as a whole, are ill-fitted. Continually shifting coalitions are not necessarily a sign that a decision-making body is composed of intelligent persons exercising their judgements independently on every issue. This problem of nonpartisan systems is observable not just in city councils but also in the Nebraska state legislature. It must be admitted, though, that this has not been the case in all nonpartisan bodies. Studies of the Minnesota legislature, in the period when it was nonpartisan, revealed that the ideological caucuses within it were associated with party organizations in the state. In Nebraska, however, Welch and Carlson concluded that there was relatively little structure in voting in the legislature:

> This suggests not only that party is the most important reference group in structuring legislative behavior but also that in the absence of party, no other kind of reference group serves a similar purpose. Even though strong constituency differences exist . . . constituency is not a strong factor around which voting can be consistently organized.[20]

The authors argue quite plausibly that the lack of consistency in legislative voting combined with the usual levels of voter information about their representatives provides for an unconvincing form of democracy.

In this brief survey of the American experiment in abolishing parties from some levels of politics, two conclusions surely emerge. Legislation against parties does not always remove them, though in many cases it would seem to weaken their influence. Moreover, to the extent party influence is reduced, democracy does not seem to be much enhanced. Whatever the abuses of power practised by parties, and these were extensive in nineteenth-century urban America, nonpartisanship does not represent a major advance in extending citizen control over leaders or over the policy agenda.

ELECTIONS AND THE CONSTRAINTS ON PARTIES
IN GOVERNMENT

In turning to consider how party competition may restrict the activities of parties once they are in government, it is useful to distinguish three rather separate issues. The first is whether the possibility of opposition at some future election prevents governments from pursuing a policy of extreme oppression. To put it crudely, it may be asked whether Hitler's Germany or Stalin's Russia, or some similar regime, is possible when opposition parties are at least permitted to form and to contest elections. The second issue is whether, in general, potential competition leads parties to modify their policies and objectives. Finally, there is the question of whether there is a direct relationship between the degree of competition in a party system and moderation in the policies pursued by parties. We examine each of these issues in turn, but before doing so it is important to recognize several difficulties we face in our discussion. The total number of examples which can be invoked is actually rather small; we are examining 'counterfactuals' – what would have happened if there had (or had not) been potential competition from other parties; in many instances the need to form a coalition government prevents parties from implementing the policies they have 'presented' to their electorates. Moreover, and this is a point we examine later when considering consociational democracy, the knowledge that there will have to be compromise solutions in a governing coalition may encourage parties to offer more extreme policies to their supporters, because this is the best means of securing the support of loyalists, while at the same time the party elite knows that it will never have to deliver on its promises. It is within the limitations posed by these problems that we must now examine the constraints imposed by party competition.

The argument that the most extreme forms of political oppression cannot be practised against groups which have the right to form parties to oppose a ruling party at an election has some merit. The Third Reich and the Soviet Union under Stalin have had no counterparts in regimes where opponents can mobilize for electoral competition. Undoubtedly, the use of terror by the state is more likely to provoke a reaction when opponents can organize and communicate with a wider public; knowledge of this will incline those who control the state to modify their objectives, or to find other means of realizing the objectives. Obviously, in the immediate post-war years the spectre of a repeat of mass oppression led many to believe that, even if it could offer nothing else, liberal democracy at least had the great merit of preventing the excesses of 'totalitarianism'. Yet we must be careful not to overstate the claims which can be made in this context. The terror against which political competition is a barrier is an unusual phenomenon. It has been practised only rarely even in those states where one party has a legal monopoly of power and obviously its practice can better be related to certain historical developments than to the absence of electoral competition *per se*. Again, the potential for competition, or even competition itself, does not prevent regimes from collapsing into forms in which extreme oppression is possible: oppression developed very rapidly in the wake of the collapse of the Weimar Republic in Germany. Thus, while the possibility of competition might be a formal condition for the prevention of mass oppression, it is not necessarily a stable institutional form. Moreover, it is not merely the potential for opposition parties to form that is required, but a franchise embracing those who might be oppressed.

This last point becomes apparent when we consider the case of South Africa. This is a state which has engaged in widespread oppression of its non-white population. Yet, it is also a state in which white opposition parties have not only been allowed to form but have actually formed and actively contested elections. (Indeed, the limited political reforms of the early 1980s have also permitted the formation of parties by non-whites which are able to contest elections that give their interests a small input into the political process.) But this has not been any kind of barrier against state oppression. The Nationalist party has been sustained in power by an electorate that has been highly supportive of its policies towards non-whites and the use of oppression has not led to a fragmentation of that support. To the contrary, the major electoral threat to the Nationalists has come when government policy has sought to modify the policy of apartheid; such moves have prompted splinter parties to form from the right-wing of the Nationalists. The South African example exposes one of the major problems in Joseph Schumpeter's attempt to redefine democracy. For Schumpeter democracy was merely a method for selecting leaders – a method which involved party competition. But in his discussion of eighteenth- and nineteenth-century British politics it is clear that Schumpeter believed it was the existence of a competitive mechanism alone, rather than one which operated with an extensive franchise, that was characteristic of a democracy. Even with a relatively small electorate democracy was possible because of the constraints competition of any kind would impose on those who governed. But, while competition might place some constraints on the activities of government, the South African example suggests that this might not prevent the oppression of those who cannot display opposition through elections.

This leads us to the second issue. Does competition between parties tend to produce a moderating influence on governing parties? There is at least one argument derived from the rational choice approach which suggests that it should. This is the theory of the minimum winning coalition first advanced by William Riker in the early 1960s.[21] Employing some fairly standard assumptions used in rational choice analysis, Riker deduces that there will be a tendency for coalitions which are only just winning coalitions to form; if, for whatever reason, oversized coalitions have come into existence, they will tend to collapse into minimum winning ones. At the heart of Riker's argument is the assumption that coalition members will wish to do as well as possible for themselves and that they do so when their share of the winnings is as large as possible. This argument formalizes a point which has long had currency in political debate: that the losers of elections will try to devise ways of garnering the support of the most marginal members of a winning party's electoral coalition. This kind of argument has some plausibility when the winnings are goods which people want for themselves and are goods which are capable of being distributed on an individual basis. Thus, the distribution of wealth and income is often regarded as the kind of conflict over which effective competition could occur. But what if the voters are more concerned with keeping 'particular groups in their place' within a social stratum or have a particular view of the proper identity of the state which relates it to the dominance of certain values and groups? Here the 'other regarding' aspects of what is wanted or its non-distributory character might form the basis of a permanently entrenched majority. This would be a majority that knew, no matter how much free competition was permitted in the political arena, the majority party would always win. The classic example of this was the Unionist party in Northern Ireland during the years of the Stormont parliament.

Both at the provincial level and in local governments the Protestant majority discriminated against Catholics in a number of areas – such as in the allocation of council houses. While in some cases Unionist majorities were bolstered by gerrymandering and other such practices, the party's majorities were essentially the result of Protestants being the majority group in the province. Parties which attempted to seek support in both communities made few inroads into Unionist territory. The Unionist party was able to govern the province as it wanted to, because its majority was never under threat and because successive British governments chose not to intervene. However, could it be argued that more extensive deprivation would have been imposed upon the Catholics if they had not had at least a 'voice' in electoral politics? A proponent of this view might point to the fact that Catholics were left free to be taught in church schools whence they acquired a distinctly Irish nationalist view of history; surely this would have been eliminated in a non-competitive state. This example is not especially convincing, though. Northern Irish Protestants had what they wanted: they did not have to compete against Catholics for jobs in the Belfast shipyards; and they were advantaged in policy areas like council housing, so that little purpose would have been served by assaults on the practice of Catholicism itself. Indeed, it might have sparked a more activist policy against the province by the government in Dublin. There were constraints on what the Unionist party did, but these were not those of electoral competition but of the limits of toleration in London and Dublin. In fact, the veneer which openly contested elections gave to the Unionist regime arguably made it more difficult for Catholics to present their case effectively before a wider audience.

If the restraints of competition are not always effective in societies divided by non-economic cleavages, then what of the point that competition for the marginal vote does moderate policy where the main conflict is social class? We have suggested that it seems plausible that competition does generally exert a moderating influence. However, the evidence is difficult to interpret because of the rules under which most national elections are contested. In many countries the rules help to produce coalition governments which inevitably depart from the constituent parties' particular policy objectives. But, even when single-party government results, the electoral rules may restrict the competition for votes in which parties must engage. In Chile, for example, we find a radical social policy being pursued by the Allende government between 1970 and 1973. Yet this does not yield a convincing case against the moderating effects of competition because of the circumstances in which Allende was elected president. Chile had a multi-party system in which parties regularly tried to outflank each other and in which 'unholy' alliances were quite possible. Moreover, the rules governing presidential elections meant that Chilean presidents could be elected with a relatively small proportion of the vote – in Allende's case 36.3 per cent.

This leads us to a significant point about the constraining power of electoral competition. Popular advocates of competition often claim that it will discipline political parties into challenging for the 'middle ground'. But this assumes that there is a particular kind of connection between voter preferences and electoral outcomes, one in which all parties can only 'win' by competing for the support of centrist voters. But in a multi-party system there will be no incentive for some parties to do this, because they will merely lose the support of their loyalists while failing to make up these lost votes from those in the centre. (In addition, the centre may be unstable. This is a crucial idea in Sartori's idea of pluralized pluralism. He argued that in Italy there was 'a fluid center crossed by several possible lines of cleavage and consensus. In practice this implies that people who could agree on concrete policies are divided by their ideological or religious affiliation.')[22] In many cases this will mean that the policies pursued are only indirectly influenced by the electorate and thus the main political forum involves bargaining over the formation of a coalition government. However, under some kinds of constitutional arrangements, as in Chile before 1973, outright victory was possible for a party which did not attempt to move towards the centre. We should not conclude, however, that this exposes a peculiarity of party competition not present in economic competition. As was suggested earlier, oligopolistic competition in an economy can produce a variety of relationships between the firms involved, and one of these is the concentration by each firm on its own, specialized, sector of the market. We might conclude, then, that while some constitutional arrangements do enable competition to have a moderating influence on parties, this is not true of other arrangements and, what is more, with certain kinds of social conflict the 'rules of the game' may have little influence in moderating the behaviour of an entrenched majority party.

The difficulty we have had in reaching firm conclusions about the general impact party competition has on the policies and objectives pursued by parties suggests that efforts to resolve the third question we raised at the beginning of this section seem doomed. How can we tell if more competition is associated with greater restraints on parties? In suggesting that we cannot, we must realize not only that differing constitutional arrangements make comparisons problematic, but also that there is a fundamental ambiguity in the idea of competition, at least as it is usually employed in economic or political debate. On the one hand, by competition we sometimes mean situations that in game theory would be described as *strictly competitive* – what one competitor gains, another (or others) must lose. In economics perfect competition is strictly competitive; while in British football the FA Cup competition (a 'knock-out' tournament) is an example. On the other hand, the term 'competition' is also used to refer to situations which are primarily conflictual in character but which also embrace cooperative elements. That is, in relation to politics and economics we often identify situations which have the characteristics of *mixed-motive* games with competition. In oligopoly there are pressures to collude as well as to compete. Equally, in the English Football League there have been occasions when what are normally strictly competitive situations have been transformed into ones where collusion is an optimal strategy.[23] Party competition is normally not strictly competitive; indeed, I have argued elsewhere that, even two-party competition, with its apparent 'knock-out contest' qualities, can involve collusive strategies.[24] Where there is a mix of conflictual and co-operative goals, the introduction of further actors into the situation will affect the existing participants' optimal strategies, but without knowing the existing pattern of relations we cannot determine whether this will generate more competition. One possibility is that an increase in the number of parties may not produce greater competition for votes but may instead make parties more conservative electorally in protecting their loyalist base. In turn, this could generate issue extremism. More competitors may not mean more competition – that is, greater conflict between parties – but may rather produce greater co-operation, in the sense that parties restrict their search for votes to certain sectors of the electorate. While this might yield greater choice for the voter in terms of the range of policy programmes offered, it may also entail weaker constraints on the parties.

As a device for restricting what parties in government can do, therefore, both potential competition and actual competition seem rather blunt instruments. They can work in certain socio-economic conditions and with certain electoral and political structures. This is scarcely surprising. Political scientists have long-known that the structure of social cleavages was a central factor in the viability of liberal democracy and in influencing the type of party system that would develop in particular instances.[25] The failure of British efforts to impose Westminster-style politics on many of their ex-colonies in the 1960s provided a practical demonstration of the limits of party competition in restricting ruling elites. What is more surprising is the survival of the belief that competition actually does have such independent force, and that, therefore, it is useful to distinguish between regimes either in terms of their competitiveness or their potential to throw up competitors to ruling parties. The reason for the survival of this belief seems to lie in the failure of conservative defenders of liberal democracy to find a more adequate basis for its defence, and in the failure of more radical democrats to analyse the logic of the 'electoral connection'. The latter have tended to be more concerned with democracy in industry, or in neighbourhoods, to the exclusion of parties and party competition.

But what of the argument that competition stimulates innovation? Considerable emphasis has been given to this by some economists, but the evidence in relation to oligopolies, the economic form which most closely parallels party competition, is complex. In some industries oligopolistic firms generate considerable product innovation, while in others they are willing to let product design stagnate and to maintain their current share of the market. If competition between parties were to have a similar effect, we would expect that in some party systems the parties are seeking to find new ways of defining divisions within society but in others parties tend more to reflect long-established political cleavages. Now this point becomes important in the next section, when we consider voter choice, because we argue that parties can, and do, help to determine the political agenda in a state. But that they have this power does not mean that they use it – some parties may find the cosy relationship between themselves is preferable to the risks of attempting to radically redefine the political universe. It has been argued, for example, of the British parties that cleavage alignments which became fixed in the 1920s remained so until the 1970s because it suited the two major parties not to attempt to 'innovate'. As in the economy, if competition does encourage innovation among parties, it does not do so uniformly.

PARTY COMPETITION AND VOTER CHOICE

When we turn to consider whether competition between parties does indeed generate choices for the electorate, there are three rather separate sets of issues which it is necessary to examine. The first is whether, leaving aside problems of voting cycles and so on, party competition does serve to connect voters with what a government is likely to do subsequently. The second issue is whether the choices offered directly reflect the structure of conflicts within a society, or whether political institutions themselves lead to certain choices being filtered out of the electoral arena. The third issue is whether what the electorate does in casting votes amounts to exercising a choice at all. These issues are the subject of this section. They form the basis for a discussion, in chapter 7, of the connection between voter preferences and government policy – the debate which is popularly known as the 'Does Politics Matter?' debate.

CONNECTING VOTES AND OUTCOMES

Even if we accept, for the moment, that parties do offer alternative sets of public policies to the electorate and that the voters make decisions between parties on this basis, the connections between alternatives offered and policies implemented is still an indirect one when compared to the similar relations in most economic markets. On the one hand, policy programmes are collective goods so that voter C can only get what he wants if a sufficient number of other voters go along with him. Of course, some collective goods are provided through economic markets, though they are a less common phenomenon there than non-collective goods. On the other hand, in some circumstances the outcome could be one which no one voted for or, perhaps, would find acceptable. This could occur when coalition governments have to be formed after an election, and when the composition of the government and its policy priorities are dependent on the election results themselves. This has no counterpart in the economic market – the failure to realize a collective good there does not entail the provision of some other collective good for which no demand has been displayed. Obviously, not all coalition government is of this type. In Ireland and West Germany, for example, there is agreement between two of the parties in advance of an election that they will form a coalition government should they secure an electoral majority between them; in these cases the electorate can be said to know the choice they are faced with, even though more than one party controls government. But in cases where the composition and policies of a government depend on post-election negotiations it is arguable that the choices facing voters are not 'real' ones, because none of the programmes offered by the parties can be implemented intact.

If, then, we took as a test of voters' ability to exercise a choice in voting that elections must normally bring to power either single parties or parties which have contested the election as a 'team', how many liberal democracies do provide for voter choice? One of the problems in answering this apparently simple question is knowing how to deal with the newly democratized regimes (such as Spain or Portugal) and the many small, island democracies created from British colonies in the last twenty or so years. I propose to ignore these 'difficult cases' and to take only the established liberal democracies – for example, the twenty-five regimes identified by Sartori in his analysis of party fractionalization.[26] Of these twenty-five, four can be omitted immediately because they no longer exist as liberal democracies (Chile, Uruguay, Turkey and the French Fourth Republic). Of the remainder, two others (Japan and India, at least at the national level of politics) might be omitted for our purpose because the dominance of one party in the system is so institutionalized that it is arguable that voters there are unable to exercise an effective choice. Among the other nineteen regimes in only about half do we find a *possible* connection between what is offered to the voter at an election and what he will receive from a government. These cases are Ireland, West Germany, France, Norway, Sweden, Australia, Austria, New Zealand and the United Kingdom. Canada represents a marginal case because in six of the last fourteen general elections there a minority government has been returned to power which has been dependent on the support of minor parties. It is important to emphasize that we are talking only about 'a possible connection' because it may be that the parties do not really have programmes or that their major issue concerns, or the major interests supporting them, are similar. Certainly, in the case of Ireland it has been argued that party politics since independence in 1922 has been dominated by non-programmatic parties with widely overlapping electoral bases. Of the other nine regimes, two (the United States and Switzerland) do not yield voter choice. In the United States this is because of the separation of powers – between 1952 and 1988 American presidents found themselves facing opposition party majorities in a least one of the two chambers for twenty-two of these thirty-six years. In Switzerland elections have no impact on government formation; since the early 1940s (with the exception of a few years in the 1950s) Switzerland has been governed by a coalition of four parties, which have constituted more than a minimum winning coalition and which have demonstrated virtually no interest in competing with each other. In the remaining instances, with the partial exception of Finland, we find multi-partism where post-election bargaining is usual (Italy, Netherlands, Israel, Denmark,

Iceland, Luxembourg and Belgium). (The Finnish case is unusual in that the president acts more like a French president; he invites a party leader to negotiate to form a government, but, because of the nature of the country's relations with the Soviet Union, negotiations with the Conservatives, for example, were usually not possible.) Consequently, if emphasis is to be given to the choices which party competition supposedly throws up, then we must recognize that in many competitive regimes the electorates do not have choices in the same way that they have choices in economic markets.

However, this is not quite the end of the matter. Even in those countries where the link between party programmes and government output is indirect, the interaction between the parties is not so irrational or opportunistic that the electorate could have little idea of what might happen afterwards. Increases in support for particular parties usually do increase their claims to inclusion in government and to greater weight being given to their programmes. The practices of the Swiss parties, the total exclusion of the Communists from government in Italy since 1947, or the great power exercised by the small religious parties in Israel, are not typical of the connection between voters and policy results in most multi-party systems. The extreme form of detachment between electoral activity and elite response, as found in the French Fourth Republic, is comparatively rare. Rather than seeing liberal democratic regimes as divided between those where the voter can exercise choice and those where he or she cannot, it is more useful to see the availability of choice in terms of a continuum: at one end of this would be a state like New Zealand with two programmatic parties, one of which always assumes office and attempts to implement its programme; and at the other end would be a regime like the Fourth Republic.

DO POLITICAL INSTITUTIONS DETERMINE VOTER CHOICE?

However, if the power of the voter to choose varies from one regime to another, then we must surely ask how the choices presented to voters are determined. It is here that we encounter one of the great debates in political science: between those who argue that the parties found in a political system reflect directly the social base in which they operate, and those who claim that institutional structures can lead to the 'filtering out' of both the parties and the interests they represent. Perhaps the most famous arguments connected with the latter position have concerned the differential effects of various kinds of voting system. In its crudest form this was the claim that proportional representation produced multi-party systems, while two-partism was the result of using majoritarian or plurality systems. In this chapter we do not have space to devote to examining this or many of the other arguments which have been much discussed in the 'sociology' versus 'institutions' debate. What we can do is outline some of the key issues in that debate, at least as they bear on the question of whether party competition can filter some issues, values and objectives out of politics.

Just as parties were the subject of the first books of political science at the beginning of this century, so they were at the centre of the sociological revolution in political science in the 1950s. Samuel Eldersveld, James Q. Wilson and others were, perhaps, the counterparts of Ostrogorski and Michels.[27] By the mid-1960s a number of important and subtle models of the relationship between social structure and parties had emerged. Perhaps the most important of these was that of Lipset and Rokkan. They related party systems to the historical development of four lines of social cleavage: centre–periphery; state–church; land–industry; and owner–worker. The cleavages which had emerged, the time of their emergence in relation to each other, and the ways in which these conflicts were resolved were the main influences on contemporary party systems.[28] In focusing attention on social strata and on historical development, such analyses helped to weaken further the legalistic and institutional tradition in political science. The importance of this for democratic theory was two-fold: In a sense, it helped to undermine the argument that voting was akin to choice, because it involved the continuing struggles for supremacy by different social groups. Yet, if the voter was not a conscious decision-maker, of the type advocated by John Stuart Mill, he or she was at least not at the mercy of institutions that could filter issues out of party politics.

In these 'sociological' analyses electoral institutions could modify but not fundamentally change the character of party systems. The challenge to the 'sociological approach' did not come from those who wished to revive the narrow debates about the impact of electoral laws, but from a new generation of sociologically informed political scientists who sought to demonstrate that political structures themselves determined parties' relations with their electorates. There were a number of influences on the 'new institutionalists', but one who was especially important was E. E. Schattschneider. The leading proponent of responsible party models in the United States, Schattschneider in his later work came to examine the process of conflict formation. He did not accept the claim that political elites merely responded to conflicts in society. Rather elites determined which conflicts came onto the political agenda, and a key element in party strategy was deciding whether to displace existing cleavages from that agenda. As Schattschneider argued:

> To understand the nature of party conflict it is necessary to consider *the function of the cleavages exploited by the parties in their struggle for supremacy.* Since the development of cleavages is a prime instrument of power, the party which is able to make its definition of the issues prevail is likely to take over the government.[29]

The more immediate impact of Schattschneider's analysis, on its publication in 1960, was not on the study of parties but on the then growing debates about the nature of power and about its distribution in American communities. His ideas about the 'mobilization of bias', of course, were taken up by Bachrach and Baratz in their development of the idea of a 'second face of power', and in turn they were influential in the development of Crenson's ideas about how elites can control a political agenda.[30] However, while part of Crenson's account of agenda control in relation to air pollution does involve an explanation of the role of different kinds of party organization found in the cities he studies, his is not primarily an analysis of parties. The influence of Schattschneider's framework on the study of parties is more directly seen in the work of Walter Dean Burnham. Burnham followed Schattschneider in analysing the dynamics of American electoral realignment and of the role played by elites in bringing this about.[31]

Another influential 'new institutionalist' analysis of parties has been expounded by Martin Shefter.[32] Shefter has demonstrated the interaction between structures of the state and the methods used by political parties to obtain electoral support. Both the state and parties influence what is presented to an electorate. As Theda Skocpol, herself a 'new institutionalist', says of Shefter:

> Unlike many students of voting and political parties, Shefter does not see parties merely as vehicles for expressing societal political preferences. He realizes that they are also organizations for claiming and using state authority, organizations that develop their own interests and persistent styles of work. Lines of determination run as much (or more) from state structures to party organizations to the content of electoral politics as they run from voter preferences to party platforms to state policies.[33]

This general theme, that political institutions are major determinants of how parties compete in electoral markets, is one which
I have also attempted to develop in *The Logic of Party
Democracy*.[34] The main thrust of the argument outlined there was
that because they were oligopolists, parties had a degree of
autonomy that was not possible under perfect competition and
that, consequently, parties were often misunderstood because an
analogy with perfect competition is usually employed in relation to
them.

For our purposes, the importance of 'new institutionalist' arguments is that they pose a greater threat than the 'sociological
approaches' to the claim that party competition necessarily provides
voters with choices, or at least choices that are worth having. The
particular institutional frameworks within which a party operates
determine what sort of choices are made available. For Schattschneider, for example, party competition could only work properly
with highly integrated parties – for him, the loose party structures of
the kind found in the United States prevented the parties from developing programmes, and without such programmes there could not
be effective voter choice. Similarly, Shefter has provided an account
of why patronage-based parties, which were not especially programmatic, emerged in the United States and Italy though, of course, in
many respects his analysis is very different from Schattschneider's;
but the impact of this kind of analysis is also different from
Schattschneider's. Analyses such as these enable us to explain the
dynamics of elite control of policy agendas. With them, for
example, we can begin to account for the consensual approach
adopted by the British parties towards Northern Ireland, nuclear
defence between 1962 and 1979, and (to some degree) race relations
during the 1960s and 1970s. But in doing so are they also serving to
undermine the claim that elections involve 'real' choices offered to
and made by voters?

The answer to this is that 'institutionalist' arguments clearly do
pose further problems for those influenced by liberal economics
who see electoral competition as a mechanism for aggregating preferences optimally. It is also evident that, where state structures
and party structures can restrict the scope of competition extensively, voter control can be rather narrow in scope. But few, if
any, of the 'institutionalists' have ever supposed that institutional
structures determined absolutely the nature of policy agendas, or
that they always acted as collusive oligopolists. It leaves open the
possibility that voters *could* be choosers between significant
alternatives, whilst recognizing that there may be considerable

variation between states in the ability of institutions to structure policy agendas.

DO VOTERS REALLY CHOOSE?

The third issue we posited at the beginning of this section, whether the actions of mass electorates do amount to the exercising of choice, takes us again to another major debate about parties. In this case it was one which was especially prominent in the 1960s. On the one side were those who argued that, since their advent in the 1950s, voting studies had demonstrated that, whatever else they were doing in casting votes, voters in liberal democracies were *not* making choices.[35] On the other side were those who argued that this cynical conclusion about mass electorates was only possible if overly stringent conditions were introduced when defining choice. The first group could marshall several arguments in support of their claim. One point was that elections were contested by parties offering *packages* of policies to voters, and the only common bond to these policies was that they could be derived from a particular ideology. If voters were generally ideological, then they could be said to be choosing between packages to which they could give a rank ordering. But if voters were not ideological, then they might be faced with packages that contained some policies they wanted and some they did not. The sort of package they wanted might simply not be available and, if it was not, voters could be faced with having to decide whether they felt more concerned about one issue than another; this exercise might tax even the most diligent of citizens. And, in fact, surveys of voters showed that most, and especially those in the United States, were only weakly ideological. A further argument was that most voters were ill-informed about politics – they did not conform to the ideal of the voter in democratic theory; their knowledge of the politicians and policies associated with particular parties was low. Again, surveys confirmed these findings. Moreover, support for parties was so deeply ingrained in most voters that only a few ever reported changing their vote from one party to another, and indeed one British survey reported that sixty-nine per cent of voters could not even think of anything which would make them think of voting differently.[36]

Opponents of this view challenged the conclusion that these arguments demonstrated that voters were not choosers. Studies such as V. O. Key's demonstrated that, irrespective of the knowledge that American voters could articulate about politics, when they did switch their vote from one party to another this was compatible in most cases with their views on issues or politicians. Thus, even the relatively uninformed voter was not usually an irrational voter.[37] It could also be shown that the problem of 'packages' under party competition was little different from the problem faced by consumers in economic markets where products are complex. It is not just a voter who might find that the package (of policies) he or she really wants is not offered by any supplier. With complex goods and, more especially services, the particular combination of qualities desired may not be available. The purchaser of a car may also have to decide whether, say, braking power or acceleration are the more important concern for him or her when different models vary with respect to these qualities, and he or she cannot obtain the precise product he or she wants. Yet the problems involved in making an informed decision about cars does not mean that choice cannot be exercised. That a particular product or party has highly loyal purchasers or supporters does not mean that these individuals are not really *choosing* it. My own preference for Mars Bars over Twix is almost as strong as my loyalty to a particular political party and in both instances my preferences have very complex causes; but that there are such causes, and that my preferences are strong ones, does not invalidate the claim that in the sweet shop and in the polling booth I am making a choice.[38] This is not to deny that there may be other functions performed both by the market and elections but such functions would not undermine a choice function.

On balance, the evidence of those who have asserted that in some sense voters choose seems more compelling. Even by the mid-1970s there was evidence that the particularly low levels of voter awareness found in the studies of the 1950s and early 1960s in the United States was more a reflection of the relatively apolitical environment of the time.[39] Moreover, since the 1960s the weakening ties of voters to parties in most liberal democracies has made competition for votes that much more difficult and has made parties even more aware of the different ways in which they could attract voters. The need to compete for the marginal vote was always a factor weighing in party strategies but now there are many more marginal voters. This point brings us to a consideration examined more fully in the next section: what is contained in the choices offered to voters? The mix between personality and issues characteristic of modern election campaigns prompts the question of whether competition between personalities represents a choice, or rather a 'real choice', for voters. Taken to an extreme, the cult of the leader, as for example it is manifested in Jamaican parties, does seem to detract from the democratic character of the electoral process.[40] But on the other hand, leadership style is inevitably intertwined with the presentation of issues to mass electorates, so that an emphasis on leadership qualities is not necessarily incompatible with choice over matters that are connected to the resolution of conflict within societies. However, since this link between personalities and issues is central to the educative effects of party competition, it is to this that we now turn.

PARTY COMPETITION AND POLITICAL EDUCATION

Political competition can be seen as a device creating a citizenry that is more oriented towards shared objectives than special individual or group interests. By focusing on shared interests, parties will develop a more public-oriented citizenry. However, for the most part a concern with the educative effects of competition has not come so much from those democratic writers who have given prominence to civic orientation, but more from those who have given greater priority to the idea of voters choosing between party programmes. If parties did not discuss political issues or policies at all, then it is difficult to see how any kind of education could emanate from competitive elections. Thus, one point to consider is whether parties could contest elections without raising matters connected to public policies. Of the major democratic theorists, Schumpeter comes closest to advocating this position: competition is needed solely to provide a means of restraining politicians and the cornerstone of parties is the organizational structures which provide electoral machinery, while platforms and ideologies are merely means of attracting voters. The need for platforms seems more related to what voters expect than to some essential characteristic of competition for public office itself. But even he appears to stop short of claiming that competition over platforms and issues could actually be abandoned and replaced by competition over which leader or set of leaders was most competent to govern. Indeed, it is difficult to see how voting on competence could not but involve substantive policy disagreements. The other possibility would be that policy discussion could be replaced by campaigning wholly based on the personal qualities of leaders. The widespread use of television campaigning in the 1960s fuelled such fears, but once again it is difficult to see how campaigns totally devoid of political issues could be conducted. If we examine those accounts of elections where charges have been made about the low level of political content, such as in the 1974 gubernatorial campaign in California,[41] or if we look at serious attempts to parody the growth of issueless politics, as in the film *The Candidate*, it is not an arena without issues which we find. Rather, the problems are those of issue ambiguity, of candidates manipulating the media and of personality politics marginalizing issues rather than removing them completely from the political arena.

However, if this suggests that those who reject the claim that elections can provide for mass political education need to construct their case carefully, it also provides little comfort to its proponents. That debate over policies is at least in the background of all campaigning in liberal democracies does not show that it is educative. This is why the argument that it can and should be educative is usually linked to the idea that parties should be 'responsible', in terms of presenting clear and simplified accounts of conflicts within the polity and of the most appropriate means of resolving them. Conflicting messages, ambiguous stances and the obliteration of particular issues by transforming them into some other issue are all ways in which parties can create 'white noise', which can both distort immediate electoral choice and fail to contribute to the longer term political education of the electorate.[42] This brings us to an important point. For proponents of the educative role of party competition it is the longer term considerations which matter; clear alternatives and clearly focused debate are essential for voter choice, but they also promote public understanding of the nature of the political universe voters inhabit. Most nineteenth-century writers were dissatisfied with the achievements of parties in this regard. But it could be argued that there were two developments, one in the late nineteenth century and one in the mid-twentieth century, which might have been expected to provide for a greater educative role – the mass membership party and television.

The mass membership party was one in which members had some form of control over leaders, and there were two reasons for supposing that this might promote political education through party competition. The issue-orientation of members would act as a constraint on leaders who might otherwise neglect disputes in favour of competition over leadership qualities. Moreover, members, unlike the patronage appointees of political machines, would themselves be more interested in 'educating' the electorate in periods between elections. There are grounds for arguing that in the early years of this century mass membership parties did play such a role. Despite Michels' account of oligarchy in the German

SPD at the beginning of the twentieth century, it was not for fifty or sixty years that this party and other social democratic parties became overtly catch-all parties. The parties also had large memberships and in some cases penetrated their communities quite deeply. Nor were the socialist parties always the most successful – Pugh, for example, has shown how the Primrose Leagues attached to the British Conservative party had both large memberships and provided a highly formalized political education for their memberships. [43] Their activities far surpassed those of the formal constituency Conservative parties. Again, mass membership parties did not attempt to restrict the electorate and to limit party competition in the ways that the American parties had after the mid-1890s in their attempts to preserve newly created local political monopolies. [44] But this was not a long-term solution to the problem of how to ensure parties could provide political education for the masses. On the one hand, the search for power did lead many socialist parties to become 'catch-all' parties – the classic example is the German SPD which after 1959 abandoned even its claim to be a socialist party. The problem with this was not that the socialists were trying to expand their electoral coalitions but that the forces of the electoral market seemed to be pushing parties towards the obscuring of political issues. On the other hand, as we see later, changing social conditions meant that the parties could no longer provide organizations and activities which could attract large numbers of activists. Without activists the link between the parties as educators in elections and as educators between elections would be broken. In turn, this would weaken the impact of the former.

At first glance television too might seem to have had the potential for allowing elections to effect political education – after all, information could be acquired through the passive act of watching, rather than involving the costs of going to speeches and meetings, and the concentration involved in reading newspapers or magazines. But it has not always worked out this way. What evidence there is suggests that levels of political information are not noticeably higher because of television, nor are public views on issues or political problems markedly clearer. Indeed, television has had two effects on relations between party leaders and voters which, if anything, have increased the 'white noise' which the latter experience in relation to politics. Television tends to emphasize campaign *events* rather than issues in its coverage of news. In the United States in 1976, for example, 63 per cent of television's coverage of events and issues was devoted to campaign events, while only 51 per cent of newspaper coverage was devoted to this. [45] The mounting of events and controlling them in ways which maximize favourable television coverage, has become one of the hallmarks of modern campaigning. Television has also accentuated the role of leaders' personal characteristics in campaigning at the expense of issues. However, we must be careful not to exaggerate the extent of this development, nor to make the age before television appear too much of a 'golden age' of party politics. Personality did matter then, and Gladstone, for example, was as much selling himself on the hustings as he was attempting to promote political debate. Nevertheless, television has not only altered the sorts of personal characteristics required of party leaders, but it has also enabled personality to intrude far more. Obviously, this is most pronounced in the presidential systems of France or the United States, but even in Norway with its tradition of serious political debate about issues the requirements of television campaigning seem to have affected the selection of party leaders.[46]

We must be careful, too, not to underestimate the considerable variations between countries in relation to the effects of television on the potential for political education. There are significant differences in elite attitudes to television. Generally in Scandinavia it is still regarded as an educational rather than an entertainment medium, so that there are pressures to resist American trends in its use in campaigning. Again, state regulation of party access to television varies. In the United States both parties and individual candidates can advertise, and this has tended to weaken parties as vehicles for popularizing coherent platforms. But the free market in political advertising is comparatively rare. In Britain, the formal 'party political broadcast' is a major device while in Germany and Norway formal 'grand debates' are often the centre-pieces of television campaigning. None of these devices, however, are likely to enthral mass audiences, and indeed the main weakness of television campaigning is not so much that it drives issues out of political debate, but that the parties (even in America) lack the kind of access to television that would enable them to develop appropriate mixes of entertainment and information which could be educative. Parties cannot run their own entertainment programmes on prime-time television, for example. Indeed the price of effective political education by parties might be a far higher penetration of television by parties than would otherwise be thought desirable.

Within the present, restricted, access to television now available to parties, there are still enormous variations in its educative impact. Despite the large number of elections and the widespread use of political advertising, voter information about parties and candidates in the United States remains very low. Graber reports that in 1976 43 per cent of those surveyed in a poll could comment on the strengths and weaknesses of only one candidate.[47] In America television helps to accentuate the decentralization of the parties so that it is difficult for the citizen to pick out themes and issues which can help to re-form and shape his own political judgements. In states with more centralized parties this problem of the intensity of the 'white noise' competitive politics generates is that much less.

Thus far we have considered the potential for activities connected with electoral competition as educative devices. But there is another argument to consider: that electoral competition, far from educating the electorate, serves to inflame demands and expectations in the electorate that can never be met. This line of argument has been developed by Brittan. In essence his point is that competition between parties leads them to make more and more unrealistic promises about what government can achieve; an electorate incapable of seeing through these illusions correspondingly comes to demand, and to expect, more of government; hence what Brittan describes as too much 'back-seat driving'[48] occurs with political leaders being 'pushed' by the demands of organized groups and by the electorate more generally. This model of party competition seemed to fit well with the experience of electoral competition in England between 1950 and 1975, with parties regularly being voted out of office and with opposition parties claiming to be able to meet a wide range of objectives that present governments were alleged to have failed to pursue or to meet. There is clearly something to this argument because, unlike economic competitors, opposition parties have no 'product' (except their previous periods in office) against which promises for the future can be evaluated. While there are some limits as to the promises parties can make to the electorate without appearing to be rogues, these limits are not severe restrictions on them. However, there are two problems with the model. Competitive 'outbidding' by parties in the 1950s, 1960s, and 1970s has been replaced by a rather different style of electoral politics, at least in Britain. Electorates seem more sceptical about the sorts of claim made earlier and parties make more cautious assertions about the ability of governments to provide decisive solutions. Brittan also saw elites within parties as being pushed by party and other structures into attempting and promising too much. A conservative democrat, he did not see that under some conditions party structures could be a device for constraining party leaders from engaging in the politics of 'outbidding'. In other words, to use his analogy, some back seat drivers might encourage use of the brake rather than the accelerator.

Very often party organizations are seen as groups of activists whose issue extremism leads them to demand policies that leaders do not wish to be saddled with in the electoral market. That is, they are regarded as another source of pressure on leaders, and for a writer like Brittan, who took an avowedly Schumpeterian view of parties, it is not surprising that party structures did not figure as a possible source of restraint on leaders. Yet the kind of out-bidding which worried Brittan, of responding to inconsistent demands and expectations, is precisely the kind of behaviour advocates of party programmes have sought to limit. Indeed the argument is made that internally democratic, programmatic parties would limit it in two ways. The programme itself would constrain the leaders in terms of how they choose to fight elections. But pro-grammes and elections fought on programmes, would help to reduce the excessive expectations of voters, because of the need for internal consistency in programmes. It is the weakening of pro-grammatic parties which produces inconsistent promises to the electorate. Yet, if this is the basis for a case against the Brittan model, it would require a detailed analysis of the kinds of party structures which might provide this checking mechanism on party leaders. Certainly, in the period covered by Brittan's study, British political parties could not have played this role and, arguably, they accentuated the problem of group pressure on government.

We have seen, then, that a case can be made out for party com-petition having an educative function. But one of the major problems for those who would have parties perform this function is that of constructing arrangements both within parties, and between parties and voters, that will enable such education to develop. For all the advances in information technology this century and despite the great increases in formal education, levels of conceptualization about politics and about socio-economic conflicts remain relatively low. While the educative effects of party competition may be desirable and possible, they have not been realized yet.

CONCLUDING REMARKS

We began this chapter by considering the idea of competition and examining how restraint and choice were linked in theories of economic competition. We then examined how, in political com-petition, restraint might be exercised on parties and whether party competition involves choice by the voters. Finally, we turned to examine whether in the political market competition could have an educative function. What has emerged is that the simplified view of political competition, expounded in the writings of Schumpeter and others, of competition having a definite restraining function but not being a mechanism for effecting choice or political education, is ill-founded. Neither potential competition nor actual competition seems to constrain parties as much as most conservative democrats would have us believe. On the other hand, while the question of whether voters exercised choice in the electoral market was a complex one, our analysis has not forced us to conclude that voter choice is impossible. A similar conclusion was reached in connection with the educative effects of party competition. But in regard to both 'choice' and 'education' the nature of intra-party relations seemed to be significant in determining whether parties could provide these objectives. Before we can turn to examine intra-party relations, though, we must examine the nature of parties in liberal democracies and their relation to other kinds of organization.

4

PUBLIC AND PRIVATE DIMENSIONS OF PARTIES

For reasons discussed in chapter 2, the primary focus of this book is parties in liberal democracies. In this chapter we are concerned with the issue of what kinds of institution parties in liberal democracies are. We shall see that parties are both private and public institutions; this is a feature they share with many other organizations. What is unusual about them, though, is the particular mix of 'public' and 'private' they exhibit. To understand this point we must first distinguish four different dimensions of the 'public–private' dichotomy.

THE PUBLIC–PRIVATE DICHOTOMY

Control Some organizations are controlled by, or are responsible to, the state; in others, control or responsibility rests with private individuals or with other private organizations. One element of control is legal status. Some bodies are legally part of the state, or are owned by the state. The American Department of Justice and British Coal (formerly the National Coal Board) are examples here. Equally, there can be little doubt that General Motors or the British charity Shelter have the legal status of private organizations. However, while legal status is important in any account of who (or what) controls an organization, it is only one element in this. Some organizations which are unambiguously public, in that they are part of the state, may actually be far more responsive to certain private bodies than to other state institutions. One of the criticisms of some of the federal regulatory agencies in the United States has been that too often they have been overly responsive to the interests they are supposed to regulate. Again, some organizations which are legally private may receive a great deal of direction from state agencies. This can be because they are heavily dependent on resources supplied by the state or because there is little scope for independent action in their co-operation with state agencies. British universities are legally charities, and hence private bodies, but since the early 1960s they have been subjected to increasing government direction in a variety of areas. There are also a number of types of organization which do not fit easily into the public–private dichotomy. At the end of the 1970s there was a major debate in British politics about the proliferation of Quangos (Quasi Unofficial Nongovernmental Organizations), although the term itself tended to be used rather broadly so that it came to include bodies that were not really hybrids between public and private organizations.[1] Further complications have been introduced by government regulation of organizations. In some cases government regulation of the way an organization conducts its affairs may be sufficiently extensive that its legal status is only a partial guide to whether it can be considered 'private' or not. For example, in some countries so-called public utilities (such as water, gas and electricity) are supplied by private companies, but the pricing policies, relations with customers and safety standards are all controlled by the state or state agencies. In sum, while there certainly are organizations which could be described as highly private, or public, in character, there are many instances ranging from genuine hybrids to largely private (or public) bodies where control is at least partially shared.

Resources A second dimension involves the origin of the resources which organizations acquire. While financial resources are the most important in many cases, some organizations rely heavily on labour or more specific resources. For some the state is the principal, or the only, supplier, while for others resources come mainly from private individuals or organizations through, for example, gifts or sales of products. Of course, bodies which are private under law and which may also be relatively free of government influence or direction, may still receive a large proportion of their resources from the state. Conversely, some government agencies may be heavily dependent on sales or on voluntary labour. In the former category we find many kinds of 'voluntary' organizations; as various studies in the United States have shown, there has been an increasing reliance by non-profit suppliers of social services on sales to government and on government grants.[2] On the other hand, while it is true that departments of central government do not usually obtain much income from sales to private persons or organizations, there are many kinds of government bodies which do. To take one small example. In Britain polytechnics are most assuredly part of the public sector of education, being institutions which are the responsibility of local authorities, but they are now being encouraged by central government to earn more income from contracts for research and innovation from industry. A better known example is the recent trend in many American state universities to have extensive fund-raising of the kind traditionally practised by private universities.[3] They are using their reputations and their 'pull' with alumni to general donations from individuals and corporations. Certainly in the United States there seems to have been a growth in the size of the 'private sector' which is funded heavily by governments and of governmental bodies which raise income from sources other than taxes. A full account of why this should be occurring cannot be attempted here, but one of the more interesting explanations of the former is that governments find it cheaper to have non-state agencies to supply certain services than to provide it themselves.[4] In the social services labour costs may be expected to be lower because non-governmental employees are less likely to be unionized and because many of these agencies also rely heavily on volunteer workers.

The first two dimensions of the public–private dichotomy we have discussed have involved identifying 'public' with the state and contrasting this with that which is non-state. The third and fourth dimensions have a very different focus. Here the contrast is between that which is private and wider ranging persons or considerations. The connexion between these two sets of dimensions is that in liberal (but not libertarian) political theory the state has usually been accorded a central role in protecting or advancing these broader interests. Of course, this is not to suggest that all, or even most, liberal theories have advocated an interventionist role for the state; in the pluralist theory of the American David Truman, for example, the state is really a mechanism for balancing interests – both private and wider ranging ones.[5] But even here, in protecting the 'rules of the political game', it is the state which is the lynchpin in preserving the environment in which interests can be mediated.

Objectives Once again the initial distinction between private and public seems relatively straightforward: there are organizations, such as businesses, which are engaged in the promotion of the private interests of their owners or members, while there are other organizations, such as many charities or state agencies, which aim to promote the interests of others or of very general interests in society. Whereas General Motors aims to make profits for is shareholders, Oxfam is not engaged in making money or otherwise advancing the interests of its trustees, employees or donors, but rather seeks to prevent famine and to ameliorate its effects among others. Yet, as with the other two dimensions, there are many examples of organizations where the goals have become mixed – either formally, in the way that the organization defines its objectives, or informally because of the concerns of those who control it. For example, even though we should disregard comparatively recent attempts by firms to link their retailing efforts to charitable causes (by offering to donate money to a particular charity for each item of a product sold), there are instances of for-profit enterprises having other-regarding objectives. Law firms which provide services for the poor are usually run by individuals who have to earn a living by practising law, but equally have social objectives which means that they are prepared to subsidize legal work for certain kinds of clients. On the other side some charities have been captured by private interests and government agencies which provide as much a service to particular interests as they do to the wider public. In the eighteenth century many English public schools were transformed from their original purposes as providers of education for the poor to being largely fee-paying institutions for the middle classes; in the post-war years the British Milk Marketing Board is an example of a government agency involved in promoting both public and private interests.

Externalities Some organizations internalize all the costs and benefits they generate – other persons or organizations who are not directly connected with the activities do not share in any of the benefits or disbenefits produced. In British towns there are often many shoe shops, all of which sell very similar shoes; the opening up and operating of an additional one will, in most cases, have little impact on the trade done by other stores, on the goods made available to customers in that town, and have little effect on persons other than those who choose to buy there and those who own it. In contrast to this, there are bodies which provide either benefits or costs to people who are not part of the direct operations and in some cases these benefits and costs may be very large – both in relation to the scale of the operation itself and in comparison with wider social benefits or costs. The cost of industrial waste is usually externalized; a wider public than the firm itself, or its customers, suffers the disbenefits of smog, or whatever. Equally, in helping to preserve open countryside in Britain, the National Trust provides benefits shared by far more people than the million or so members of the Trust. Now two of the central arguments in liberal democratic theory have concerned the extent to which the state should be involved in ensuring that costs are internalized by persons and organizations, and the role of the state in fostering 'public-regardingness'. On the one side this has spawned debate about the mechanisms appropriate for regulating the externalization of costs, and on the other it has produced arguments about the virtues of voluntarism and how the state can affect its development. One popular argument among political conservatives was that state provision of welfare services tended to decrease people's willingness to contribute to charitable causes; but studies such as those by Obler have demonstrated that the charitable spirit can thrive in a welfare state, although contributions are more likely to be directed away from areas where state provision is extensive.[6]

In this chapter we are examining parties in the context of each of these four dimensions of the public–private dichotomy. In the first section we shall see that, while parties are legally private bodies in all liberal democracies, the extent of state regulation varies greatly, and in the United States it is sufficiently great that some central aspects of the parties clearly fall within the realm of state control. In the second section we consider the forces in a number of liberal democracies which have led to the state becoming a source of funding of parties and their activities. While this development is not universal, many parties are now dependent on the state, a development which we shall see (in chapter 6) has consequences for the way parties organize themselves. In the third section we show that parties embrace a peculiar mix of private and public objectives. Indeed, the very complexity of this mix has led to controversy among political scientists as to how to conceive parties and their objectives, and how to construct models of party behaviour. Finally, in the fourth section we examine the benefits parties are thought to provide for a society. This is an issue which is often embraced within discussions of alleged party 'functions'; one of the most important aspects of these 'externalities' generated by parties – those resulting from competition between parties – has already been discussed extensively in chapter 3, but further ramifications are examined here.

PUBLIC AND PRIVATE ASPECTS OF CONTROL OVER PARTIES

The parties which emerged in the nascent liberal democracies of Britain and the United States in the eighteenth and early nineteenth centuries were private gatherings of individuals. The authors of the *Federalist Papers*, together with many of their fellows at the Convention in 1787, may have been worried by the prospects of faction and tried to devise institutional structures which would hamper it, but they did not attempt to regulate it. Regulation came much later when the abuses of machine politics led to far greater state control of parties and their activities than in virtually any other liberal democracy. In Britain the decline of electoral corruption, with the advent of the secret ballot and effective curbs on election expenditures by candidates in the late nineteenth century, meant that such controls were never needed. Any British person, or group of people, can call himself (or themselves) a party and can contest an election if they so choose without having to register or comply with any special regulations relating to its internal structure or financing. The result is a variety of bodies calling themselves political parties, ranging from the large ones represented in the British parliament, to one-person outfits such as Screaming Lord Sutch's Monster Raving Loony Party. In the rest of Europe, where there is a much stronger tradition of the idea of the state, there are usually more formal requirements to be met before a political grouping can become a party. In Norway, for example, parties must be registered:

> An application for registration must be supported by the minute book of the constituting meeting, the names and signatures of those elected to the party's central committee, and the signatures of at least 3,000 electors who declare they wish the organization to be registered as a party. Registration will be refused if the proposed name is too close to, or likely to be confused with, that of an existing party.[7]

Parties are de-registered in Norway if they fail to provide any candidates at two consecutive elections, though they cannot be denied registration on grounds of their beliefs or ideology. But, even these sorts of requirements are not stringent and certainly do not compare unfavourably with, say, the kind usually found for commercial firms that want limited legal liability.

In brief then, with the exception of the United States and to a much lesser extent West Germany (we shall explore these cases in more detail shortly), parties in liberal democracies have remained very much private institutions. The idea that they should be controlled, or even influenced, by the state is contrary to the liberal idea of competition of ideas, leaders and policies. It is worth noting, however, that the separation of state and party is also advocated in orthodox Marxism–Leninism, where the Communist party is seen as controlling the state rather than being absorbed by it or there being mutual penetration of the two bodies. In liberal democratic theory, though, one of the principal justifications for the separation of party and state is not applicable in Marxist theory – that *competition* between parties provides certain benefits (benefits which we examined in the last chapter) and competition would be undermined by state influence. Consequently, in liberal democracies we do not find restrictions on how parties may compete with each other, and where restrictions have been imposed these have related to how they organize their internal affairs. (In fact, in many cases devices like the direct primary have, indeed, affected inter-party competition.)

In West Germany parties have been required since 1956 to meet certain conditions in their procedures for nominating candidates at both the *Land* and federal levels. In comparing this regulation with the American experience, Ranney argues that legislators:

> must be chosen in the constituencies by direct secret vote of the enrolled members of the party, or in a nominating convention of delegates chosen by members. If the party's management committee for the *Land* objects to the list so chosen, a second vote must be held, and its results are final.[8]

Seen in a comparative perspective, these restrictions on the operation of a private organization are not extensive: public limited companies are legally required to proceed in certain ways in relation to their shareholders, for example, and trade unions in many countries are similarly restricted in relation to members. (In Britain, there is now a provision for secret ballots when strikes are proposed.) Although there has been a growing acceptance in postwar Germany that there is now a *Parteienstaat* (a party state), this does not mean that German parties are perceived as *part* of the state; rather, they remain as private organizations which work closely with the state and which give it its character.

This is very different from what has happened in the United States. There certain aspects of parties are now quite clearly within the public domain and, because of this, the American parties are

Janus-faced. On the one side, they remain highly decentralized groupings of notables, of whom the candidates themselves are now the most important element. Individuals are linked by informal arrangements and not by formal ties found in mass membership parties. On the other side, some of the internal arrangements have been controlled by state laws for the last seventy or eighty years, and this state control of procedures has contributed to the difficulties American parties have in running their own affairs. In some ways American parties cannot control what they do or how they operate. This unique combination of public and private control is one of the main causes of misunderstanding of American parties by European observers. Equally, though, it contributes to a general failure by American specialists on American parties to appreciate the complexity of parties found elsewhere. (When these two groups of experts meet at conferences, not surprisingly, they tend to 'talk past each other'.)

Although some states in America had attempted regulation of parties' internal affairs earlier in the nineteenth century, it was not until the end of that century that a major move towards regulation commenced. By 1920 this system was largely in place and has endured without any threat to it since then. As Ranney has noted:

> First came laws requiring the use of secret ballots in all intraparty elections of officers and candidates. Next came laws laying down the qualifications for party membership by stipulating who could participate in intraparty elections. These were followed by statutes specifying the number, powers and composition of party committees and conventions. And the climax of the Progressive reforms [was] the direct primary.[9]

In fact, Ranney's judgement that direct primary elections were the key element in the transformation of American parties into what he calls 'public agencies' is suspect. Requiring parties to hold direct primaries no more converts them into public agencies than would laws requiring trade unions to hold secret ballots, or companies facing takeovers by others to ballot their shareholders. Instead, the most significant elements in the transformation were the requirements relating to party committees, and (in some states) primary laws enabling virtually any would-be candidate to enter the primary ballot and any would-be voter to vote. The first of these innovations meant that parties could no longer control who was to participate in their affairs. Those who were selected to serve on party committees could not be expelled for, say, incompetence, supporting candidates of the opposing party, or publicly propounding views which were totally contrary to agreed party policy. Once a person was qualified to serve on a party committee, usually in a direct primary in a geographically defined constituency, he or she could not be removed. Even in the most tightly controlled parties, such as the Democratic party in New York City, the most severe sanction available was to expel a member from a high-level committee – in 1965, for example, this sanction was called for (but not agreed to) in New York when two members of the Manhattan Democratic party's Executive Committee publicly supported the Republican mayoral candidate.[10] There were ways of limiting the influence of dissidents in a party in New York and many of these were highly effective until the Second World War, but dissidents could not be removed.[11] Once the resources which made some party control possible declined, the inability of an American party to determine who could participate in it, and hence what kind of party it would be, was fully revealed. The second innovation, the primary open to virtually anyone, would not have completely destroyed the private character of American parties if the parties had been able, at least, to restrict the electorate to which the candidates appealed to those who actually participated in party activities. But the parties could not so restrict their electorates. Despite attempts in some states to have 'closed' primaries, ones limited to loyal party voters, in practice there was often little difference between these kinds of primaries and 'open' ones. Efforts at restricting the electorate, by for example requiring a sworn affirmation of loyalty, proved generally to be unenforceable. While there were obvious and straightforward procedures in mass membership parties for 'kicking out' unwanted members, there was no such option in the American parties.

The central point about state regulation of American parties, then, is that it could stop them from becoming the kinds of parties that those who were actually active in them might have wanted. By 1920 the parties were public agencies in the sense that state law prevented private individuals from shaping a party as they wanted it. But they were not public agencies in the strong sense we discussed at the beginning of this chapter: the state did not control the kinds of policies or candidates a party might put forward. It was for this reason that we described American parties as Janus-faced. But this complexity is not unique to parties. There are a number of kinds of organizations, ranging from universities in Britain to privately owned 'public utilities' in the United States which cannot be fitted into a simplified dichotomy between public and private.[12] While American parties are unique among political parties in liberal democracies, they are strikingly similar, in terms of how they are controlled, to a wide variety of other organizations.

Having outlined the general framework within which we can understand American parties, it is now necessary to draw attention to four important aspects of this complex mix between private and public. The first is that not only is it unique among parties but the forces which produced it were also unique, so that it provides no model which can be employed in understanding party developments elsewhere. Along with the advent of nonpartisan elections and other devices, the drive to control the internal affairs of parties in the Progressive era drew on a much older tradition of anti-partism which had been prominent periodically throughout American electoral history. Such tendencies have been much less deeply rooted in other liberal democracies. Again, in no other liberal democracy has there been such a long history of party corruption in the years before reform movements gained momentum. Even with their own domestic examples of electoral malpractices, English Tory observers in the 1820s were worried by the American experience.[13] With the advent of urban party machines from the 1840s onwards, this venality became even more evident to domestic and foreign observers alike. Moreover, the partial dismantling of American parties as private organizations could take the form that it did because there were no major mass membership parties in the country. In all other liberal democracies such parties became important political actors within a few years of the granting of the franchise to elements of the working class. The growth of socialist parties in most other countries had an impact on parties, and with this form of party structure becoming so widespread any attempt at public regulation of internal party affairs would surely have produced very different outcomes from those in the United States.

A second aspect of the 'American hybrid' which is worth mentioning is that in some states minor parties are not required to comply in the same way as the major parties with the legal structures imposed on them. It is recognized that minor parties which recruit members may simply have no need for and be unable to operate a complex structure of precinct committees usually found in the two major parties. However, while some states do allow minor parties to nominate their candidates in conventions, others still require that formal nomination occur in a primary election. More significantly, though, whatever the concessions made to minor parties, the very institutionalization of the major parties as public agencies is one factor (if not the most important one) which has helped to 'freeze out' minor parties in the United States. Democratic and Republican parties retain organizational structures 'on paper' even when they cannot fill positions or can fill them only with people who are really uninterested in party work. Together with a presidential system, plurality voting and committees in legislatures organized entirely around the two parties, this has helped to stifle the growth of third parties in America.

Third, public control of parties was found only at the state level of politics. Although the federal government regulated some of the activities of parties, including requiring the reporting of campaign expenditures by candidates, it did not intervene to regulate their internal affairs. There were no grounds for such intervention because, nationally, the parties were little more than gatherings of state parties. National Conventions were meetings of autonomous state parties, and the National Committees had few powers so that membership of them gave politicians little additional 'leverage' in relation to their own state parties. It was not until the reforms instituted after 1968 that the national Democratic party laid claim to any authority over state parties, and, even then, it sought merely to provide rules governing the selection of delegates to National Conventions.

Finally, in addition to state legislatures regulating the way in which parties are organized, the courts have also intervened in certain respects to regulate how participants in a party make use of these structures. The most important decisions have been those making primary elections *public* contests, and not just the required nomination procedures of private associations. As Ranney argues:

> In *U.S. v. Classic* (1941) the Supreme Court held that, where state law makes the primary election 'an integral part of the procedure of choice' of U.S. Representatives, 'or where in fact the primary effectively controls the choice, the right of the elector to have his ballot counted at the primary . . . is protected just as is the right to vote at the general election'. In *Smith v. Allwright* (1944) the Supreme Court employed this doctrine to declare unconstitutional a rule of the Texas Democratic party excluding Negroes from voting in its primaries, thereby ending the venerable Southern institution of the 'white primary'.[14]

Nevertheless, the Supreme Court has placed limitations on both state control of primaries and public access to them. In *Tashjian* v.

Republican Party (1986) the Court struck down a Connecticut law which required parties in the state to have closed, not open, primaries. The Republican party had opposed the law on the grounds that a primary which permitted independents to vote would help to build party strength in the state. At the same time the Court stated that the ruling did not mean either that members of the public had a right to vote in any party's primary, or that a party was entitled to have a primary which permitted members of another party to vote.[15]

As Epstein has pointed out, the limits of state intervention were reached perhaps in the case of *Terry* v. *Adams* (1953). In that case the organization involved was not a formal party organization but an unofficial body at the county level, the Jaybird Democratic Association in Texas. This had existed since 1889, and its all-white membership would meet in May of each year to decide whom they would endorse in that year's Democratic primaries. Hardly without exception, their nominees won both the primary and subsequent general election in the county, and the Supreme Court found that it had been 'the dominant political group in the county since organization'.[16] Because of its central role in the electoral process, the Court held that it could not lawfully exclude blacks from its membership. But this kind of intervention, in turning a party's internal affairs into a public forum, has been limited. In two later decisions of the American Supreme Court – *Cousins* v. *Wigoda* (1975) and *Democratic Party* v. *State of Wisconsin* (1981) – it was held that the American Constitution guaranteed the rights of freedom of speech and freedom of association to parties, and that courts could not require individuals or parties to support candidates or policy positions. These limitations on court intervention were illustrated dramatically in 1986 in a case involving the Democratic party in Illinois.

As a result of the primary elections that year, two supporters of the bizarre, and sinister, right-wing politician Lyndon H. LaRouche, Jr, were nominated as Democratic candidates; one of the two was the party's candidate for Lieutenant Governor. The LaRouche supporters were totally unacceptable to the party's gubernatorial candidate, Adlai Stevenson III, and to most Democratic activists; unable to remove them from the ballot at the general election, Stevenson ran as an independent, with another running-mate for the Lieutenant Governorship. State and local parties failed to provide any resources for the LaRouche supporters and did not support them in any way. The two candidates then sought a court injunction to require the Illinois

Democratic Party to support them actively, but this was denied.[17] The judge in the case took the view that members of the party could not be compelled to support candidates of whom they disapproved, and the only rights possessed by the candidates were to be the *Democratic candidates*. They had no claim to the use of party resources merely by being candidates. In a very clear way this illustrates the sort of boundary we find in America between parties as private associations and parties as public agencies. Both state legislatures and courts have been careful not to dissolve completely the private character of parties.

SUPPLIERS OF RESOURCES TO PARTIES

Until the past twenty or thirty years political parties in liberal democracies drew virtually all their resources from private individuals or organizations. Many parties had large incomes from membership dues, some had enterprises (such as newspapers) generating money from sales, nearly all received gifts (in money or kind) from interest groups, and a few were still supported by wealthy patrons. In addition to their financial dependence on the private sector, parties also obtained the workforce they needed to perform political tasks from that sector – volunteers, employees and 'clients' of patrons. This is not to deny that in some cases the state was crucial to a party being able to accumulate resources. Parties based on patronage very often could maintain their patronage only because of their control of government contracts or employment. Equally, and on a much smaller scale, some parties have raised money for party coffers by requiring those who draw a salary from holding public office to pay a portion of this to the party. But neither of these sorts of arrangements involved the state as a direct supplier of resources to parties. More recently, though, there have been two important kinds of initiatives in some liberal democracies which have drawn the state in as a direct supplier.

The less significant development has been the growth of staff, research facilities and other resources made available to legislators and other public officials. It has been quite widespread, and even the relatively ill-provided-for British MPs now have far more 'back-up' facilities than they did in the 1960s. Of course, many of these cannot be used directly for political purposes, but they do help parties in several ways. They enable representatives to maintain better contact with their constituents, a facility not available to defeated or prospective candidates of other parties. They enable the party to maintain a higher public profile. And they provide jobs which, in conjunction with those directly under a party's control, help to create a political career structure which 'ties in' party loyalists. In most countries increased administrative assistance and funds for elected politicians have helped to strengthen the existing parties – but in the United States it has had a very different impact. There, individual politicians have used these resources to weaken further their links with party organizations; they have been able to rely even more on their own personal organizations, and election experts of various kinds are often taken onto the public payroll when a politician comes into office, only to be released on unpaid leave for political work when re-election contests are approaching. (In fact, the situation is slightly more complex than this, because in California, a state where candidates' links to parties have traditionally been weak, greater staff resources have contributed to certain forms of co-operation between candidates of the same party.)[18]

The principal justification presented to the public for this expansion of facilities has usually been that it better enables political representatives to perform tasks for their constituents. While this ignores the fact that the self-interest of representatives and parties are also served by it, it is, nevertheless, true that elected representatives have become less able to provide services for their constituents. There are several reasons for this. Nearly all legislatures in the western world have had an increasing amount of legislation with which to contend and this has made it more difficult for representatives to act as agents for constituents in dealing with state bureaucracies. The demand for intervention by legislators has also grown with the increase in services provided by governments. The firm which believes that, unfairly, it was not awarded a government contract, and the person who fails to get a state benefit to which he or she is entitled, both turn to the political arena when they fail to gain satisfaction from state bureaucracies themselves. Moreover, party organizations have not increased in size and in resources to be able to play a major role in meeting this demand for assistance. Consequently, the most obvious way of filling the vacuum has been to provide more funding and staff for legislators.

The more significant development, however, has been the emergence of state funding of parties. By the 1980s ten countries (Austria, Belgium, Canada, Finland, Italy, Norway, Spain, Sweden, United States and West Germany) had adopted some form of public subsidy of parties, while the Netherlands had adopted a limited subsidy for research and education institutes.[19]

The proportion of party income emanating from the state varies between countries and between parties within a particular country (see table 4.1). In Sweden in 1980 all the major parties received between 54 and 79 per cent of their income from the state; in Italy the range was much greater, with the Communists' state subsidy accounting for only 30 per cent of their income, while the MSI (Movimento Sociale Italiano) was far more dependent on the state, with the subsidy comprising 89 per cent of its income. Moreover, in the United States it is the party's candidates, rather than the parties themselves, which have been the main beneficiaries of the limited public funding which is mostly confined to presidential politics. (At the state level, there has been some funding of parties.) Generalizing about the origins of public subsidies is difficult, as it is in connection with the forms the subsidies take in different countries. It is not surprising, therefore, that von Beyme should argue that 'the attitude parties have taken in the argument over public aid is not uniform right through the *familles spirituelles*',[20] though he shows that social democratic and left-centre parties have generally supported the idea. However, it is possible to identify four main sources of the move towards state aid, although only some of them are applicable in particular cases.

Public funding of parties has been especially popular in those regimes in western Europe where democracy collapsed in the inter-war years, and where the reconstructed democratic regimes have accorded a major role to strong parties in the working of the new state. West Germany and Austria are the outstanding examples of

Table 4.1 Income derived by parties (or party candidates) from public subsidies as a percentage of total party income

| Country | Public subsidy per party | | |
	Highest	Lowest	Median
Austria	54	32	39
Canada	29	23	27
Finland	78	26	65
Italy	89	30	74
Spain	91	44	89
Sweden	79	54	67
USA	19	19	19
West Germany	33	2	22

Data taken from von Beyme, *Political Parties in Western Democracies*, p. 206.

party penetration of the state (a subject we examine in chapter 7), but parties have also played a major role in the reconstruction of liberal democracy in Italy and Spain. West Germany was the first country to introduce state aid to parties, in 1959, but the system of 'freely disposable subsidies' was declared unconstitutional in 1966 and has been replaced by aid given for specific purposes.[21] (This has now become the more common form of subsidy in western states.) The law in Spain provides a good example of how state funding is linked to the perceived need to rebuild democracy. The initial law on public funding was passed in March 1977, before the first post-Franco general election; the impact of the law was to affect adversely small parties. Subsidies to parties were based solely on the results of the general election: a party received one million pesetas for each seat it won in the Congress of Deputies and the Senate, 0.45 pesetas for each vote for successful Congress candidates, and 0.15 pesetas for every successful Senate candidate. Quite clearly, one aim of the policy was to prevent extreme multi-partism emerging in Spain, and after 1977 parties which had obtained no seats were virtually driven to bankruptcy. This policy was reinforced in 1978 when a further law provided for state funds for the annual operating expenses of parties. Only parliamentary groups were eligible for money and to form a parliamentary group a party or alliance had to obtain five per cent of the popular vote. Each parliamentary group received one million pesetas every year and a further 60,000 pesetas for each of its deputies and senators. Once again, the policy reinforced the position of large parties and weakened that of small parties. In Spain, as in West Germany, democracy was equated with the existence of a relatively small number of strong parties, and state funding was to help bring this about.

Another source of pressure for state aid is the increasing expense of elections, which can result in parties becoming heavily dependent on particular interest groups. Scandals which arise from these connections can produce pressure for alternative forms of funding which will reduce the incentive for politicians to enter into arrangements with interest group leaders. Obviously, among the best-known scandals were those involving President Nixon in the 1972 election, and which became apparent during the unfolding of the Watergate scandal. Large sums from individual and corporate donors to the Nixon campaign had been 'laundered' by his own election campaign organization so as to evade the existing restrictions and reporting requirement. Public and congressional indignation at the revelations led to a limited form of public subsidy to presidential candidates (at both the nominating and general election stages) and to much tighter reporting requirements on income and expenditure by all federal election campaigns. Together with the West German experience, though, this case helps to expose some of the limitations in public funding as a way of breaking candidates' financial links to interest groups. Far from group funding to candidates declining in the United States, there was merely a partial switch by organized interests from presidential to other kinds of elections. Indeed, it has been widely argued that the reforms introduced in 1974 actually encouraged greated interest group participation in elections, by drawing attention to how easily it could be done. The second half of the 1970s saw the rapid rise of political action committees (PACs) organized by business corporations, a development completely unforeseen in 1974. In West Germany, too, public funding did not help to prevent a series of financial scandals (including the so-called 'Flick affair') in the 1970s and 1980s – scandals in which all the major parties, except the newly formed Greens, were implicated.

In the West German experience also we see a further source of pressure for public funding linked to the second one – the desire to prevent corruption on the part of elected politicians. The argument is not only that ties to interest groups may become too close, but also that politicians may actually sell favours to those on whom they are dependent for finance. This problem is endemic in Japanese politics, for example, in which the 'Lockheed scandal' is only the best-known of many such arrangements.[22] In Japan, though, the dominance of one party has prevented serious attempts at reforming the funding of party activity. Where a party is less dominant than is the Liberal Democratic Party, public criticism of corruption can create pressure for state funding.

Finally, state funding taps a central democratic value – that competition for the people's vote should occur without particular competitors being unduly advantaged by the support of small elites. Normally, uneven distributions of money and other resources in elections (such as access to a favourable press) do not produce widespread resentment among the electorate. However, there are circumstances, as in the Watergate scandal, when voters are peculiarly sensitive to issues of fairness, and this provides the opportunity for those who favour state funding to attract support for the issue.

We can understand the possible impact of these four factors by considering why public funding of parties has failed to get onto the political agenda in certain countries, and we can take Britain as our example. In 1976 a government committee, set up under the chairmanship of the former Labour minister Lord Houghton, reported favourably on the idea of some form of public subsidy being given to parties.[23] Although a number of countries had recently adopted public funding and the Labour government was to remain in office for another three years, the report met a rather critical response and was 'shelved' more or less immediately. The issue has not been revived since then. In Britain the regime has not collapsed in modern times and parties are not widely regarded as being essential for the preservation of democracy. Again, there have been no scandals involving corruption by the parties or leading party officials on a scale which rivals those in, say, West Germany. The issue of unfairness in the distribution of resources has not surfaced as politically salient at the mass level of politics for two reasons. The most significantly disadvantaged party, the Liberals, have not yet achieved the 'electoral breakthrough' at general elections which would be necessary to force any aspect of electoral or party reform onto the policy agenda; and in Britain restrictions on expenditures by individual candidates, though not by parties nationally, have been rigorously enforced since the late nineteenth century, so that there have been no individual examples of 'unfairness' at the constituency level to stir public imagination. The one element favouring the adoption of state subsidies is the overwhelming financial advantage business support gives to the Conservative party. Yet this has failed to become an issue taken up by the Labour party, partly because of its own dependence on funding by trade unions and the stake the unions have in preserving the status quo in the Labour party, and partly because business support for the Conservatives seems to be declining.

However, the disappearance of the issue in Britain between the mid-1970s and the mid-1980s does not mean that it might not re-emerge rather suddenly. A corruption scandal would be one obvious cause of this, but in any case the decision by the Conservative government to require unions, but not companies, to hold ballots before they create political funds has disturbed the status quo which was itself a powerful force in keeping public funding off the agenda. It is not too difficult to imagine that, after a future general election, with no single party obtaining an overall parliamentary majority, a deal might be struck with the Liberals and Social Democrats which included some element of state funding. And, of course, one of the features of an issue like state funding of parties is that, while it may be resisted initially, once it has been introduced virtually no established party believes it has an interest in removing it entirely. Few organizations like denying themselves 'free' money. Any debate then more likely focuses on the extent of state funding, the limitations (if any) imposed on private funding, and the purposes for which funding is given. Consequently, in the long term, we might expect the slow spread of public funding, though it is likely (as now) to take very different forms in different countries.

But, if state funding of parties may be expected to spread, it is important to ask whether it does in fact help to maintain competitive politics and minimizes the power of social and economic elites. It is, after all, the ethos of fairness in competition which often provides momentum to the introduction of public funding. However, as we have already noted, in Germany and the United States state funding has not lessened interest group ties to parties. Equally, when it does not involve matching funds with those raised from membership dues, state financing yields a *relative* disadvantage for those parties that are most successful in attracting large numbers of members. The Italian Communist Party is an example of this, and it is difficult to reconcile such a consequence with democratic norms. The parties most usually advantaged by state funding are those which have demonstrated electoral support but which cannot, or do not, wish to recruit many members, and which have relatively little access to interest group funds. Of course, public funding also usually advantages parties that have obtained significant support at the time such funding is introduced; it is very much a matter of the so-called Matthew effect, 'to those that have shall be given', and this was quite deliberate policy in the case of Spain. Forms of funding could be devised that did not relatively disadvantage parties with large memberships, but it is more difficult to see how safeguards to protect new parties, which might be formed in the future, could be introduced. But the real problem with state funding is that it does not deal directly with the power of special interests, unless it goes hand in hand with prohibitions on private funding and very strict screening of the financial affairs of party elites. When these sorts of provisions are omitted, public funding may well fail to address the issue of fairness in electoral competition.

PUBLIC AND PRIVATE OBJECTIVES OF PARTIES

One of the major problems in the study of any institution is in understanding how the conflict between the overt objectives of the institution itself and the private objectives of those who control it generally affects the behaviour of the institution. In the 1950s, for example, the work of Simon and others on organizational behaviour contributed to the debate as to whether for-profit enterprises actually attempted to maximize profits, as they were supposed to do in traditional economic theory, or whether the desire by administrators for a 'comfortable' existence led to 'satisficing' behaviour by organizations.[24] Again, in relation to government agencies, Niskanen devised a model of bureaucratic behaviour in the early 1970s in which the pursuit of their own self-interest by bureaucrats results in their agencies having overly large budgets.[25] There are two main problems in specifying how institutions will behave: knowing exactly which objectives those who run them pursue (income maximization, satisficing with regard to personal stress and so on, or whatever); and knowing how much the private objectives modify the formal objectives of the institution. These difficulties are also evident in the case of parties, but there is an additional problem here – specifying the objectives of a party itself. As a result, there has been considerable disagreement among those who have sought to develop a formal theory of party interaction as to the objectives parties could be presumed to have. Anthony Downs, for example, disregarded any distributional aims parties might have – he assumed they sought to maximize their vote; for Riker, on the other hand, the relative shares to be had from whatever it was that government could distribute was all-important. And for another of the early 'positive theorists' of parties, Joseph Schlesinger, it was the career ambitions of individual politicians which were crucial.[26] The result is that there is no theory of party behaviour comparable to the theory of the firm in economics, and even attempts at classifying different types of parties in terms of their behaviour (such as Schlesinger's later distinction between office-seeking and benefit-seeking parties) are disappointingly primitive.[27]

Even if we exclude those publicly oriented goals which are simply rhetorical devices for gaining electoral support for a party, the objectives of parties are a mix of those which are oriented towards private interests and those which are directed towards benefiting a wider public. And, of course, this balance between the two kinds of objectives can shift. Agrarian parties in Scandinavia and some parties in former consociational democracies have become more like 'catch-all' parties – wanting to garner votes from wherever they can, rather than relying on a particular interest in society. Equally, in the 1970s the British Labour party became identified with a policy of subsidizing various declining industries –

favouring particular interests, that is, at the expense of others. Of course, the boundary between a private interest and a wider public interest is not easy to draw, so that in particular cases the distinction can be rather artificial. For example, over sixty per cent of British households are owner-occupied, the form of occupancy which provides the largest kind of subsidy (through income tax relief on interest payments) available in the housing sector. None of the major parties, with the exception of the Social Democrats, have questioned the maintenance of this subsidy. From one perspective, home-owning households are a special interest, though if home-ownership becomes even easier for all social classes the category would take on some of the characteristics of 'a public'. Nevertheless, it is uncontroversial to claim that virtually all parties have had some public-regarding objectives, just as most have also had objectives which are designed to benefit certain special interests. Now in this respect parties are rather unusual. Whatever the purposes of those who run them, the formal objective of companies remains that of making as much money for the owners as possible – although, obviously, the maintenance of income in the long term might dictate non-profit maximizing strategies in the short term. Conversely, the objectives of a charity like Oxfam are publicly oriented, regardless of, say, the career ambitions of those who run it; the charity aims at relieving poverty, although there may well be disagreements as to the best strategies for bringing that about.

However, while many kinds of organization do not have 'mixed' formal objectives in the way that parties do, parties are not the only kind of organization which have this characteristic. One example is the non-profit teaching hospital in the United States. On the one hand, these organizations compete for paying patients with other kinds of hospitals, and they try to maximize their profits (which they cannot distribute to any individuals or persons) so as to increase the standing and business of the hospital. That is, they behave in a very similar way to for-profit firms. On the other hand, many of them were originally founded for the benefit of the poor, or to advance medical knowledge, so that, far more than for-profit hospitals, they tend to cross-subsidize the research they conduct and are more willing to admit 'charity cases' for hospitalization.

Just as the overt goals of parties are more difficult to specify than are those of most organizations, so specifying the objectives of elite-members of a party is more problematic than is, for example, specifying the objectives of the managers of businesses. Not only may there be differing self-interested objectives among such elites (for example, some may be more committed to 'maximizing' their careers in the party in terms of the level of office they reach, while others might be 'satisficers'), but many, if not all, may have social objectives as well. Whatever social objectives business managers themselves might have, the usual assumption is that these do not have an impact on the goals pursued by the organizations they run. But this is likely to be less true of organizations seeking to promote non-private interests, and we would expect that they would attract as participants, leaders and employees, people whose social objectives are broadly similar to those of the organization but may differ from it in some significant respects.

In looking at the goals of party elites we must separate three distinct elements: The first is the *social objectives* they have – the public policies they would promote when in office. The second element is their *private objectives* – to attain high office, possibly, or to reap an income from the patronage resources available, or whatever. And the third element is the *concessions* they must make, because of the pressure of electoral competition, in relation to the first two elements. As can be seen by comparing figures 4.1 and 4.2, the factors likely to affect the behaviour of party elites are far more complex than those affecting the behaviour of elites in economic enterprises. The logic of the electoral market affects both the public and private goals politicians may wish to pursue; this is the same kind of constraint as for the business executive who must trim the pursuit of personal goals to the requirements to meet (at least) some minimum level of profitable operation for the firm's shareholders. However, the additional, and crucial, problem in modelling party behaviour is that we have no means of knowing whether assumptions we make about the balance between their social and private objectives, for which party elites aim, correspond to those found in the real world. Now for some purposes we can construct formal models for which we do not have to worry about this. For example, the series of studies influenced by 'ambition theory' assumed that American politicians were motivated purely by maximizing their political career opportunities, and the result was important information about the difference ambition makes to behaviour. As with all 'rational choice' modelling, it was only by abstracting from reality, and excluding other goals politicians might have, that the impact of career goals could be studied. However, these studies would

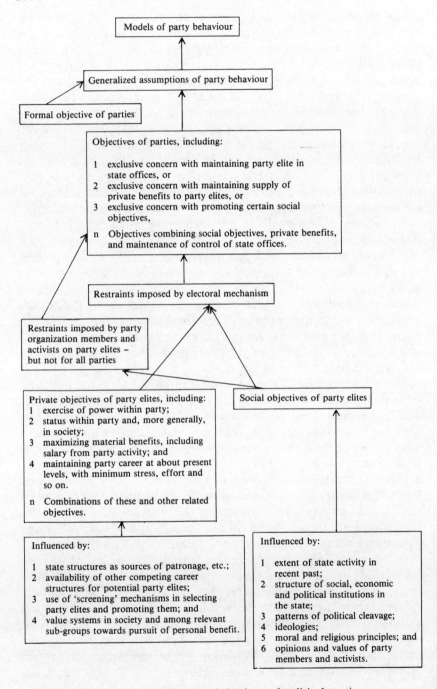

Figure 4.1 Modelling the behaviour of political parties

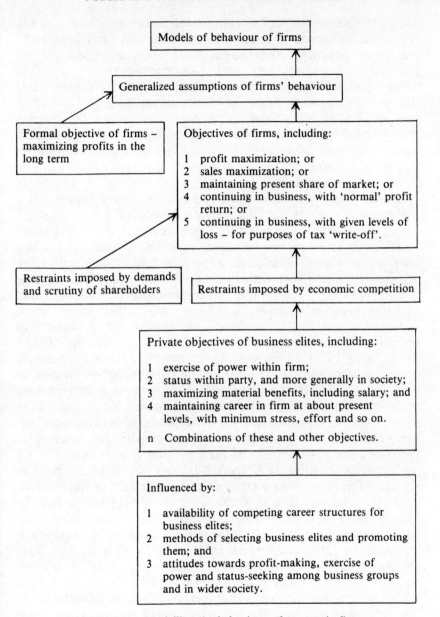

Figure 4.2 Modelling the behaviour of economic firms

never be able to tell us how important career ambition was for American politicians in relation to the other private objectives or the social objectives they might have. Nor, *a priori*, are we justified in assuming, say, that American politicians give less weight to social objectives than politicians elsewhere. Yet the claim that we can do so is to be found in several studies – including that of Wright, who argues that American parties lie towards the 'rational – efficient' end of his 'rational – efficient/party democracy' continuum of party types.[28] (A brief discussion of the way Wright relates both types of party to the electoral mechanism is presented in chapter 6.)

Indeed many studies of parties have wrongly assumed that, for example, the social and private objectives of party elites necessarily conflict. This is not so. There are instances of patronage-based parties, as in late nineteenth-century Detroit, providing progressive social policies; the private and social objectives of party elites can complement each other. In fact, for studying single political systems, and more especially in making comparisons between regimes, we have only rather fragmentary evidence as to the assumptions we should make about the objectives of political elites. Elected politicians in the United States in the 1980s do not seem to have *entirely* private goals, and nor do policy differences between them seem explicable entirely in terms of differing electoral constraints. Equally, in British politics in the period 1965–76 the two major parties were led by politicians widely regarded as careerists, for whom social objectives were less important than for either their predecessors or successors. However, the vast amount of material that is now available on leaders in both political systems still does not make it easy for agreement to be reached on the goals of politicians for the purpose of devising models similar to those for the theory of the firm in economics. This suggests that rational choice approaches to the study of parties are likely to be far more difficult to operationalize than in the study of commercial enterprises. In studying the public and private objectives of parties, it seems we must rely much more on in-depth historically informed studies of particular regimes. What these studies indicate is that there is considerable variation in the objectives pursued by politicians, both within (and quite possibly, between) liberal democratic regimes.

EXTERNAL BENEFITS AND COSTS OF PARTIES

As we suggested at the beginning of this chapter, organizations can create benefits and costs for people other than those who are directly part of the activities of these organizations. Because of their likely impact on public policy, parties have generally been regarded as organizations which will generate very large externalities, and in this sense are often seen as among the most public of organizations. For much of the nineteenth century, many political theorists and writers focused on the costs of party politics rather than on any possible benefits that it might yield. Because they necessarily divided societies, parties were a source of political instability; the temptation to expand the scope of political conflict for short-term advantage would lead to longer term demands for the enfranchisement of the working class, a development regarded as highly destabilizing until the end of the nineteenth century; the dominance of parties would lead to preferment for special interests in a society, at the expense of more general interests; parties posed problems as to how individuals could be properly represented in parliaments; and parties might lead to the 'wrong sorts of men', and especially the self-interested, getting into positions of influence. These were among the concerns of those who discussed parties.

The expansion of the franchise in Britain and the rest of western Europe did not, however, produce the predicted political instability, nor did the European parties generally exhibit the excesses of venality characteristic of American parties. The result was that, especially among elites, attitudes to parties were to change radically in the twentieth century. By the middle of this century, they were widely regarded as one of the cornerstones of liberal democracy; this was to culminate in the central role accorded to parties in the 'reconstructed' regimes in West Germany and Austria after 1945. Democratic theorists, like E. E. Schattschnieder in the 1930s and 1940s, argued that, far from being the perpetuators of special interest politics, parties were the principal device for countering the influence of pressure groups.[29] Moreover, idealized accounts of how individuals could be represented in industralized societies and of how non-party regimes would best 'throw up' people of talent into governing positions were now discredited. These developments, together with the growing influence of structural–functional explanations in the social sciences in the 1940s, led to the growth of the idea that parties in liberal democracies performed certain functions – functions which were essential for the preservation and stability of these regimes. In less than a hundred years, parties had been transformed from being one of the main costs which might have to be paid for expanded political representation to being the principal mechanism for providing democracy in a modern state.

In the 1950s political science became preoccupied with the functions parties allegedly performed. Writing in 1969, King said of the lists of functions which appeared in many books 'at least one list is to be found in almost every book on political parties, usually toward the beginning. No definitive compilation exists, and the functions generally cited are often inter-related and overlapping.'[30] King then identified and discussed the six main functions which appeared in most such lists:

1 structuring the vote;
2 the integration and mobilization of mass publics;
3 the recuitment of political leaders;
4 the organization of government;
5 the formation of public policy; and,
6 the aggregation of interests.

In an interesting, and provoking discussion, King argued that, to the extent that these functions are performed in liberal democracies, parties themselves have only a very limited part in this. His article parallels the similarly titled book by Epstein, published two years earlier, in suggesting that parties are far less central to liberal democracy than the then conventional wisdom suggested.[31] While Epstein claimed that the parties of the future were more likely to reflect developments in American parties – in the growing reliance on new campaign techniques, rather than on activists and organization – King extended the scope of the debate by arguing that, in any case, parties did far less now than political scientists usually imagined. The article was important in drawing attention to the unquestioning attitude towards the relationship between parties and liberal democracy then adopted by many in the discipline, but King's selective use of evidence enabled him to draw more far-reaching conclusions about party weaknesses than was really warranted. In particular, he paid little attention to those states (especially West Germany, Austria and Italy) where strong parties had developed in the post-war years. Nor, of course, could he foresee that, after its first ten years, the Fifth French Republic would witness the growth of far stronger parties than had developed in the Third and Fourth Republics.

What, then, are the 'externalities' which parties provide in a liberal democratic society? At the price of considerable over-simplification, we can identify several main kinds of externality. There are those related to competition between parties, which we have already considered when analysing the idea of political competition in chapter 3. Then there is the role parties play in counteracting special interests in a society, and in protecting more general interests. Finally, there are the externalities which result from parties acting as advocates and conciliators of interests – activities which tend to facilitate social integration rather than fragmentation. In the remaining part of this section we consider briefly these last two externalities.

The argument that parties are a bastion against the dominance of special interests in a polity was developed most fully by Schattschneider, following his study of restrictive tarriff legislation in the United States in the early 1930s, but the logical underpinning of the argument has been expounded more fully with the use of game theory in political science in the 1960s.[32] Essentially the argument is as follows:

1 Special interests, particularly business interests, find it much easier to raise political resources than more general interests in a society.
2 The closer the decision-making structure of a state approximates that of a simple-majority system, the more difficult it is for special interests to make their resources 'count'. The more the decisional system approaches that of unanimous voting, the easier it is for these resources to 'count'.
3 The more cohesive parties are internally, and the more the party system approaches that of a two-party system, the greater is the resemblance to a simple-majority decision-making structure.

The core of the argument is that parties have to aggregate interests (the sixth of the 'functions' identified by King), and that requires them to take account of interests which may be 'under-organized', or possibly not organized at all. The greater the incentive for them to aggregate, the weaker the claims special interests can make of them. However, in rejecting the American parties as being too weak to withstand the pressure exerted on policy-makers by business interests, Schattschneider seemed to adopt an idealized model of British party government in suggesting how parties might act as a counter-force to pressure groups. Now, in evaluating the 'counter-force' argument, we necessarily touch on a number of arguments about the nature of party government discussed more fully in chapter 7. Nevertheless, without pre-empting this discussion, there are several possible limitations to the 'counter-force' argument we can examine here.

The first of these is the rarity of the two-party system, which Schattschneider and, later, Barry seemed to regard as a central element in forcing parties to take account of weakly organized interests. Indeed, von Beyme has said of two-party systems: 'These are more of an abstraction than reality: even Great Britain, Canada and New Zealand have only been two-party systems in some phases of their history because they were clinging to the idea of alternating governments to avoid coalitions.'[33] In his own classification of parties, he regards only the United States and New Zealand as two-party systems. A second possible limitation is that in quite a few liberal democracies, parties are operating in conditions where there is only a restricted incentive to compete aggressively for marginal voters, and hence, in doing so, to take account of wider interests in society. Excluding the case of Switzerland where parties behave in a non-competitive way, there are three main types of party system in which this incentive is likely to be restricted: those where one party is electorally dominant (Japan and India, for example); those which are examples of what, Sartori called 'polarized pluralism' (such as the French Fourth Republic); and those consociational democracies in which 'catch-all' electoral strategies are eschewed in favour of elite co-operation in government (the Netherlands and Belgium, until the 1970s, for example).[34] Finally, there is the argument that parties are not always separated from the interest-group system in the way indicated by proponents of the 'counter-force' argument. For example, there are parties such as agrarian parties which exist to promote a particular economic interest, just as many socialist parties are closely tied to trade unions; and the growth of liberal corporatism, especially when this produces the inter-penetration of parties and groups of a kind evident in Austria, further weakens the independence of parties in protecting broader interests in a society.

However, these considerations are less devastating for the 'counter-force' argument than they might appear at first sight. For one thing, the number of states in which parties have little incentive to appeal to a wide electorate on the basis of shared interests seem to be rather fewer than some have suggested, and this category is arguably getting smaller. Today, arguably only Japan and India remain of those liberal democratic states where one party dominated; as von Beyme points out, Israel had left this category by 1977 and it can be argued that Ireland has now as well. Again, while Sartori believed that there were a number of instances of 'polarized pluralism' among liberal democracies, von Beyme has argued that his classification conceals two rather different types of party system.[35] There have been a very small number of cases (including the Weimar Republic and the Second Spanish Republic), where entrenched opposition to the regime by parties on the flanks of the ideological spectrum has meant that centre parties have been incapable of governing and parties preserve their electoral 'ghettos'. But there is a much larger group of supposedly 'polarized pluralist' party sytems, including that in Italy, where opposition to the regime itself has weakened and where centre parties can govern. Furthermore, social change, and especially the growth of groups in the middle class, has made it difficult for the politics of elite accommodation practised in the consociational democracies to survive. 'Catch-all' electoral strategies have been emerging in these systems. But these social changes have also put pressure on many parties with close links to particular interests to weaken these ties, and to attract other kinds of voters. This is evident in both agrarian parties and in socialist parties with strong links to trade unions. And, of course, with the partial exception of nationalist parties which revived in many parts of the western world in the 1960s and early 1970s, the newer parties have rarely been tied to particular interests in their regimes.

Yet, in any case, the need to govern, or at least to take a stance towards governing, forces parties to behave very differently towards more general interests in a society than do organized special interests. This is one of the reasons why 'flash' parties organized around particular economic interests (such as the Poujadistes in the French Fourth Republic) can find it difficult to sustain initial electoral success. Whatever the electoral strategy pursued, acting in a national legislature pushes parties towards giving greater consideration to broader interests than is necessary in other kinds of political organization. The real threat to the 'counter-force' role of parties, then, does not come so much from the absence of two-partism, or from limited electoral competition, but from internal party weakness which leaves individual party leaders open to pressure from organized interests. It is this problem of internal discipline in the American parties which worried Schattschneider, and which, if anything, has become worse during the last twenty or so years.

The second kinds of 'externalities' we are considering in this chapter relate to the effects parties have in their role as advocates and conciliators of interests. These are connected to two of the 'functions' of parties discussed by King – the integration and mobilization of mass publics, and the recruitment of political leaders. Even though parties vary in the extent of their penetration of society, and this is a subject we examine in chapter 7, they are, nevertheless, crucial institutions in establishing the frameworks within which grievances and demands are articulated. An important aspect of this is that, with the minor exception of a few fringe organizations calling themselves parties, most parties in liberal democracies help to socialize mass publics into accepting certain means as the most appropriate for articulating demands. In this way, if in no other, parties can develop indirectly a civic-orientation within the polity. The Italian Communist party (PCI), for example, which Sartori saw as the source of intense polarization in Italian politics, has socialized its members and voters into using the 'normal' procedures of liberal democracy. Or, again, the French Communist Party stood aside from the student and worker unrest in May 1968, believing that (because of its own interests) the normal political process should not be abandoned then. Whether they are Eurocommunist, or loyally pro-Moscow, Communist parties, like virtually all other parties, have a stake (and generally a very large stake) in the maintenance of regularized procedures for articulating and alleviating grievances. This acceptance of the 'normal political channels' is one of the main values which parties help to convey to mass publics. For parties, direct action tactics and other strategies outside 'routine politics' are a 'double-edged' weapon. While they help draw attention to issues and help to maintain the enthusiasm of activists, they make it more difficult for parties to control the development of a conflict at a time when this may be important for getting their way on an issue. This, indeed, is one of the possible sources of tension between parties and single-issue groups with which they are loosely allied. One of the more interesting aspects of the West German Greens is how they would be able to manage their supporters at a stage when the basing of American nuclear weapons in Germany became a possible issue for negotiation. In such circumstances some forms of direct action may well maintain pressure for the issue to be on the state's policy agenda, while other forms might help to weaken support for the issue among wider publics. Unlike other parties, the Greens have not attempted to set up the kind of bureaucracies which might help it better to control such activities, but even they are strongly committed to many aspects of 'routine politics' which enables them to further their objectives.

Related to this vested interest which parties have in routine political procedures is the need to have leaderships that can best advance the issues they support. This too has an impact on the political system, in that it provides a further filtering device by which those who cannot handle routine politics well are usually excluded from the highest party offices. That particular kinds of leader are usually to be found at the apex of parties means, therefore, that there is a further 'dampening' of anti-system movements in the state and of political styles which further the disintegration of the state. This, of course, is one of the main reasons why those nineteenth-century writers who thought that the rise of parties might herald the rise of demagogic politics proved to be wrong; parties have an interest in keeping demagoguery in check.

In making these claims, about the 'public' effects of parties, we are not suggesting that parties are the main instrument in liberal democracies by which mass publics are socialized into accepting the values of 'routine politics'; nor are we claiming that parties can always control entry to positions of political leadership, nor that they always select those who extol the virtues of 'routine politics'. Rather, we are making the more modest claim that parties usually do make a difference in this regard, and that, consequently, they do provide what many regard as significant benefits for a society.

CONCLUDING REMARKS

In this chapter we have explored the four dimensions of the distinction between 'public' and 'private', and we have seen the particular set of characteristics parties have. For the most part, they have remained private organizations with respect to how they are controlled. Although there has been a growth in public funding of parties in some states, many of them still rely on private sources for money, as they do for other kinds of resources. Parties themselves, and those who run them, have a mix of public and private objectives. And parties and party competition produce external benefits which are important for the stability of a regime. No other organizations have quite this profile. Among the closest, perhaps, are privately owned water and electric companies, of which there can only be a restricted number in a given locale, and which (like parties) provide external benefits through their operations and in which too there may be an ethos of serving a community as well as engaging in profit-making enterprises. Yet, one of the most noticeable differences between these two kinds of organization is that, with public utilities, state control often supercedes private control, and, even when it does not, very close regulation is usually practised. The services are too important to allow market forces to predominate. With parties, fears about how state control or state resources might affect competition between parties has tended greatly to restrict intervention. When the state has intervened, it has generally been in response to a crisis – whether it be the widespread corruption in nineteenth-century American parties or the collapse of liberal democratic regimes in the inter-war years. Regimes do not want to disturb the way parties operate, or the way they interact in a party system unless it is essential to do so; the fear is that any intervention may encourage state–party relations of a sort incompatible with the practice of representative democracy.

However, this approach has one adverse consequence: If there are factors which are more slowly undermining parties, the ways in which they compete in the electoral market, or the 'externalities' they provide, it is unlikely that this can be regulated until it reaches a crisis point. One example of this is the increasing cost of elections which the revolution in campaign technologies has helped to create. Except in those states where there are very rigid restrictions on the use of these techniques, or on campaign expeditures, there is a pressure on parties to make use of these techniques whenever possible, and this helps to escalate the cost of elections. The more financial resources increase in importance relative to, say, the labour resources available to parties, the more parties are likely to develop links with and obligations to organized interests. Not all of these sorts of ties are incompatible with democracy, of course, and in many of them influence may be a two-way process. However, the balance between special and more general interests in a society is likely to be threatened the greater the access organized interests have to parties. It is precisely these kinds of conflicts, between the self interest of the owners of public utilities and the common interests of those they provide for, that has been one of the main forces leading to the regulation of public utilities. Yet, as we have suggested, intervention in the case of parties tends only to emerge in response to a crisis, and this indicates an important potential weakness in the ability of states to preserve an environment in which parties and party competition can provide the desired benefits for a society. But, if regulation of parties is problematic, what of the possibility of some form of checking mechanism within parties themselves? This brings us to intra-party relations, and we begin by examining participation in parties before turning to look at the related issue of who controls political parties.

5

PARTICIPATION IN POLITICAL PARTIES

The concept of participation is strangely elusive. Superficially it seems considerably more straightforward than, say, the concepts of rights and freedom, and this has led Geraint Parry, one of the leading authorities on participation, to argue that 'there is no problem as to the meaning of the word "participation"'.[1] Parry then defines participation as 'the act of taking part or having a share with others in some action', and he suggests that it is *political* participation which raises problems. There are, however, objections to this claim. While the concept of 'the political' is indeed a complex one, there are many other areas of action where the problem of identifying the boundaries of the action makes for difficulties in distinguishing participants from non-participants. Again, the 'contribution' of some persons may be causally necessary for an action to occur, or to occur in the form that it did, but the relationship of these persons to others raises serious doubts as to whether they constitute participants or not. In particular it is market relations which pose the doubts. Consider the case of a party which conducts most of its campaigning through direct-mail leafleting and billboards and suppose that it employs one firm to print this material. There is a clear sense in which the printing firm is sharing in the action but normally it would not be regarded as a participant in the party or its election campaign. This qualification – 'normally' – helps us to understand the standard case. When the printers have a monopoly and do not accept work from other parties, or when they are involved in the design of the literature, or when they offer a financial discount to a particular party, the case for them being regarded as participants becomes much stronger. But in the standard case of a market relation, the suggestion that they are participants in party activity would seem a peculiar one.

Two features of market relations underlie this distinction between the actor in a market and a participant. On the one hand, the former is indifferent to the activities and ends of those with whom he enters into a transaction. The printing firm's decision to take on the work of a party or candidate is based on a commercial judgement about profit-maximizing, sales-maximizing, or whatever commercial objective the firm adopts as an operating principle. This does not preclude the possibility of the firm's owners or managers having personal preferences for the party whose work they undertake, but it is only when such considerations have entered the decision to undertake the work that the question of the firm being a participant in the party or its activities might arise. On the other hand, when the firm has a monopoly in a particular product and when the product is available to only one party, the issue of a market relation constituting something akin to participation also arises. Consider the example of advertising firms or campaign consultants. The particular talents and style of one firm are not open to rivals of the party or candidate that employs them. Even when they are employed to give purely technical advice, and not to develop advertising themes or to run the campaign, such firms have become more like participants. (Usually, though, the relationship between these firms and their clients does extend beyond technical matters, and in the United States there have been occasions where complete responsibility for a campaign has been left in the hands of campaign consultants.)[2]

In relation to parties, the significance of this distinction between the participant and the actor who has a purely market relation with party activity is that, in one kind of party, market-based relations could be extremely important. Such instances raise the question of whether the people involved are best regarded as participants in the party or not, and has led to disputes as to who should be allowed to exercise influence within the party and through which channels this should be done. To understand this, it is necessary to draw a distinction between elite-based parties and membership-based parties.

The first political parties – in the United States and in Britain – were organized by social elites which were active in legislatures. In Britain parties in parliament emerged and declined at various periods from the late seventeenth to the mid-nineteenth centuries. When party division was important, as in the period leading up to the first Reform Bill in 1832, this still did not mean that there was extensive electoral activity in the country. Many elections remained uncontested, and where there was competition it was not national parties which were involved but the dominant local elites.[3] The people they utilized in campaigning would be brought in by a variety of incentives: there are those who were tied by social obligations to particular members of the elite, others who felt allegiance to a particular tradition or style of politics and hence to a party, and finally there were those who were paid to undertake certain tasks.[4] How extensive a campaign was depended on the degree of conflict between the local elites and on the size of the electorate, and of course the latter varied enormously, especially before the passage of the 1832 Bill. The central feature of such a system was that important decisions, such as who would be the candidate, were taken by a very small group of people, while if there was competition a much larger number of people might be needed in some constituencies for campaign tasks. In many respects the situation was the same in the United States until the late 1820s – of course, the main difference lies in the relatively smaller reliance placed on social obligations in building up support there. In the late 1820s the political power of American social elites was reduced. The cause of this was the success of the Jacksonian revolution in the Democratic party and the subsequent emergence of party competition in many parts of the nation. The Jacksonians decentralized power within their party and, for example, initiated party conventions in the selection of presidential candidates, thereby replacing the role of congressional caucuses. As important was the rise of genuine two-party competition, something which had flourished briefly in the 1790s, and which, because of the size of the electorate, meant large numbers of people had to be involved in campaign work. In the 1830s the United States became the first state where parties had to organize mass electorates.

A central feature of the original, legislature-based, parties was that they depended on regular co-operation between those who were powerful locally. While a certain shared view of the world, as well as shared traditions, bound individuals together into parties, it was their elite position in a locale which gave men access to the parties. The effect of Jacksonianism was both to make for more formal intra-party arrangements and to break up some centralizing tendencies. The guiding principle, that the central party structure itself should not determine *who* should exercise power in the party in a particular locale, remained. In the continental European countries a similar pattern of elite-based parties developed in the nineteenth century. In the early 1950s Duverger was to use the concepts 'caucus' and 'cadre' parties in analysing them.[5] One of the main differences between the American parties and their European counterparts was that the former had to mobilize a mass electorate much earlier, towards the beginning of the period of industrialization, and without competition from other kinds of political party. By the time the European bourgeois (liberal) and conservative parties had to engage in mass mobilization, at the end of the nineteenth century and in the early twentieth century, they faced opposition very quickly from socialist parties whose antecedent organizations and trade union allies had gained experience in the political mobilization of the working class.[6] These socialist parties organized themselves on very different lines from the older parliamentary-based parties, and in the twentieth century this was to prompt changes in the way caucus–cadre parties organized themselves. However, although the socialist parties were generally the most influential in changing the organization of party politics, they were not always the first to develop mass bases. Some Catholic parties in Austria and Belgium, and most especially in Germany, developed highly structured mass membership organizations at the same time as, or before, the emergence of large socialist parties. By the 1870s a Catholic party had developed in Germany with an organization embracing much of the Catholic population.

In place of informal alliances between the locally powerful, which relied on material rewards and social obligation, as well as commitment to a cause, to raise the needed workforce for electoral activities, the socialist parties relied on the principle of mass membership. The party's work would be undertaken by dues-paying members, who would be the main source of party income too, and who in return for becoming members would be able to exercise some control over the running of the party. This principle of co-operative effort and shared power had been a feature of many of the earlier forms of working-class organization in economic concerns – such as consumer co-operatives and (in Britain) building societies.[7] Yet if there was decentralization of power, at least to some extent, to the members, socialist parties were also centralized in that their branches were subservient to the party as a whole. Thus, unlike the caucus–cadre parties, local 'units' were not completely autonomous, and they did not have to rely on social deference or material reward for supplementing the electoral activities of those committed to the cause.

At the beginning of the twentieth century, then, there were two main kinds of parties in liberal democracies. There were the socialist parties (and some religious parties) where the main participants were the members of the party, although some supporters who were not members would perform a limited number of electoral tasks. The principal complicating factor here was those parties (such as in Britain or Norway) which provided for indirect membership, through the membership of trade unions, so that there were people who were members of a party but not necessarily supporters of it and who, indeed, might be supporters of another party. However, this kind of indirect membership did not usually bestow on such members the kinds of rights associated with individual membership. The other kind of party had various types of participants within it, in regard to their reasons for participating, as well as some individuals who were employed to do party work for financial reward and who in some cases could scarcely be described as participants. In order to deal with the threat posed by socialist parties, several parties had already created alternative structures to the informal hierarchies of the local elites, as a way of recruiting the large workforce needed for mass mobilization. The British Liberals had directly incorporated the party organizations which had sprung up in the 1870s following the franchise extension of 1867, while their Conservative counterparts had effected a more indirect relationship with the locally based, mass-orientated Primrose Leagues. In the United States, the caucus–cadre parties had gone much further than the European parties in creating party organizations to garner the votes of the masses without ceding formal control to them. The patronage-based machines of the cities, developing from the middle of the century onwards, constituted in a sense elite politics on a much larger scale than anything found in Europe, and with non-traditional elites often controlling these operations. As was also the case in some southern European countries, such as Italy, material rewards fuelled machine politics, but these were not usually straightforward market transactions; the party workforce was rewarded with jobs and other favours to create mutually reinforcing systems of obligations, while typically the use of government contracts to secure financial contributions from business also did not involve open, market transactions. Politician and contractor were bound to each other by having entered into transactions that might well be illegal and, if made public, would probably generate bad publicity for both.

During this century there have been several changes making more complex this distinction between socialist, mass membership parties, on the one side, and the non-socialist, caucus–cadre parties on the other.

I

During the first half of the century the non-socialist parties required more workers to undertake party and election tasks than at the end of the nineteenth century, and this meant that even less reliance had to be placed on direct market transactions to recruit these people.

The causes of the increased demand for personnel were further franchise extensions and the growing competitiveness of socialist parties, both of which put pressure on other parties to improve their means of mobilizing voters. The largest increases to national electorates came from the enfranchisement of women, but even by 1900 there had still been categories of adult men in many countries who had not been entitled to vote. Consequently, by the 1930s electorates in some states were much more than double the size of thirty years earlier; in Britain, for example, the electorate increased four-fold between 1900 and 1929 – from 6.7 million to 28.6 million. During this period, also, socialist parties began to expand beyond their original bases in the larger urban areas and in most states they were assisted in this by the growing density of trade union membership. Again, the British example illustrates the increased electoral pressure on non-socialist parties. In the late nineteenth century a high incidence of uncontested seats at some general elections was still common, although, as in 1885 and 1892, some general elections did involve competition in the vast majority of seats.[8] At the general election of 1900, 185 MPs (excluding Irish Nationalists) were returned to office unopposed – that is about 30 per cent of MPs in England, Scotland and Wales. But gradually, though with great variation from one election to another, the rise of the Labour party eliminated the uncontested seat as a feature of the British parliamentary system. In 1929 only seven MPs were elected unopposed. In 1918 (the first election at which there was direct competition between Labour and Liberal candidates nationally) the Labour party had 388 candidates; by 1929 they were able to enter 571 candidates – about a 50 per cent increase.[9]

Non-socialist parties had to respond to this challenge. In rural areas this was often less of a problem. Social networks, and especially deference to social elites, could generate the necessary political activity; the Conservative party in Scotland, for example, was able to rely heavily on such networks until the 1960s. Again, and primarily though not exclusively in rural areas, more explicitly 'exchange relationships' between patron and client could continue to provide electoral resources in some countries. The main problems for the non-socialist parties were in the urban areas and in suburbs. Here, unless they had been able to increase their funds massively, caucus–cadre parties would simply have been unable to 'buy in' a party workforce, and in a number of countries very restrictive campaign finance laws made this impossible anyway. If non-socialist parties were to get campaign tasks performed, it would have to be by non-market means. Even in parties where funds were available for paying for campaign work, we find that increasingly this money came to be used to supplement other incentives to activism. In the United States, where payments were often made to party canvassers, poll-watchers and others, these were jobs that were now preserved for faithful party organization members and their families rather than given to non-party types. Money was thus used to bolster a network of mutual obligations. In fact, after the 1950s local parties had much less money to spend in this way and there has been a great reduction in the proportion of campaign work done 'for money' in America. The reason for this lies in the growing relative importance of the individual candidate as the main actor in campaigning, and candidates have tended to rely far more on *volunteers* than did the local parties.

II

Because of their need for much larger party workforces, many non-socialist parties have either modelled their structures on the socialists', or have taken over specific elements of socialist organization. One consequence of this has been a proliferation of 'hybrid types' of party – parties with elements of both the elite-based party and the mass membership party.

This 'contagion from the left' in regard to party structures was analysed by Duverger in the early 1950s, and it led him to conclude that the socialist form of organization was the most advanced.[10] We shall see that this judgement was incorrect, but for the moment it is necessary to distinguish between two rather different factors leading to the emergence of mass membership structures in non-socialist parties. The first is that there are parties other than socialists possessing an ideology in which the party is merely one arm of a wider social movement. The purpose of mobilizing, therefore, goes beyond the mere winning of public office and involves a notion of the individual's connection with the party as more extensive than that of a campaign worker. Where participation is conceived as being more than simply instrumental to electoral success, a party will tend to be more committed to the

notion of participant input into the party, even when the party's
ideology is supportive of deference and hierarchical structures.
This is true of many religious parties, and another obvious
illustration of the point is the Nationalist party in South Africa.[11]
This party has been set in a political culture which values status
distinctions and is certainly not egalitarian in style; but the
development of Afrikanerdom is a goal requiring participation by
Afrikaners and the party is seen as one of the forums in which this
can be achieved. Consequently, party members have had more
influence over their party than non-elite participants in the
successive white opposition parties in South Africa; but this
influence is not exercised in the same way as in European socialist
parties because there is not the same support for the formal
systems of accountability valued by socialists.

   This use of the mass membership form of organization has to be
distinguished from the adaptation of elements of this from by
caucus–cadre parties in order to attract party workers. One of the
problems facing elite-based parties at the beginning of the century
was how to retain loyal activists who would undertake party work,
especially in cities and suburbs. In the absence of the patronage
resources available in American local government, more use had to
be made of political ideology in attracting individuals and this
entailed creating organizations to which they could belong. In
some cases, as with the Primrose Leagues, the organizations were
attached to the parties rather than being directly part of the party
structure. There were problems with this sort of arrangement,
though. At some point the most energetic and political of the
activists were likely to become dissatisfied with mere 'supporters'
clubs', and alternative structures meant the possibility of conflict
within the party but with no formal means of regulating it.
Consequently, there was a tendency for non-socialist parties to
adopt the socialist idea of *membership*, in which the fee-paying
member acquired certain rights in the party in return for his money
and, hopefully, his labour. However, often these rights did not
amount to the (theoretically) full control of the socialist members.
The British Conservative party's annual conference passes motions
on policies but does not claim to be able to mandate the party, for
example. However, if the growth of membership-type structures
was a pronounced tendency, it was no more than this. Some
parties could survive without members. As von Beyme suggests:

   In continental Europe an effective party organization could co-
   exist with an ideological rejection of the modern form of organis-

ation. This was manifest among the Swedish government supporters right into the twentieth century. It was some time before the rise of other parties (peasants, Liberals and Social Democrats) began to erode the privileged position the Conservative 'gentlemen' had enjoyed for so long. But the Conservatives did succeed in maintaining their power position largely without a formal organization right in the twentieth century. It was the rise of a professional class, a counterpart to the nobility in its ability to escape at least at times from occupational ties, which created the pre-requisites for the rise of the modern party organization.[12]

It was not until the 1950s, therefore, that Conservative parties in Sweden and Finland developed a mass organizational base.

Moreover, the concessions to the modern idea of membership may be slight: the Gaullist party in France gives few formal rights to its members.[13] And, even when the idea of membership is taken seriously by a party, it may not subscribe to the original idea of the socialist parties that a large membership is desirable. For reasons which become apparent when we consider the impact of new technologies, some parties prefer to have a relatively small membership. The West German Free Democrats pride themselves on being 'small but select'. Nevertheless, there are only three examples of major liberal democracies where socialist party organization put *no* pressure on other parties to adapt. (This was also the case in South Africa. There the Labour party ceased to be a major political force in the 1930s, being undermined by Afrikaner nationalist mobilization. In this case, though, one of the major parties, the Nationalists, had already organized themselves on mass membership lines.) Highly structured parties in Ireland had developed by the beginning of the twentieth century, and at that time they were arguably better organized than those in Great Britain. While a social democratic party did develop there after independence, it has never attracted anything like the electoral support of the two largest parties in that party system. (The largest share of the general election vote obtained by the Labour party was seventeen per cent in 1969.) Moreover, the adoption of the single transferable vote as the method of election in Ireland has accentuated the tendency for candidates (especially incumbents) to develop networks of personal support. In many ways, his or her fellow party candidates are a greater electoral threat to a member of the Irish Dail, than are candidates from other parties. Thus, while in one sense there is well-developed party organization in Ireland, it is very much geared to personal links between legislators and constituents and owes little to the mobilizing power of a working-class party. In the United States a socialist party was still-born in the first two decades of this century. However, we see later that, even here, the issue of 'membership' and of the rights of different kinds of participants in the American parties was to become a major issue in the mid-twentieth century. Finally, in Canada, a socialist party did emerge in the western provinces in the inter-war years, but it was not typical of socialist movements, in that its key element was an agrarian and not an industrial base. It made relatively little impact in the more populous and industrialized provinces of Ontario and Quebec. At the national level the party, which was later called the New Democratic Party, was similar to the Labour party in Ireland – it was never able to become even the second largest party in the country and it propounded an especially moderate version of social democracy. As a result, Canadian party organization, too, has been relatively free of pressure from a successful, mass membership socialist party. Unlike the United States, though, Canada had inherited both British parliamentary institutions and some of its traditions of political organization in the second half of the nineteenth century.

III

Continuing urbanization, the decline of peasant agriculture and increased and improved mass communications have posed increasing difficulties for social elites; they are less able to obtain work for their parties from those people who were bound to them in systems of mutual obligation.

As studies of, for example, Britain have shown, at the beginning of the century many of the newly enfranchised working class were socially deferential and took on the voting habits of their 'betters'. In states with large peasant populations the management of electoral politics could be even easier. With the decline of the peasantry, and also of domestic service, in western Europe the ability of elites to control elections through traditional means generally declined. In turn, this made it necessary to employ other ways of mobilizing voters. Nevertheless, clientelism – a system of personal, but unequal, relations in which favours are exchanged between the people involved – has survived, and continues to be a means by which some parties can ensure that electorally related tasks are performed. A full explanation of the factors which enable clientelism to survive would be very complex, and involve evaluating the differential effects of political structures, patterns of social values and access to economic resources.[14] For our purpose it is necessary only to point to the major factors enabling clientelism to thrive in some liberal democracies.

One consideration is that liberal democratic structures have developed, or been imposed on, regimes which are less industrialized than mid-to-late twentieth-century western Europe. In Colombia, for example, Schmidt has analysed the role of *gamonalismo* in rural and small-town areas:

> It consists of a network of individuals who have access to scarce resources like jobs, money or goods as well as the ability to sponsor events that entertain . . . or connections with important institutions like the police. These individuals are plugged into the national political party system . . . In some cases the gamonal is in the service (paid or not) of a nationally prominent patron who needs help in mobilizing local votes and thereby retaining political power. Such gamonales assume the day-to-day responsibility of politics in the community and carry out the routine tasks of supervising the constituency.[15]

In Jamaica too both of the major political parties have strong clientelistic features, especially the more right-wing Jamaica Labour party, and here clientelism is pervasive in the trade union movements which are an important source of linkage with the working class.[16] Affluence, and the divorce of market relations from social ties which tends to accompany industrialization, makes these sorts of relations more difficult to maintain, but they are still an obvious and relatively cheap way of organizing an electorate in less economically developed regimes.

Another factor facilitating the maintenance of some patron–client relations is control of government. Continuous access to governmental power gives a party the opportunity to exploit resources from which relations of mutual obligation can be developed.[17] These can take several forms: the placing of party supporters in government jobs; mutual penetration of parties and powerful economic interests; and the creation of personal organizations attached to individual politicians. In states where one party has controlled the liberal democratic goverment, or has been a member of a coalition government for a long time, long-term relationships can be sustained. In Italy, where the Christian Democrats have been in every government since the second world war,

> the Christian Democratic party has developed and used its control over patronage (especially jobs) to accomplish two ends, the

maintenance of voter loyalty and party domination of all branches and agencies of government. That party's capacity to survive . . . may be explained in large part by the success of this form of linkage.[18]

On the other hand, in Japan the continuing control of the Liberal Democratic Party (LDP), again since the war, has helped its leadership to develop close links with major industrial concerns; this policy has produced a number of scandals relating to bribery. Moreover, the power of the LDP has enabled its individual members to develop strong personal electoral organizations, in which the distribution of largesse plays an important role.[19]

Then again, there is the rather different experience in Sweden, where the Social Democrats were in power from 1932 until 1976, and which provides a useful contrast with traditional patron–client relations. There the dominance of one party helped to bring about the inclusion of interest organizations in national politics in a form to which the term 'corporatism' has been applied. These relations are certainly not ones of patron and client, but they are similar in that a socialist party made use of ties to other actors (in this case, interest organizations) to create indirect resources with which to preserve its electoral successes. The argument is not that the party used control of the state either to place 'its people' in state bureaucracies, or to generate funds from interest groups, but rather that its inclusion of the groups helped to stabilize politics to the advantage of the ruling party. As Ruin argues,

> First, valuable information can be obtained through such an inclusion. The interest organizations possess expertise in many different fields; also they can convey to the government the attitudes and wishes of different segments of the population. Second, valuable *mobilization of support* can be achieved. By including interest organizations in the political process they easily become responsible for governmental decisions taken. The process receives, one might say, an extra dimension of legitimacy . . . Potential opposition is pacified.[20]

What is evident about the Italian and Japanese examples is that patron–client relations are arguably more important in modern parties at the elite levels of the parties than in providing direct links with the masses. This presents a notable contrast with the American urban machines in their heyday, when the provision of low-level jobs was as at least as important as government contracts in sustaining the machines. In part, this emphasis on elite-level patronage in parties in advanced economies reflects changes in campaign technology which have made new forms of campaigning possible; we examine these changes shortly. However, the modern state has generally made government less valuable to parties as a source of patronage than it was at the turn of the century.

One development has been the gradual ceding of areas of responsibility to professions and to possessors of new skills who claim 'professional' status. Professions have their own codes of conduct and their objectives may depart from those of would-be political masters. As professions have come to run and administer more areas of policy for which the state is financially responsible, so it has become more difficult for parties to penetrate the state completely. In the case of the United States, the Progressive reformers were often members of professions, and one of their prime objectives was to take responsibility for various policy areas away from government and to place it in the hands of independent boards and agencies on which the professions would have much greater influence.[21] While this has been taken further, perhaps, in the decentralized American political system than elsewhere, it remains true that the expansion of state activity in the twentieth century has often taken forms which help to reduce party influence – over both policy and in the development of patronage. Another point is that modern forms of welfare provision typically involve *rights* for the recipients which make it difficult for the control of welfare to be used as the basis for creating patron–client relations. Indeed, Hamilton has argued that in the United States the low levels of voter mobilization by Blacks can be related to the growth of 'patron–recipient' relations under the Great Society programmes. Unlike the patron–client relations fostered by the machines, these new arrangements gave black leaders in the institutions established under the various programmes neither the resources nor the incentives for political organization in the communities.[22]

The general impact, then, of changes in the availability of patronage has been to force elite-based parties to diversify in the way they recruit activists and get election tasks performed. Except in the less economically advanced states, the patron–client relation can only play a rather limited role in electoral mobilization. It still survives and is important in some regimes where there is a dominant party, but, even in the cases of Japan and Italy, we find well developed membership-type organizations supplementing the patronage operations. In contrast, the most well-developed examples of elite-based parties competing in elections at the turn of the century, the American parties, could operate without *volunteers* for the most part. So that we can see how the caucus–cadre form of party has had to adapt, and the result has been the emergence of 'hybrid' parties with features of both elite-based and mass membership-based parties.

IV

There was a marked decline in the ability of parties to use social and recreational facilities as an inducement in recruiting party workers. This affected both elite-based and mass membership parties, and again contributed to the growth of 'hybrid' parties.

At the beginning of the twentieth century the social facilities, such as clubs and outings, provided by some parties were a major incentive for potential party workers. In many American cities the political clubhouse was as much a social as a political centre, while most European socialist parties, along with trade unions, organized all forms of recreational activities for their members. Perhaps the most well-known examples of this were the stamp-collecting clubs organized by many local branches of the Austrian and German Socialist parties. In Britain this tradition is maintained by the presence (and often dominance) of political club teams in local snooker, bridge and other sporting leagues. Nor were socialist parties the only ones to provide extensive facilities; Catholic parties, such as the party in inter-war Czechoslovakia, often did so as well. The success of parties in attracting workers because of their social and recreational facilities was partly the result of there being relatively few other large organizations attempting to do the same, but there was also a lack of inexpensive leisure activities. Increased affluence, the mass-produced motor car and changing social values affecting how people should interact with each other, undermined this important resource for the parties. By about the 1960s the social aspect of most political parties in western Europe and North America was in serious decline. For parties which were mainly of the caucus–cadre type, this meant that a relatively higher proportion of their party workforce was likely to be attracted to the party by its policies or ideology, and in turn they would expect a greater input into the party. This did not necessarily mean demands for full democracy of the kind found (in theory) in socialist parties, but it did mean that discussion of issues and policies, as well as influence in the selection of leaders, could no longer be a preserve of the party elite. The growing importance of politics in these parties meant that many had to adapt their *modus operandi* to cater for those who would regard themselves as members. An example of this sort of shift is the British Conservative party which abandoned its traditional way of selecting the party leader in 1965. Discussion within the party hierarchy was replaced by an election process – albeit one making MPs the only voters. But the point about this process was that it gave the average party members some sense of a connection between their own activities and the directions which the party would take.

Obviously, the effect of the declining 'pull' of social facilities was different in socialist parties. On the one hand, as in the British Labour party, it both reduced the size of the party membership and helped to facilitate a shift in the ideological composition of many constituency parties. Party management became more difficult, as it did in some other northern European socialist parties.[23] On the other hand, it provided an incentive for parties at least to consider employing new campaign technologies in place of older labour-intensive means of campaigning. Resistance to this was often considerable, and socialist parties have frequently been the slowest to adapt to the 'new campaigning', but without an army of workers upon which to call electoral survival may depend on successful use of the media, direct mailing and so on. In turn, this can lead to an increased role for the party's central leadership and for the experts they employ; but, especially where parties are strong in local politics, this need not entail a reduced role for party organizations at all levels.[24] The new campaign technologies are less easy to employ at that level of politics, so that there would seem to be limits to the erosion of the mass membership base.

V

The rise of new campaign technologies since the Second World War has introduced a new kind of participant into political parties – the campaign specialist organized in independent firms.

At first, in California in the 1930s, the people employed to provide specialist services to party candidates were experts in public relations or advertising who 'took on' a candidate as they would take on any other client. There was a clearly defined *market* relationship, and the firms were no more an element of the party than were the printers of campaign leaflets or the manufacturers of campaign buttons. In some areas of campaign technology this business relationship survives. Many of the major polling firms, for instance, will do polls for anyone and regard themselves as providing a purely technical service. But the growth of campaign consultancy has seen a proliferation of the kinds of relations which can develop between parties and party candidates, on the one side, and the consultants and experts on the other. In the United States many of these firms work only for candidates with whose ideology they are compatible. The successful firms always have clients and this has led to the consultant choosing his candidate as much as the candidate choosing a particular firm. However, as Sabato argues, often it is not so much ideology as the 'personal mesh' between consultant and client to which the former looks when deciding for whom he will work: 'There is a sort of ritualized mating dance when consultants and prospective clients meet, a mutual sizing-up and testing of one another that can be quite intense for all parties.'[25] Moreover, the campaign consultant's aims are to make money so that the revenue earning potential of a campaign partly determines whether a given candidate will be taken on.

Outside America the possibilities for a close relationship between party candidate and consultant in which the latter is dominant are rather limited. Closer ties between party and candidate, restrictions on access to television broadcasting and, in some cases, much stricter controls on campaign expenditures all contribute to consultants being employees of a party rather than, in effect, being participants in it. Yet there is an obvious sense in which even Saatchi and Saatchi (the consultants employed by the British Conservative party in 1979 and 1983) have a rather different relationship to the party than the firms which do their printing. The way in which a party is marketed affects how both the elite and mass members of it come to see that party. Of course, any marketing strategy draws on qualities and images valued by those in the party, but the strategy also helps to 'shape' priorities and images. The important issue, though is not whether we should regard consultants as *formal* participants in the party, but that they must be recognized as having an influence on the party.

As we have already suggested, one of the principal consequences of the new technologies has been to modify the activities of mass membership parties, with a centralizing of campaign strategy and campaigning itself. This has had two important and related consequences for the leadership of parties. On the one hand, the party leader becomes a greater focal point in campaigning. On the other hand, it has had a severe impact on the earlier practice in some European parties of the party leader not automatically being regarded as the person who would head the government should his party win an election. In Austria the party leader was often not even a parliamentary candidate; indeed, in central and eastern

Europe there was a tendency for brokerage over the most important decisions of coalition politics to take place between party leaders rather than between the leaders of parliamentary parties. While this distinction between party leader and parliamentary leader has not been eroded completely, the requirements of modern campaigning have at least forced parties to designate an individual who will head a government in advance of an election campaign. In West Germany, for example, the parties have selected a Chancellor-designate since 1961.

If these changes suggest a further narrowing of the differences between caucus–cadre and mass parties, we must not conclude that the new technologies make caucus–cadre parties the model for the future. This was a view propounded by Epstein who, in opposition to Duverger's vision of 'contagion from the left', argued that it was 'contagion from the right', from the caucus–cadre parties, that was developing.[26] The main problem with Epstein's argument is that it ignores the functions which members can perform and which the technologies cannot. Opinion polls can give detailed analyses of voter opinions, but there are aspects of these opinions which even the best-designed polls can fail to capture. Equally, television may be no match for communities and small groups in forming and moulding opinions – the absence of active party supporters in a community may mean that its case is never really heard in discussions or conversations.[27]

We have seen, then, that there has been a tendency for 'hybrid' parties to emerge and for the clear distinction between elite-based and membership-based parties to become more blurred. Nevertheless, there remain many instances where it is evident that a particular party is primarily of one type rather than the other. In the remainder of this chapter we examine the differences between parties with respect to participation in three of the most significant activities of parties: the nomination of candidates; setting of party policies and objectives; and the organizing of electoral campaigns. We shall see that, while opportunities for participation vary considerably between parties, there seem to be no set of arrangements which provide for both widespread participation and effective party control over its own procedures. This discussion lays the foundation for an examination of conflicts between elite and mass participants in parties in chapter 6.

THE NOMINATION OF CANDIDATES

Obviously, where a cadre party survives in a relatively pure form, there are no members or large groups of committed activists who might participate in, or demand to participate in, the process of nominating candidates. As with the non-Gaullist conservative parties in France, local notables are left a free hand to work out candidacies among themselves. Difficulties arise within predominantly caucus–cadre parties where there are groups of party workers who believe they have the status of members and should have correspondingly full rights of participation in the nomination process; the Democratic party in the United States provides a clear example of this. Within mass membership parties there are two main limitations on member participation. The first is that the power to nominate may lie in the hands of higher echelon bodies in the party; when this happens, members may (at most) be called upon to ratify decisions taken from above. In some cases they may simply have no powers. One example of this concerned the ordering of the SPD's list of candidates in the Weimar republic. As in any party list system of voting, the party had to provide an order of candidates and the SPD national organization took the decisions in Reichstag elections. This meant that trade union leaders, among others, had far greater influence than individual party members. This procedure changed after 1949, when all the major parties used delegate conferences in each *Land* as the decision-making body in federal elections. More commonly, the members may merely give their approval to decisions made elsewhere.[28] These may be decisions made at the level of the national party organization, or at the local level by party office-holders. Indeed, it has been widely argued that virtually all parties exhibit one of these forms of elite control, and hence exclude members from participation, but it is now recognized that there are important exceptions, including Ireland. There perhaps forty per cent of Labour party members and thirty per cent of Fianna Fail and Fine Gael members are actively involved in the nomination of candidates.[29] The other limitation is that, in any case, the power to nominate may be a power than can be used only infrequently. Generally this is not so under the party list system, where the resignation or death of members may require the entire list to be re-examined before the next election, especially where it is important to 'balance' different interests in the party; unless a principle of strict seniority is being applied, decisions about who is to occupy each position on the list have to be made. However, in single-member constituencies, for example, there is no 'automatic' requirement of this kind in relation to nominations, and party practice may preclude decisions about a nomination being taken again until the sitting member himself or herself dies, retires, or resigns. This proved to be a major issue in the British Labour party in the 1970s.

In the Labour party the power of nomination quite specifically rested with local constituency parties and there were procedures they had to follow in making nominations. But there was no requirement for these procedures to be implemented again once the candidate entered parliament. In the early 1970s there were conflicts within several constituency parties between groups that wished to remove a sitting MP and the MPs, who were usually right-wingers. (One of them, Reginald Prentice, subsequently left the part and joined the Conservatives.) While the party's rules did not preclude constituency parties from 'deselecting' their MP, it proved difficult to implement in most cases. The reservoir of patronage and loyalty on which the MP could draw were often sufficient to stall, at some stage of the complex procedures, the movement to 'deselect'. Not surprisingly, this issue of removing sitting MPs became a central one in the growing disputes within the party. In 1977 the party conference voted to introduce a system for the compulsory reselection of MPs, but its opponents delayed its introduction until 1980. Today all Labour MPs must undergo reselection before each general election. However, while this has extended the opportunities for participation in the nomination process, the Labour party still limits in another way the input of the individual members. It is general committees of the constituency parties which make nominations and not the party members *en masse*. This does not mean that the individual members lack power, for it is they who select delegates to the committees, but it does mean that the extent of member involvement depends on power structures at the ward level. Allegations of small groups of members being able to control ward parties virtually unchecked have been rife in the Labour party for years; what has changed is that, whereas in the past this worked to the advantage of the right, it is now left-wing groups which have been the target of criticism.

This example highlights one of the main difficulties facing those who wish to extend participation in the nomination process. If nominations are made at single meetings which all members can attend, there is the potential problem of 'stacking', especially by would-be candidates who would have an incentive to enrol as many of their personal supporters in the party as possible. It is easy to organize them to attend a single nomination meeting. Relatively open procedures of this kind are likely to make the candidates themselves more powerful in the nomination process and, through that, more powerful in the party. Yet, a decentralized system of nomination – involving sub-constituency level units and several meetings in the nomination process – is likely to put off all but the most committed activists and make it easier for some small groups to exclude their political opponents. This suggests that what is needed, if the aim is to extend effective participation in the party, is some combination of open and restricted procedures which provide a check on the two tendencies we have identified. In an earlier study I argued that the sort of nomination system used in Colorado, of a party assembly designating up to about three candidates with nomination being decided in a closed party primary, might be a model to consider for this purpose.[30] However, what should be emphasized is that the mechanisms required to avoid the Scylla (of candidate power) and Charybdis (of local group monopolies) are likely to depend on the particular circumstances of the political system in question. For example, party primaries in the Labour party today would not extend participation very far because of the low level to which individual membership has sunk: in 1979 members constituted less than three per cent of the Labour electorate. Yet, equally, there would be the possibility of too much influence being acquired by candidates if any self-declared Labour party voter was eligible to vote in a primary.

If the central issue facing membership parties has been *how* members should participate in the nomination of candidates, in the United States an issue at the centre of political debate both at the turn of the century and in the late 1960s was *who* should participate in candidate selection. While the Progressives in some states, such as California, resolved the issue by making the primary election with a broad electorate the main nominating arena, this was not the only solution. In some states, such as New York, party conventions continued to be used for some offices while electoral laws there also make it possible for party organizations to keep dissident candidates off the primary ballot. Elsewhere, as in Colorado, a dual system of conventions and primaries was introduced. With both these kinds of arrangements disputes arose as to who, if anyone, should play a 'gatekeeper' role in providing candidates with access to the primaries. But the office with which this controversy over nominations was to become most widespread was that of the presidency itself. While some states did introduce presidential primaries in the Progressive era, these were *indirect* primaries, in that the candidate could not be selected directly in them; at most, the primary electorate chose delegates to a National Convention. The result was a so-called 'mixed system' of nominating presidents – some delegates were chosen in primary elections but the majority were selected by caucuses and conventions. This system worked reasonably smoothly until the Democratic Convention of 1968, when the whole question of the right to participate in the party came to a head.

The Democratic party had been undergoing a gradual change in the composition of its activist base long before 1968. From the late 1940s a new kind of issue-oriented activist had started to enter the party's organizations at the local level, especially in the larger, more cosmopolitan, cities. Adlai Stevenson's campaign for the presidency in 1952 had been a strong factor encouraging this kind of activism, but the movement had grown only gradually after the failure of that campaign. It differed in several respects from earlier mobilizations of the American middle classes. It was not anti-party in character, but rather most of its members wanted to transform the Democratic party into a more programmatic party. Moreover, while some of these new activists were utterly opposed to patronage politics, this was not true of all of them, and in practice it was often difficult to draw a sharp distinction between the new 'amateur' and the old 'professional' activists.[31] The amateurs generally worked for the election of Kennedy in 1960, even though most of them had again supported Stevenson's candidacy that year and were resentful of some of the tactics employed by the Kennedys both before and during the National Convention. This slow change in the Democratic party was disrupted by the divisive political issues of the 1960s, particularly the Vietnam war. Among many of the older amateur Democrats, there was anger at a war being waged by a Democratic president, while many new political activists were mobilized by the issue of the war. Together these two groups worked for the nomination of opponents of Lyndon Johnson in 1968 – some for Eugene McCarthy and others, until his assassination, for Bobby Kennedy. Meanwhile, after Johnson's withdrawal from the presidential race, many of the leaders of local and state parties swung their support behind the vice-president, Hubert Humphrey. Humphrey did not win any primaries that year and the anti-war activists' resentment of his eventual nomination was increased by the use made of party organizational power in many cities to prevent them from fully participating in caucuses and conventions.

At the heart of this dispute lay differing views of who had a right to participate in the party, differences which had been partly concealed by the relatively peaceful assimilation of issue-oriented activists into the party in earlier years. On the one side were those who believed that the main participants in the nomination process should be the party 'regulars' – the long-serving activists who occupied party office from the ward level upwards. They did not argue for a closed party elite but rather for one open to those who were prepared to serve an apprenticeship in the party. Rather like the Communist party in the Soviet Union, full membership of the party was something which had to be earned. On the other side many of the activists who supported McCarthy and Kennedy took a view of the right to participate that was partly derived from the mass membership party model. Those who were concerned by political issues should be able to join a political party and, having joined, be able to have a say in nominating candidates. In the absence of formal membership in American parties, they took the act of mobilizing around a candidate or an issue as being the equivalent of this. But, of course, while these activists probably were the functional equivalents of members in mass membership parties, there was no understanding on the part of their opponents that this was a valid comparison. From the latter's perspective it was the 'regulars' in the organization who constituted the party. Moreover, as Ranney pointed out a few years later, within the country there was even further disagreement as to who the 'members' of American parties were.[32] The introduction of primaries had produced two other, and more inclusive, groups which had some claim to being the 'members'. The more restricted group was the 'self designated adherents' – people who declared themselves to be Democrats (or Republicans) and who registered to vote in their party's primaries. An even broader group was the entire electorate – on this view the person need not even regard himself or herself as a Democrat to have a right to participate in that party's primary; merely having an interest in doing so was sufficient to claim 'membership' of the party. (This extension of the notion of a 'member' so that it virtually became meaningless had already been put into practice in a few states like Washington, where 'free love' primaries enabled voters to vote in one party's primary for one office and the other party's primaries for other offices.) The complexity of this situation, and the fact that the dissident Democrats had no scheme or support for implementing membership on the lines of social democratic parties, meant that it was difficult for them to get their view of membership accepted. Ironically, as we see in chapter 6, having lost the presidential nomination in 1968, they did succeed in getting the party to accept reform proposals which broadly corresponded to their ideas of who should participate. However, because of the difficulty of implementing these reforms, many states opted to use primaries.

The result has been a reassertion of the caucus–cadre characteristics of American parties, only with candidates now the dominant elite in the parties.

PARTY POLICIES AND OBJECTIVES

Just as caucus–cadre parties retain elite control over nominations, so they also restrict control over party policy, objectives and ideology. In the United States both the national parties and many state parties have party platforms, to which a number of groups in a party may contribute, but the platforms are of little significance in election campaigns or in public policy-making. The candidates have their own policies and priorities and mostly they ignore their party's commitments unless these happen to coincide with their own. In mass membership parties there is, in theory, strong membership input into the setting of policy objectives and even in decisions regarding particular policies. Such input may not be formalized and, as with the Nationalists in South Africa, it may instead involve informal attempts to secure mass support for policies which have been decided by politicians. Again, a mass membership party may try to restrict direct membership participation in the development of party programmes. The British SDP emerged as a revolt against activist influence in policy-making, and it quite deliberately ensured that the influence of parliamentarians in the drawing up of an election manifesto would be dominant. Yet, even in traditional social democratic parties, procedures have been introduced to limit direct membership participation in the selection of party policies and programmes. In the British Labour party the party manifesto is decided jointly by the parliamentary leaders and the National Executive Committtee of the party. While the latter supposedly provides for the direct input of the views of the membership, the parliamentarians have exercised their veto power over the inclusion of items already approved by a two-thirds majority at a party conference. One of the aspects of conflict within the party in the late 1970s and early 1980s concerned control over the manifesto, and a move to give total control over it to the National Executive Committee was defeated only narrowly in 1981. In 1983 the manifesto was more closely linked to the policies agreed in party conference than were earlier manifestos, but the electoral landslide against the party that year strengthened the control of the parliamentary leadership and allowed it to exercise far greater discretion over the inclusion of some policies, such as that relating to nuclear power.

Superficially it might appear that the substitution of indirect influence over party programmes for direct control would be a limitation on the extent of democracy within a party. Nevertheless, a number of justifications for this have been put forward and it is important to separate them, not least because some are far more plausible than others.

> The construction of public policy requires technical expertise which most party members lack.

Certainly, if a party's programme involved highly complex proposals for, say, tax policy or social insurance schemes, then there is a strong case for allowing party members only to decide on the general principle of these policies, rather than on their details. Too much tinkering could make a policy demonstrably unworkable. However, few parties have the research resources enabling them to work out whole policy programmes in detail. While the West German parties have far greater facilities available to them than their British counterparts, even they are not effective 'governments in exile' when they are not in office. Detailed policies are usually the preserve of parties in government and opposition parties are necessarily confined to making general policy statements. Specific commitments, such as Macmillan's pledge in 1951 to build a given number of houses per year if the Conservatives were returned to power in Britain, are comparatively rare, and this particular commitment was virtually unplanned or thought out. But even parties in government tend to campaign on more general statements than specific proposals, because this is what the electorate is interested in and can understand, so that the argument from expertise is one which is unconvincing in most circumstances.

> Party members have a tendency to want specific commitments on policies, but in many cases the viability of particular proposals can only be ascertained once a party is in government.

One of the consequences of a relative lack of information for parties in opposition is that it is often difficult to assess the viability of enacting policies. Party members, though, often want the commitments given on party platforms or in manifestos to be more specific because this provides a better guideline for its representatives in public office. Here the case for 'filtering' the direct input of party members may seem more convincing. If voter choice is to be available, then the 'packages' of policies offered by the parties must avoid promises which may not be fulfilable. Of course, as we saw in Chapter 3, the problem of parties 'outbidding' each other was a feature a British party politics during the 1950s and 1960s, and there we suggested that it was the *absence* of control on leaders' promises which helped to produce this. (This point is developed further in chapter 6.) This suggests that participation in the setting of policies requires a fine balance between the influence of leaders who may exaggerate claims for electoral reasons and the influence of party members who may demand overly specific policies incapable of implementation once the party is in office.

The direct involvement of all members in setting policy objectives may result in a set on incompatible objectives being agreed upon.

This is the argument that large organizations tend to 'add on' programmes to meet the demands of particular sections of the membership and the resulting package is one which could not be implemented entirely, because of the constraints facing government. Just as decentralized bodies like the American Congress tend to enact too many programmes of expenditure because there is difficulty in getting committees to conform to budget guidelines, so would decentralized procedures within parties lead to 'overblown' policy packages. As with the previous argument, it suggests how parties can be the source of excessive and unwarranted expectations developing in the electorate. Clearly, however, what is at issue is *how* the opinions of party members should be taken into account in setting policy objectives, and extensive participation by members does not necessarily entail decentralization. Problems in parties would arise when sub-units had sufficient autonomy to impose policy proposals on the party as a whole, and when there was no co-ordinating policy unit which could set priorities among the various proposals. Overcoming this problem would preclude direct member participation in the final stages of policy formation, but only the most naive democrats have ever supposed that large public meetings were always appropriate forums for devising policy. The more significant problem for democrats is ensuring that the opinions of members cannot be by-passed or ignored in smaller forums.

Party members are more extreme in their policy preferences than ordinary party voters, so that extensive member participation in the setting of a party's policy is more likely to produce a programme which is unacceptable to the party's voters.

This argument has a long history, and its proponents in Britain often cite the experience of the Labour party in 1983 as evidence in support of it, while Americans point to the similar lack of success by the Democrats' George McGovern in 1972 and the Republicans' Barry Goldwater in 1964. Nevertheless, the argument about issue extremism is far less convincing than it appears at first sight. Unless we assume that party activists are likely to be risk-takers (a point we examine shortly), we would expect that they would wish to adapt party policy to the wishes of the electorate. Indeed, far from party activists misperceiving the electorate as having similar views to their own, Marvick's evidence from parties in Los Angeles indicates that they may be very well aware of how the views of the electorate differ from their own. Of the period 1969–74, a period of intense conflict over issues in the United States, he argues:

> In these years, changes in the way the voters lined up on . . . issues were being monitored by the party cadres of both camps. The remarkably high cognitive agreement about where each voting bloc stood on each issue strongly suggests that political realities were being skillfully appraised. It is difficult to imagine two sets of political fantasies, one for Democratic activists and the other for Republicans, that for quite different reasons could have led these men and women in rival camps – themselves with sharply contrasting policy preferences – to reach the same conclusions about the preferences of Democratic and Republican voters.[33]

This is not to deny that activists in some parties may, from time to time, misperceive the preferences of their party's voters, but it does suggest that its occurrence is perhaps more related to particular historical experiences of a given party than to any general deficiencies in party activists. Most especially, it is related to a small overall membership base, and to the issue extremists being a formerly 'out' group within the party. Again, the electoral disasters encountered by parties campaigning with 'extreme' candidates and leaders are matched by the successes of parties which have stood outside the consensus. The British Conservative party in 1979 and 1983, and Republican Ronald Reagan in 1980 and 1984, were two examples of this. In both cases electoral dissatisfaction with the operation of 'consensus politics' at the time of their coming to power meant that their ideology was not a disadvantage. Furthermore, the parties were able to draw attention to a number of personal characteristics of their leaders and thereby helped to overcome what resistance there was to the 'issue extremism' with which the party was now associated.

Issue-oriented party members are more prepared to take the risk of losing an election with an 'extreme' candidate or policy than are other kinds of participant in a party.

This argument gained credibility from some of the earlier studies of 'amateur' activists in the United States purporting to show that for such activists ideology was more important than winning. Similar reasoning would suggest that in a mass membership party the members would exert pressure towards issue extremism. This argument has been undermined by subsequent studies showing that 'risk taking' with candidates seems to be associated with being an 'out' group in a party rather than with being issue-oriented.[34] Issue-oriented activism can be closely associated with a strong commitment to a party and to its electoral success.[35] In Britain the example of the switch by the 'soft left' in the Labour party after the 1983 election also suggests that once a group becomes a dominant one in a party it may be more prepared to make compromises on policies in the interests of electoral success.

Parties are likely, then, to face a problem with issue 'extremists' imposing unwinnable candidates or programmes on them when groups which have had little influence on the party in the past find that they have an opportunity to get some of their policies accepted. One of the main circumstances when this opportunity arises is in the aftermath of a dispiriting electoral defeat, when leaders and activists temporarily have drifted away from the party leaving it open to change. However, longer term changes in a party may also be associated with 'risk taking' in its early stages. After 1960 the Republican party became increasingly a conservative party in its activist base and in the candidates it nominated; the old moderate-liberal wing of the party was virtually destroyed. But it was only in the first presidential campaign, Goldwater's in 1964, that the newly dominant element in the party produced a campaign that rejected concessions to political centrists. While Goldwater's slogan that year was 'A choice, not an echo', the continuing take-over of local party organizations by conservatives did not subsequently produce the stark choice offered in 1964. Conservatives who could demonstrate an ability to draw wider electoral support became the primary contenders for power. Austere conservatives, like Philip Crane in 1980, found it difficult to mobilize support.

With party memberships generally in decline, it is far easier for parties to be 'infiltrated' by groups which have little in common with the mainstream tradition of these parties.

It was precisely this kind of reasoning which lay behind the British SDP's decision to provide for only indirect membership influence on party policy-making; their experience of the Labour Party, from which they had 'exited' led them to believe that parties could be at the mercy of unrepresentative groups. There are, however, a number of reasons for being cautious in accepting such arguments. While as von Beyme acknowledged, 'the membership density of parties is dropping in many countries', he also indicated several considerations restricting the significance of this.[36] Again, the decline in individual membership in the British Labour party was far greater than in most other parties – from over one million reported members in the early 1950s to 280,000 less than thirty years later. It was certainly not a typical case. The British electoral system too, more than most others, encourages extreme groups to join major parties rather than fight elections under their own banners. Moreover, where there was 'infiltration', it was made possible by the basis of organization in Britain, the parliamentary constituency, which is sufficiently small to permit take-overs by unrepresentative groups. Finally, of all the mass membership parties, the British Labour party is perhaps the one where membership recruitment has been taken least seriously and this made it prone to a collapse in its membership base. While the party did not seek to actively recruit new members, it also did not adopt the opposite strategy of making sure that its members were deeply committed to the party. Annual membership fees, for example, remained low – unlike the German SPD, in which fees are related to personal income and many party members pay more than £100 a year to the party. All of this suggests that, if there is an argument about the need for limiting membership input to policy-making because of 'infiltration', it is probably not generalizable beyond the particular case.

We have seen, therefore, that while there are grounds for '*structuring*' the input of members into the policy-making of a party, many of the arguments employed against widespread member participation seem either defective or of limited application.

ORGANIZING ELECTION CAMPAIGNS

Election campaigns are relatively labour-intensive activities. Many of the means used by parties to induce their potential voters actually to vote for them involve a workforce for which there can be no direct substitute. This is most apparent with door-to-door canvassing during elections and with pre-election efforts to create a climate of opinion within communities favourable to a party. But, of course, this form of campaigning is not universal; geographical constraints, as in Norway or the hills of the East Bay in California, have long forced parties to rely primarily on other methods – such as a politicized press or direct-mail advertising. But even in these cases, there are many tasks connected with finding out the likely sources of support and ensuring supporters can get to the polls, that require people as well as capital equipment or technical skills. As we suggested earlier in this chapter, the amount of labour required has meant that parties have had to rely far more on volunteers of various kinds than on the direct purchasing of labour. Even in the classic party machines in America's cities the relationship between machine member and party was more than a transaction in which material rewards were exchanged for labour. Moreover, there is a clear sense in which many of these people were *participants* in campaigns, in that they had some discretion in their own precincts as to how they 'got the vote out'. They were expected to achieve this goal, but they were also often thought to be the best judge of what worked 'in their patch'. The participatory element in patronage-oriented parties in the United States was further strengthened by the fact that machines, like the parties in Italy later for example, recognized that electoral success was linked to party involvement in activities beyond narrowly defined electoral matters. In his study of Chicago in the 1970s, one of the few remaining Democratic machines of the old-fashioned kind, Guterbock argued that

> the key to the success of the ward club is the participation of party agents in the public political life of the local community . . . the politicians in the ward I studied commit tremendous time and effort to the meetings, rallies, ceremonies, conferences, and confrontations which are so much a part of local public life.[37]

Whatever the limitations of patronage politics, compared with issue-oriented political activism then, it did not necessarily limit political participation to the mechanical performance of orders issued from above. If it had, the relatively low salaries and rewards available to most of the functionaries would never have been sufficient to sustain their continued involvement with the party.

The main threat to electoral compaigning as the basis for a significant form of participation in liberal democracies has not come so much from the continuing availability of patronage but from the new campaign technologies. And the point is not that these technologies reduce the need for campaign labour, but that they reduce the 'creative' elements of participation for the lower level party activists. There are two main aspects to this.

In all liberal democracies television campaigning has had the effect of centralizing decisions about campaign strategies. Compared with campaigning through billboards or door-to-door canvassing, there is less scope for local initiative here and so these forms of campaigning have become relatively less important. As Criddle has said of France:

> Hastened by the process of presidentialization, electoral cam-
> paigning in France has, in common with that in comparable western
> states, deserted the streets for the television studios. Whilst French
> elections still make a visible impact on publicly provided street bill-
> boards available to all candidates, even these billboards reflect the
> changing campaign styles. The large, consensus-orientated presi-
> dentialist parties, such as the PS, RPR and UDF, have reduced
> verbiage to the minimum and now simply display their candidate's
> face above a short slogan. Only the Communist Left and the
> *gauchiste* formations retain their faith in the once traditional screed
> of words.[38]

In short, television tends to make the mechanical tasks of campaigning relatively more important because it nationalizes the campaign process. Of course, there are other forces helping to maintain the traditional participatory elements of campaigning, such as the need to maintain a party voice within communities, but the impact of television and of computerized direct-mailing techniques is wholly in the direction of reducing the participatory elements.

Furthermore, in the United States, where the new technologies have contributed to the increasing independence of candidates from their parties, the effect has been even more devastating. When they are able to, candidates prefer to recruit activists who are committed wholly to their own campaigns, rather than activists from their party's organizations because the latter are more likely to participate in a number of campaigns.[39] This tends to limit the 'participatory element' in two ways. The tasks the activists are expected to perform are more rigidly defined within the overall context of a campaign strategy where media campaigning is dominant. Again, candidates, unlike the old machines or the party-oriented amateurs of the 1950s, have no particular interest in their campaigners becoming involved in the public debates of their communities. Candidate-centred campaigning does not rely on the merging of the electoral arena with the larger political arenas but rather is more exclusively an electoral activity. In other words, the link between participation in election campaigns and other forms of participation is weakened. Once again, it is important to place this tendency in context. Television is not necessarily a catalyst for de-politicization, even if its effects are as we have described. For example, it probably makes it much easier to generate the support needed for single-issue campaigns. Rather, our argument is that it weakens the links between different arenas, even when the same individuals are participants in them. This means that political participation is more likely to be subject to the sort of difficulties of effectiveness which Hirsch identified when discussing 'the tyranny of small decisions'.[40]

CONCLUDING REMARKS

In this chapter we have seen that parties in the twentieth century have had the potential for being important arenas for political participation. For various reasons it was difficult for parties to recruit the labour they require for electorally related purposes on a strictly commercial basis. This meant that they had to recruit participants using various mixes of material, solidary (social and recreational) and purposive (ideological) incentives.[41] However, much of the potential for mass participation in parties has not been realized. As von Beyme has noted: 'members do not participate to any marked degree in internal will formation'.[42] Even in the electorally successful Swedish Social Democratic party a study reported that sixty-nine per cent of members claimed that they *occasionally* took part in internal decision-making.[43] In most other parties membership participation in their internal affairs is probably much less, although our knowledge of this is limited since there have been few attempts at cross-national comparisons. This partial success of even the formally democratic parties has produced disputes in a number of parties about the proper locus of power. In turn, this has prompted attempts to reform some of these parties and efforts to start new parties on rather different lines from existing ones and it is to this issue of control in parties that we now turn.

6

CONTROL OVER POLITICAL PARTIES

Arguments about who should participate in parties and about the best institutional arrangements for facilitating participation, have developed in the twentieth century against a background of scepticism about the feasability of mass control of parties. Indeed, there are few other areas of human activity where a theory purporting to show the impossibility of a particular objective has emerged so soon after the growth of institutions supposedly committed to the promotion of that objective. Yet within a few years of the establishment of socialist parties advocating participation in and control of a party by its mass membership, Michels claimed to have demonstrated the 'iron law of oligarchy'.[1] His book, *Political Parties*, was significant in a number of ways. Along with the work of Pareto and Mosca, it constitutes one of the major exemplars of 'classical elite theory'. Again, as von Beyme has noted, it is one of the first books that can be considered to be 'genuine political science'.[2] Moreover, it was important in setting the context in which future academic debates about the potential for democracy within political parties had to be set. Its influence, though, on how parties organized their internal relations, and on how reformers dealt with the problem of elite control in parties, was rather limited. There are several reasons for this – some of which relate to weaknesses in the arguments themselves, and some of which relate to its subject matter. Primarily, it is about the German SPD and, while other socialist parties in Europe were influenced by SPD organization, the academic debate about the distribution of power in that party had little impact on their development. *Political Parties* was not published in English until 1915, and within a decade or so Michels himself had become an apologist for Mussolini. This, together with his focus on 'soft' issues like mass psychology in the post-war years, rather than on the 'organizational' elements of *Political Parties*, further made him a marginal influence on socialist party development.[3] In the English-speaking world it was not until, perhaps, the 1950s that Michels' ideas became an important subject for analysis and even as late as 1971 Hands could argue that there was virtually no critical literature of Michels' book, even though the general thesis was known widely.[4]

Critics of Michels have produced a number of compelling objections against his claim that there is an inevitable tendency towards oligarchy in all organizations, including those, such as socialist parties, supposedly run on democratic lines. There is the argument that Michels fails to indicate precisely what oligarchy is. Not all logically possible relations between leadership and mass involve powerlessness for the latter, and the need for leaders in an organization, of course, is not sufficient to show that democracy is impossible, thought it does mean that direct democracy cannot be practised. There are, too, several different arguments introduced in the book, some of them relating to supposed 'psychological' laws while others relate to the logic of organization and the precise connection between these arguments is never outlined. Also, in rejecting Michels' claim to have shown the impossibility of democracy in organizations, Hands argues that Michels had a wholly inappropriate notion of the conditions necessary for democracy within a party. We should not expect democracy in an organization to be a microcosm of democracy within the nation-state, involving, for example, competitive factions.[5] Finally, with the benefit of hindsight, it could be argued that in an obvious respect Michels 'loaded the dice' in his favour. By choosing the German SPD as his example of oligarchic tendencies, he was studying a party set in a bureaucratic political culture and, it might be argued, institutions have a tendency to reflect the culture in which they are set; today the SPD remains a highly bureaucratized party compared with many social democratic parties in Europe. These points having been made, indisputably Michels did identify several factors which can impede, even if they do not prevent, membership control of organizations. In addition, there are other factors not discussed by Michels which also pose problems for internal democracy in parties. Even if Michels was wrong in suggesting that there is an 'iron law', he was certainly correct in arguing that democratization of an organization cannot be achieved simply by ceding formal powers to the members.

In this chapter we examine some of the more important problems connected with the implementation of mass control of a party, before turning a look at attempts at reforming practices in parties to provide greater democratic control. As we shall see, there are rather few such instances and the successes have been rather modest. Nevertheless, this does not indicate that ultimately Michels was 'right'. Rather, it shows that democracy within parties is a difficult goal to achieve, even when there is a widespread consensus that it is desirable.

CONSTRAINTS ON MASS CONTROL OF PARTIES

Only periodically can large numbers of people be included in decision-making procedures in an organization.

This argument is closely associated with classical elitism. It is also undoubtedly true; what is disputed by protagonists and opponents of democratization is what follows from it. There can be little doubt that, once an activity becomes sufficiently extensive in scope, responsibility has to be delegated to a smaller number of individuals. No member would have sufficient time to be involved in all decisions and the amount of time necessary for full participation would produce great inefficiencies within the group. Protagonists of representative democracy argue that devolving powers to given individuals is compatible with democracy, because the full body of members can still meet periodically to issue general policy directives and to check that earlier directives have been carried out. In theory, this is the role of the Annual Conference in the case of the British Labour party. In fact, as with all socialist parties, there is a gap between the arrangement in theory and in practice. However, parties are certainly not the worst case of institutionalization in co-operative enterprises producing elite domination. The British building societies, for example, are membership-based bodies and are the descendants of previously small co-operative ventures. Today individual members have virtually no power and the societies are run by self-perpetuating elite groups of managers.[6]

The question for us is whether, leaving aside resources such as patronage which may become available, institutionalization itself entails elite control. Is a small group (to whom responsibilities have been delegated) simply in a better position to out-organize a large number of members? Now, certainly, the 'Olson problem' is relevant here.[7] On grounds of self-interest there is no incentive for any one member in a large body to join in collective acts, because the likelihood of his making a difference is so small that his contribution will be wasted. (Either the act succeeds and so he would have done better to free-ride, or it doesn't and he has expended resources on a losing cause.) In a world of self-interested individuals, then, there would be a tendency for the leadership to win by default. The Olson problem does seem to be relevant in explaining the failure of membership movements in bodies like building societies. Here there are no pre-existing local organizations where members otherwise participate – unlike parties, they did not function also as social clubs – and the individual member is primarily self-interested, as an investor or a depositor. But, as we have seen, not only have socialist parties created local branches to recruit members by offering them selective incentives (such as social and recreational facilities), but they have also tried to foster 'a collective spirit'. Party members are not, for the most part, isolated individuals who are in the party for their own self-interest; the very conditions which Olson recognized as necessary for solving the 'Olson problem' are generally present in parties, or rather they are sufficiently present to make arguments from the powerlessness of the individual member implausible.

An alternative argument which might be put is one discussed earlier: those in leadership positions have access to skills and information requiring members to defer to them. Here again a convincing argument might be made with respect to building societies. It might be contended that only the managers have the relevant expertise in financial markets to know how to set interest rates and to know when to change existing rates. Membership control of such activities, it might be argued, would simply destabilize the societies' operations. But in the case of parties it is less clear that an argument from technical expertise could be convincing. The objectives of parties are often rather general in character and commitments to specific policies do not usually rely on great technical resources. Parties in opposition lack the facilities to plan in this way, and economic strategies, for example, often consist of no more than a general approach rather than being based on a full-scale alternative to the model of the economy used by the governing party. Perhaps the most extreme illustration of this lack of an alternative model was in Britain in 1964, when the incoming Labour government introduced '*ad hoc* departmental economic advisors . . . including Lord Balogh as adviser to the Prime Minister. The appointees usually had personal and political ties to the Labour party, as well as expert status.'[8] While they had attachments to the party, these appointees did not constitute a well-defined 'school' of economic thought and the party had not campaigned on the basis of a detailed, economic policy at the election that year.

In brief, then, while institutionalization might itself provide great advantages to leaders over members in some kinds of organizations, this would not seem normally to be the case in parties. The more serious problem arising in this context is that only experts may be able to decide where the boundary between general policy objectives and issues of detailed policy, requiring expertise, actually lies. But if this suggests that the expert has to be involved in helping party members to define and 'shape' objectives, it suggests too that a wide range of experts act as 'consultants' to the party base so that domination by any one group of experts is avoided.

When there is a high turnover among party activists, they are at a disadvantage in their dealings with party leaders who can use turnover as an excuse for disregarding resolutions or instructions.

Clearly, if membership is sufficiently unstable that very different people are attending successive party meetings, and if this results in frequent changes in policies or instructions, then leaders have a clear incentive to find means of by-passing party meetings. As we see later, this was indeed a problem faced by the West German Greens in their attempts to mandate their representatives in the *Land* and federal legislatures. Conflict arose because the Basis meetings at which policy was supposedly made were open to any would-be participants and participant turnover was very high. This led to earlier decisions being overturned by different groups of individuals, with the result that even the most participant-minded legislators wanted procedures that would produce more consistent policies. But what are the consequences when turnover in participants is high but not so great as this?

The first point to note is that the growing reliance on policies and issues as an incentive for mobilizing activists and members probably does lead to much greater membership turnover. Members who were partly lured by patronage or by the social facilities offered by parties were far more likely to be long-term participants because there were relatively few alternatives to the party. While we lack much quantifiable data relating to turnover fifty or sixty years ago, there seems little doubt that party membership was not something into which individuals drifted only to leave shortly afterwards. In contrast, participation in parties today can be somewhat transitory in nature. In an earlier survey of Democratic precinct committee members in Denver I found that only 8 per cent of members in 1979 had held these positions for more than 10 years, while 36 per cent of the members had done so for less than 15 months.[9] However, it is apparent that the impermanent character of the membership there is probably some-what greater than in most European parties simply because there are fewer costs to be borne in becoming a member of the precinct committee; it is more likely to attract dilettantes than would a dues-paying mass membership party.

Yet, of itself, even the high turnover of activists found in Denver would not be sufficiently great to produce the kind of inconsistent decisions to undermine leadership confidence in activist participation. Parties can withstand high turnover providing power is not shifting rapidly between groups with very different opinions or interests. Moreover, low membership turnover also poses a danger to mass control of a party. Even when there are no ties of patronage to their representatives, long-serving members are more likely to be bound to existing candidates and policies because of loyalty to individuals and causes. Since in most parties there is usually at least some connection between length of service and the occupation of senior positions, parties with highly stable memberships are likely to be in a better position to resist demands for change in candidates or policies. Loyalty was certainly one of the factors making it difficult for members to displace sitting right-wing Labour MPs in the early to mid-1970s. The impact of loyalty was evident also in the Denver Democratic party in 1972. By then the party was virtually free of patronage appointees, but many senior party officials and activists wished to nominate a long-serving conservative state senator (Arch Decker) for the vacant congressional seat. (Later he was to run for public office as a Republican.) Even though many of these officials were centrists or liberals, they opposed the nomination of a relatively inexperienced liberal candidate (Patricia Schroeder), who never-theless had substantial support among grass-root activists. In the event this strategy did not work but the successful candidate's resentment of the opposition to her candidacy by leading party officials was sufficient to produce a much greater separation of her own campaign organization from the party's than had been usual in Denver. To the extent, then, that low membership turnover is likely to increase activist loyalty (in the higher echelons of a party), it can restrict membership control. This means that any efforts at democratizing a party will have to devise means of limiting the impact of loyalty without making the party overly susceptible to the influence of all political fads and fashions. This balance can be rather difficult to attain.

When institutional procedures are highly complex, the party leadership is at an advantage in controlling dissident elements in the party structure.

As was suggested in the last chapter, when the adoption of a candidate or policy involves multiple levels of decision-making, it becomes much easier for political leaders to be influential, because of the strain long-term organizing puts on the resources of mass-level groups. The effect of this can be magnified when the rules governing the procedures are complex and facilitate obstructionist tactics by those well-versed in the rules. An obvious parallel to this is the American Congress where the need to put together majorities at each state of the legislative process poses severe difficulties for policies which are backed primarily by junior congressmen and senators. However, if we then draw the conclusion that mass membership control is facilitated by procedures, such as the taking of decisions at single mass meetings to minimize the costs that must be borne by a majority, two problems emerge. One difficulty is that parties, unlike legislatures, are bodies which recruit members, so that where joining a party is relatively easy there may be an incentive for groups to recruit members in order to 'stack' meetings. Where there are other resource advantages enjoyed by leaders in the party, they may well have a relative advantage in this regard too. Consequently, simplified decision-making structures do not always work to the benefit of ordinary members. This is a matter of which I have personal experience. Several years ago I was asked to join a party by a candidate for the party. He paid the membership fee of myself and several other people and in return wanted us to attend a party meeting and vote on a particular issue. In the event the matter proved to be non-controversial, but the personal recruits of this candidate outnumbered the others attending that meeting. A further problem is that simplified decision procedures make it more difficult to realize other objectives which a democrat values – such as consistency in policy proposals or 'balance' in the party ticket. Parties mandating their representatives at a single meeting, for which there has been no preliminary agenda building, are more likely to mandate them to pursue inconsistent or mutually unrealizable objectives. Equally, where there is no preliminary discussion, a slate of candidates may emerge which is unbalanced with respect to its composition in regard to race, sex, religion or some other electorally significant variable.

Once again, then, we see that while the initial constraint on mass control does not seem to be as effective as it might appear at first sight, the issue of how to devise decision-making arrangements to maximize member influence seems highly complex. In part, it seems to be related to the other kinds of constraints operating on the membership in particular cases.

The typical kind of relationship between voter and party in modern societies tends to weaken the position of members *vis-à-vis* leaders. This is because voter loyalty to the party *per se* tends to be as least as strong as their commitment to particular policies or causes.

On this view it is the nature of the relation between leaders and voters which helps to 'squeeze out' party members, irrespective of the formal decision-making procedures in the party. In many, though probably not all, circumstances leaders can afford to appeal above the heads of members to loyal party voters. The basis of the argument is to be found in the change in voter ties to parties when agricultural and industrializing societies became fully industrialized ones. This change has been well summarized by Carty who, having outlined the transactional relationship in political machines where voters and leaders are tied by a series of patron-client bonds, argues that

in fully mobilized societies . . . individual voters are typically tied to mass parties by a set of *socialized partisan allegiances*. The relatively enduring alignments of partisans are rooted in the fundamentally social and economic cleavages that mark a society . . . Campaigns, couched in terms of ideology or collective policy goals, seek to induce electors to reaffirm, or defect from, their partisan commitments.[10]

As Carty himself argues, the older transactional relationships can survive – in Ireland, Italy and Japan, for example – but they are unusual cases. Generally, in industrialized societies most voters are party adherents. On this argument the weakness of party members lies in their not being gatekeepers to the electorate in the way that the Colombian *gamonales*, for example, link elected politicians to voters. This is not to deny that party members are necessary for effective election campaigning, but it is to claim that they lack the power to overcome the resistance of party leaders in major disputes over policies or candidates.

There are two main objections to this argument. This first is that appealing above the heads of the members to the voters is a much safer tactic when voters are less likely to believe that internal party disputes will have an effect on the ability of representatives to perform effectively in public office. In the United States, where a candidate may distance himself completely from his party's organizations and activists, defying party activists can, on occasions, even be an electoral advantage. But in European mass membership parties both the reality, and voters' perceptions, of leader – member relations make intense disputes within a party potentially damaging. Some level of internal conflict can be sustained without electoral loss, and some commentators have noted that the Labour party survived and perhaps even thrived on levels of conflict not found in the other British parties. Indeed, von Beyme argues that in socialist parties 'with libertarian traits' such as the Italian PSI and the French PSU 'factionalism has always been regarded rather as a virtue'.[11] When internal conflict becomes too intense, however, a party becomes much less credible as a governing party and its electoral prospects can be reduced. This was the case with the British Labour party in the early 1980s. Consequently, while electoral considerations can provide an incentive for leaders to move away from the issue positions of activists, they cannot afford to move too far away for fear of reducing the credibility of the party. Of course, this may make activists more vulnerable to having *symbolic* rewards offered to them to allow leaders greater flexibility in their approaches to the electorate.[12] And, in turn, this suggests that ideology as such may be a double-edged sword for activists – while ideology can provide a basis for symbolic rewards, (rhetoric and so on) it may also weaken their position *vis-à-vis* leaders.

The other objection is that voter attachments to parties are weakening. The process, often referred to as partisan dealignment, is widespread, and many parties now have much smaller loyal electorates than they had thirty years ago.[13] In part, of course, dealignment stems from the relative decline of old social classes (such as the industrial working class) and of attachments to religions and other sources of identity, as well as the parallel rise of new social classes which, obviously, have no tradition of support for particular parties. But it is important not to exaggerate these changes and also to recognize that there are a number of variables affecting the readiness of voters in different liberal democracies to identify with parties. As von Beyme has argued:

> Taking only the major parties in multi-party systems, the decline in readiness of people to identify with them is indeed striking. But it is easy to overlook that some of the voters' readiness to identify with parties has simply shifted to the smaller parties; it has not disappeared altogether, as has been argued for the Netherlands and Great Britain.[14]

The effect of dealignment is to force party leaders to devise new strategies in competing for votes, and parties making no effort to break out of their electoral 'ghettos' can suffer serious decline. One of the most spectacular examples of this is the still predominantly Moscow-oriented Communist party in France (PCF) which always polled more than one quarter of the electorate between 1945 and 1956, but which obtained less than ten per cent of the vote by 1986. Even for a party like the PCF, which was never likely to come anywhere close to obtaining a legislative majority for itself, the failure to break out of its primarily inner-city electoral 'ghettos' was damaging. Its decline in relation to the Socialist party greatly weakened its bargaining position with its coalition partner.

It might be argued that greater competition for votes would weaken the position of party members still further, because leaders will have an even greater incentive to pursue policies which they think will maximize votes. Nevertheless, this would be to ignore the impact of party division on the electorate. Party leaders are far more likely to be sensitive to the electoral damage caused by extensive internal conflict when there is only a small loyal electorate. Concessions have to be made to members to preserve the credibility of the party. For example, consider the issue of nuclear defence policy in the British Labour party in the early 1960s and in the mid-1980s. In both periods unilateralism was not the policy supported by a majority of the electorate. In the earlier period the parliamentary leadership fought against, and subsequently overturned, a Conference resolution supporting a unilateralist approach. In the later period, and despite strong multilateral sentiments in the senior ranks of the party, unilateralism was kept as the party's policy. While other electorally unpopular policies were modified in the years after the landslide defeat in 1983, the party leadership wanted to maintain unity within the party and did not attempt to revise this policy substantially. A dealigned electorate makes it much more necessary for a balance to be maintained between the demands of members and the pressures of the electoral market.

To summarize: while the argument from 'loyal electorates' has some merit, the effect of this is probably not to weaken the position of party members very much.

Because political leaders pursue the objective of winning elections, they are placed in an antagonistic relationship with members who wish to promote policies and issues.

This is the argument that the electoral market necessarily leads to the introduction of alternative objectives to those desired by party members. It underlies a well-known distinction outlined by Wright between what he calls 'rational efficient' models of parties and 'party democracy' models. In the former model a party 'defines goals to win elections', while in the latter 'a party wins elections in order to implement goals'.[15] However, it is important to distinguish this argument – which is misconceived – from the valid argument that the electoral mechanism is likely to bring into party politics people with very different goals from the members.

One problem with the sort of dichotomy used by Wright is that it is derived from an untenable view of means and ends in relation to parties. Parties conforming to Wright's party democracy model, such as socialist parties, are like any other party in that in order to 'implement goals', they must win elections. To do this they must 'define the goals' in the best way to maximize their chances of success. Similarly, a rational-efficient party does not simply aim to win elections, it has objectives which follow from winning – possibly government patronage, the salaries and lifestyles which professional politicians can enjoy, or whatever. For both kinds of party, decisions have to be made about electoral strategy so as to connect the long-term objectives emanating from winning elections to the means, namely winning elections. Now, it is true that a purely careerist politician does not care which public policies he has to claim to support as long as they are electorally successful but this does not mean that he would never have to weigh up the compromises he must make between means and ends. For example, if his chances of victory are related to the extent of the largesse he distributes, there may be some fairly tricky calculations as to what he can get away with. (It should not be forgotten that maintaining a parliamentary career in eighteenth -and early nineteenth-century Britain, for example, could be extremely expensive.) The point is that while the objectives pursued by 'rational-efficient' and 'party democracy' parties might be very different, the electoral mechanism has a similar relation to them both.

A second problem with Wright's framework for studying parties is that the whole notion of 'winning' an election is problematic. In the case of the two-party system in New Zealand, or of the system of pre-election alliances in West Germany, there is little difficulty in 'unpacking' the notion of winning. But in some other liberal democracies, the precise objectives to be pursued by parties are more difficult to specify and have little to do with whether the parties are issue-oriented and internally democratic or not, as Wright seems to assume. Under the coalition arrangements in Switzerland, where there is a traditional formula for allocating the various government ministries, the competitive electoral spirit is largely absent. And what of the parties' objectives in the highly fragmented party system in the Netherlands, or more especially in a country like inter-war Czechoslovakia, where no party ever got much more than fifteen per cent of the vote? Usually, having more seats in a legislature does increase a party's bargaining power in government coalition formation, so that expanding the electoral base may be important for the party. But 'winning' may have as much to do with how close rivals, competing for the same sorts of voters, fare, or how extremist parties, which would never be allowed to become partners in a coalition government, perform. In this context 'winning' consists, possibly, of increasing the chances that the party will enter government or, if a party is in permanent opposition (like the Italian Communists), increasing its influence over government policy.[16] The connection between this objective and vote maximization is certainly not direct; nor is the connection (to use Wright's expression) between 'goal definition' and 'winning' a direct one. Goals may be defined in such a way as to simply preserve traditional sources of voter support or to spoil the electoral chances of particular party rivals, but whether they are is unlikely to have very much to do with whether the party espouses intra-party democracy or not.

Once we have disposed of these points, we can see that what the electoral mechanism does is to help generate further selective incentives for some kinds of participants – incentives which may lead to the introduction into the party of people who have little interest in the collective goals being pursued by the members. This is the familiar problem of the 'careerist' politician or the patronage-oriented politician who uses electoral politics to promote his own goals. (This can also be a problem in a caucus-cadre party, as well as in membership parties, where the elected politician appropriates resources for himself of herself which might otherwise come to his or her fellows in the caucus.) Now there are basically three main mechanisms for dealing with this – screening, accountability, and the electoral mechanism itself – and all have their disadvantages. Screening involves checking that the person is not likely to act in a self-interested way before he or she is allowed to run for office. The most effective form of screening is long service in the party, so that those who become its representatives have been well socialized into, and hence share, the communal values of the party. This was a device used by both communist parties (and originally socialist parties) and also by urban machines in America.[17] There are two main limitations with it. It may deprive the party of dynamic leadership and make it unresponsive to new elements in the party and the electorate; but it might also not prevent the pursuit of self-interest in areas which are hidden from the party. Indeed, the older party functionary who now finds himself in public office might be more inclined to accept the discrete pay-off from an interest group because he has so few high-earning years left. Systems of accountability can work if they cover full disclosure of personal income, for example, but there are many aspects of 'careerism' which it is difficult to prove in individual cases: the fact-finding mission and the 'boon-doggle' are often difficult to separate, as are many other instances. Moreover, effective methods of accountability would often require investigation and surveillance of a kind which many parties would regard as incompatible with freedom; one of the many controversial areas would be possible requirements of disclosure by the spouse and family of a politician. In theory, the electoral mechanism itself can serve as a check on the politician who moves away from the goals of the party; he may be denied renomination (in a primary election, as in America) or defeated at the polls. In practice, of course, this is a rather limited weapon. Nevertheless, it is important not to overlook the fact that the need to be re-elected does provide some kind of check on office-seekers; as studies in America have shown, the politician who is not seeking re-election does behave differently from others, and he is more likely to follow his own judgement.[18] This suggests a problem for those, like the West German Greens, who have advocated the rotation of politicians or fixed terms in office: the outgoing politician has nothing to lose.

Organization necessarily brings into existence party offices, and office-holders have an incentive to abrogate to themselves some of the most important powers in the party.

As we noted in chapter 5, it has been believed widely that either national party organizations or local party functionaries assume control of the nomination of candidates. Indeed, there are few examples where political elites did not take advantage of their positions in a party during the early stages of political mobilization and thereby reduce the powers of ordinary members. In many cases national organizations can impose candidates on local parties, or party rules allow ordinary members to be excluded from the crucial stages of decision-making. Nevertheless, there are important exceptions which enable us to understand that democrats are not contending with an 'iron law' of organizational control.

In some parts of the United States, where primaries were used in conjunction with party conventions, ordinary party activists remained an important element in mobilizing support for candidates. Neither the candidate themselves, nor party officials, could mastermind a nomination for someone without mobilizing a significant section of the membership – first to get onto the primary ballot and then to win the primary election. In Ireland, too, Gallagher has argued that:

> Constituency party office-holders, who in many countries in effect select candidates, are to a considerable extent bypassed in the Irish selection process because of the need for aspirants to have strong and direct links with the party membership. Ordinary party members know that the important decisions on all aspects of party policy and strategy are made at higher levels, and that their only real power is that to select candidates.[19]

Gallagher's explanation of the Irish experience is that the localistic outlook of voters, combined with the use of the single transferable vote, creates a tension between candidates and party interests, and this has produced ties between candidates and members which partly 'freeze out' party functionaries from the nomination process. What is interesting about Ireland are the parallels with the institutional tensions I observed in studying nominations in Colorado.[20] In both instances it was the need for direct links between candidates and activists that served to weaken the ability of central and local party functionaries to assume powers for themselves. The existence of this countervailing power seems to be essential if members are to be included in major aspects of intra-party decision-making.

However, if candidates can become too independent in the nomination process, members again lose out. This can occur if (1) candidates can recruit their own members or activists to secure their nomination, or (2) can appeal above the heads of the party to a wider electorate. This latter alternative is available when there are no preceding party conventions which control access to the primary ballot, or when candidates can threaten to run under another party label at the general election. In Colorado the use of new campaign techniques in the 1970s allowed candidates effectively to circumvent party activists in many cases. In Ireland the problem has been that the highly localized character of politics and the relatively small electorate (despite the single transferable vote) has enabled incumbents to develop their own organizations which survive while they remain in office. The threat to leave the party is so strong that only three incumbents were unseated by their parties between 1937 and 1980. Maximizing the power of party members requires the maintenance of a balance between candidate autonomy and candidate dominance and this can be difficult, but is not impossible, to achieve.

Occupying leadership position results in politicians becoming middle class, and in turn this inclines them to pursue policies which are very different from those of the memberships of working-class parties.

This is one of the oldest arguments made in support of the claim that members' control of their party can only be very limited. In fact, there are two elements of the argument. One is that working-class members take on bourgeois values when they assume leadership positions; the other is that the original working-class leaders are replaced eventually by those with middle-class origins. Both tendencies, it is claimed, help to produce a leadership with objectives different from those of the members, so that the party's objectives and policies are, at best, only partly promoted. Before we address the argument directly, there are several points to bear in mind in assessing its importance. One is that it is a gross simplification to see all working-class parties as having had only working-class electoral and membership bases. The Communist party in Italy (PCI) is one example of a party which has had both urban and rural wings, and it allied itself with a wide range of occupation associations in rural areas to help retain support for the party. In addition, some socialist parties have long-lost their working-class base, both in the electorate and among members. This occurred where a Communist party was able to become a major electoral force; an obvious example is the French Socialist party. The more orthodox Communist parties were also among the most successful at retaining a working-class base, but parties like the PCI in Italy have a growing element of urban middle-class members.[21] Not only have the Italian Communists had intellectuals among their members in the past, but 'More recently the PCI and its conveyor organisations have actually attracted members of the intelligentsia who, driven by the high unemployment in their class, are hoping to make a career with the party. Party work has become more scientific and the cadres more professional.'[22]

Furthermore, in the northern European socialist parties participation by elements of the middle class has been increasing and, indeed, has made party management more difficult. In Britain those employed in middle-class jobs in the public sector have become increasingly important in the Labour party – in the Sheffield party, for example, 62 per cent of the membership is middle class.[23] This development is also apparent in Germany where the proportion of members who were working class fell from 60 per cent in 1930 to less than 30 per cent by the 1970s.[24] (More controversial in the case of the SPD has been the claim that the party has always had a weak *electoral* base in the German working class: the argument on the evidence for this goes back as far as the early 1930s.[25]) This rise in middle-class activism must be placed in context though; the traditional urban working class is a declining element of the electorate in every advanced industrial society and, at least in the case of Germany, most middle-class members have some connection with the working class. Most especially, many of them grew up in working-class households. Nevertheless, both socialist parties and some communist parties have experienced the embourgeoisement of their membership and this has had an impact on the policy preferences of members – for example, on defence and on moral/conscience issues. It would not be surprising, therefore, if the leaders of these parties were to adopt 'bourgeois' policies.

But, of course, what the advocates of the embourgoisement thesis have in mind is not the radicalization of socialist parties, through the participation of radical elements of the middle class, but the very opposite – the dilution of socialist policy objectives by leaders who espouse more traditional middle-class values. One problem with this argument is that it ignores basic divisions within the middle class, divisions of experience and outlook which we might expect to affect behaviour in office. As Kavanagh argues:

> In Britain . . . one may demonstrate the gradual erosion of MPs
> from working-class backgrounds in the Labour party and a similar

decline of the aristocracy on the Conservative benches. Yet, not-
withstanding the growth of university-educated middle-class politicians in both parties, there are still differences between MPs of
the two parties. The middle-class Labour politician tends to be
drawn from the teaching, lecturing and social welfare professions,
employed mostly in the public sector, and is often first-generation
middle-class. The Conservative MPs are in law and business, usually
in the private sector, and come from secure middle-class back-
grounds.[26]

However, it might be claimed that the issue of leaders' back-
grounds is irrelevant – it is the experience of office itself and of the
possibilities for self-advancement that produces embourgeoisement
in leaders. But what precisely is it that causes de-radicalization?

One argument is that it is the income, and hence lifestyle, which
accompanies public office. This is a point taken seriously by the
West German Greens, who allow their legislators to retain only a
portion of their salaries – a portion equivalent to the income of the
average skilled worker in the country. As we shall see, however,
there are potential difficulties with this solution. Alternatively, it
might be argued that it is working with the bourgoisie in the state
– with other legislators and with senior civil servants – that leads to
the modification of goals. Quite simply, leaders come to share the
dominant values in the institutions in which they work. But, if this
is so, how – short of dismantling the state – can parties insulate
their leaders from such influences? One solution might be to
'rotate' legislators, a proposal we have mentioned already. But in
addition to the absence of a constraint on their behaviour during
their 'lame duck' periods in office, there is a further possible difficulty with this – the loss of expertise to the party when 'rotation'
occurs. Again, the Greens tried to counteract this by having the
legislators emply their successors (*Nachrücker*), so that the party
was not ill-served by 'rookies'. Another solution, which the Labour
party introduced in a small way in the 1974 government, is to have
party 'members' enter the bureaucracy when the party comes to
power. The danger with this solution is two-fold. Mutual penetration of the bureaucracy and party could develop and this might
well lead to administrative values permeating party decisions. This
is the case in West Germany, where Paterson argues of the SPD,

The over-representation of public officials in the party membership
is even more apparent among party office-holders, delegates to the
party conference, and party members who hold public office. This
over-representation of public officials among party members is

normally associated with a hostility to party democracy and an identification with administrative rather than political values.[27]

The other danger is that it increases the patronage available within the party and its bureaucracy. This is an issue we turn to shortly; for the moment we must emphasize that, if the argument from embourgeoisement is taken seriously, then counteracting it may be rather difficult.

But should it be taken seriously? The popular belief is that it should. In most episodes of the British television series *Yes Minister*, the civil servant first found ways of preventing a policy from going ahead and often ended up by getting the minister to accept the civil service rationale as to why change in policy was impossible. However, as Dyson suggests, the values of a senior civil service can be changed, and he argues that in Germany party politicization has produced a service which is no longer the most conservative leadership group.[28] Furthermore, the gullibility of television's Jim Hacker seems more that of a particular *kind* of party politician, and it might be argued that the growing dominance of public sector professionals in the Labour party will result in there being rather fewer party 'hacks' of the traditional kind in leadership positions in that party. This having been said, the question of how party leaders may be socialized into elite values remains controversial because of the difficulties of empirical investigation in this area. For the most part we must rely on the usually biased and self-serving accounts of ex-party representatives.

> The very occupation of government office tends to isolate a party's representatives from its membership because they became pre-occupied with the management of short-term policies; in turn, they can claim in party debates that members cannot appreciate the constraints under which their government operates.

This is not an argument based on either embourgeoisement or careerism, but rather on the fact that the perspective from government is necessarily different, and that in intra-party conflict this argument constitutes 'a trump card'. Certainly, the experience of most socialist parties is that once in office leaders are more free to ignore certain demands from within their parties – as both Callaghan and Schmidt did in the second half of the 1970s. In opposition they are more likely to take on commitments because the 'constraints of power' are less apparent. This point comes out in Hine's discussion of the Swedish socialists' (SAP) adoption of a new policy on employee investment funds:

> It should be added, of course, that the SAP enjoyed the luxury – if such it be – of exclusion from power between 1976 and 1982, and this enabled it to make a series of radical statements on labour-market policy and public expenditure, as well as on the investment funds issue, which doubtless kept its followers content. In office once more, party unity is facing a sterner test as party leaders begin to doubt the wisdom of the party's policy commitments.[29]

Obviously, what worries the democrat is not that a party's representatives may sometimes argue that certain policies cannot be carried out, but that the 'privileged position' is invoked in cases when a policy could be carried out but the representatives have their own reasons for not doing so; Callaghan and Schmidt, it might be argued, simply had different policy preferences from many members of their parties. Leaving aside the problem of 'careerism' in such cases, there remains the problem of how to ensure that party objectives get their proper weight in relation to the demands of short-term state management. Once again, 'rotation' and an input of party values and ideas from a party bureaucracy would appear to be the possible means of effecting this, but these bring with them problems for mass control.

Organization necessarily produces patronage resources for party leaders, and large party bureaucracies are likely to weaken mass control of a party.

We noted earlier the usual distinction, reiterated by Carty, between the transactional relations between voters and leaders found in more traditional societies and the 'socialized partisan allegiances' typical of industrialized regimes. In the former, patron–client links help to provide a high degree of autonomy for the leadership. We have also noted that in countries like Japan and Italy control of the state has given the dominant parties the opportunity to produce extensive, and arguably more important, networks of patronage at the elite levels of politics. Nevertheless, powerful party patronage can emerge in states where the traditional forms of patron–client relation are largely dead. This can occur when party membership becomes a basis for appointment to agencies of the state or private associations. In other words, the expanding scope of party influence in state and society may indirectly weaken membership control of party leaders. The liberal democracy in which parties have the most extensive networks is Austria. Here we find the most developed form of corporatism, with widespread interpenetration of parties and interest associations; the basis of this was the so-called *Proporz* system which existed formally until the collapse of the governing grand-coalition in 1966 and has continued on an informal basis since then. Under the *Proporz* system, which was developed to prevent the intense conflicts of the inter-war era, government positions and services were distributed roughly in relation to the parties' share of the vote. This has meant that the Austrian Socialist party (SPÖ)

> itself controls quite large financial resources and several large economic enterprises. These – in addition to the professional party bureaucracy and the new access which the Proporz gave the party to patronage positions in the national bureaucracy – have meant jobs and salaries for loyal party members. This in turn has meant that the party can exercise more leverage over potentially recalcitrant individual elites.[30]

Perhaps an even better example of this form of patronage is in West Germany, because, under corporatism, the Austrian parties have arguably lost some of their pre-eminence in the policy process. In Germany too we find *Proporz* patronage at lower levels of government and it also operates in appointments to state enterprises. However, another form of German patronage is *Herrschaftpatronage*, which is the placing of party members in key positions in the administration in order to extend party control.[31]

There are several points to emphasize about party patronage of this kind. Even the most skeletal parties, like those in Britain, have some form of patronage (such as in the nomination of magistrates, for which some attempts at party 'balance' are made). And, clearly, patronage does enable party elites to exercise some leverage within their party. Again, as Paterson argued about West Germany, the influence of state bureaucrats who are party members on their parties is likely to be a conservatizing one in that they bring with them administrative values. But, if party patronage is minimized, there is the problem that in government the party may lack the essential support to push through its policies effectively.

We thus arrive at one of the great dilemmas for the democrat. On the one hand, the possibility of embourgoisement together with the problems of leaders being isolated in an administrative culture suggests parties require personnel and expertise which can be 'grafted onto' the state to assist the party's legislators when they enter government. This is a way of maintaining party input into government. Moreover, if it is to be effective the party must presumably maintain relatively large research staffs and facilities, for otherwise they will be unable to compete with the advice proferred by the state administration. On the other hand, such personnel are likely to be far more dependent on party elites than on members, and thus provide an additional instrument for elite control. Then there is the possible complication that state and party career structures may become entwined, a development further weakening mass membership control. In drawing attention to this dilemma it is not being asserted that it cannot be resolved, but it is contended that any proposed institutional structure which is designed to provide for party input into the state is likely to have to be complex and subtle. This point is important when we come to examine the apparent failure of many attempts to democratize parties.

In regimes where populist influences are strong a 'cult of leadership' is likely to develop so that internal party procedures are undermined.

In the ex-British colonies in the Caribbean the influence of the British parties on party development has been tempered by populist influences which have their origins in both traditional African social structure and in Latin American political styles. A good example of the impact that populism can have is the People's National Party (PNP) in Jamaica.[32] This party came into being in the late 1930s and European social democracy, and especially the British Labour party, was a major influence on the organizational form which it took. However, faced by the electoral success of its main opponent, the Jamaica Labour Party (JLP), in pre- and post-independence elections, the PNP took on more of the style of the government party. It developed a trade union wing, depending heavily on clientelist relations, and it focused attention on the charismatic qualities of its leader, Michael Manley. Its campaigning relied far more heavily on slogans than on specific programmes. Nevertheless, the PNP did not completely abandon its social democratic party structure and party influence over the leadership continued to be far greater than in the JLP, which remained a predominantly caucus–cadre type of party.

The point to be emphasized is that where populist styles of politics are electorally successful, there are pressures on party leaders to utilize charisma and this necessarily weakens the position of members. One modern European state where populism has helped to undermine the role of the party membership in a socialist party is Greece. The party, PASOK, was founded in 1974 and it did not have its roots in earlier socialist parties. As Hine has observed, although it had a very similar structure to other European social democratic parties, the organization has largely been under the control of the party leader Papandreou:

> the control exercised by the party organization has been almost exclusively bureaucratic and personal, rather than democratic, and the most eloquent testimony to this is the fact that the Party Congress met for the first time only in 1984, no less than a decade after the party was first formed.[33]

Although Hine argues that generally in southern Europe leaders of social democratic parties have been more able to manage their parties than have northern European leaders, today it is really only in Greece that we find that the direct appeal to the electorate of the *charismatic* leader is the main source of this power. Indeed, in this regard, it is more appropriate to view Greece as a Balkan, rather than as a southern European, state. There is a strong tradition in the Balkan states of personality being the dominant element of parties, and of parties even becoming family dynasties. As Rothschild has said of pre-war Romania:

> All Romanian parties were led by members of the intelligentsia and most of them were congeries based on personalities and clans. This was true not only of the minor parties but to a considerable extent also of the Liberals, who were very much the creature of the Bratianu family, and the National-Peasants, whose leaders . . . each had his own retinue.[34]

Public financing of parties results in party leaders being less dependent on the income generated by members so that they are more prepared to allow dissident groups to leave the party, and less likely to seek a compromise with them.

The growth in the public financing of parties since the 1960s does tend to make membership dues relatively less important, and this probably does have a negative impact on recruitment to parties and on the incentive to keep existing members in them. But this development must be put into perspective. Public financing of parties, or party-related activities, has been adopted in about ten liberal democracies since the 1950s. However, in some states, such as Britain and India, the idea of a public subsidy to parties has met substantial opposition, so that by no means has it gained universal acceptance. And, as we noted in chapter 4, among those states which have introduced it, the reliance on state funding varies. At one extreme there are countries, like Norway, where the pattern of party financing has changed dramatically. In 1950 membership dues constituted between 37 per cent and 80 per cent of party income for the various parties. By the 1980s no party received more than 10 per cent of its income from subscriptions. In Canada, though, public subsidies provide little more than a quarter of party income (see table 4.1).[35] Moreover, in the US the party's candidates, rather than the parties, have been the recipients of public funds – at least in the case of the most important subsidies, those relating to presidential elections. Consequently, it becomes rather difficult to make generalizations about the impact of public funding on leader–member relations. But a good example of the influence it can have in some circumstances concerns the West German Greens. Although they are committed to a high level of participation in the party, they have the lowest membership density of any party in Germany and virtually depend on public subsidies for their income. Yet such results are produced by the *particular* form that public subsidy takes and there are ways of giving money that might actually strengthen the position of members. In the United States one of the main characteristics of funding at the pre-nomination stage has been 'matching' – presidential candidates receive an amount equivalent to the funds they have raised from individual donors, but only relatively small donations are permitted. Thus, to maximize their 'matching' funds from the government candidates must find as many small contributors as possible. This places a premium on local organizing and some commentators have argued that it has helped to slow down the centralization of presidential campaigns. The application of the 'matching' principle to membership-based parties, so that parties had an incentive to maximize their membership rolls, might be one means of preventing public funding from being a leadership-enhancing device. Parties would both have to recruit members and would have an incentive to prevent members from 'exiting' because of disagreements over objectives or policies.

What has emerged from this overview of the constraints on mass control of parties is that there are a number of rather complex problems connected with democratizing parties. Establishing procedures which *formally* cede power to members is insufficient to guarantee that there will be strong member influence in the selection of leaders and policies. These problems include:

1 loyalty by long-serving senior members to leaders;
2 the weighing of simplified decision-making procedures against the need for consistency and 'balance' in party policies or slates;
3 the inadequacy of devices for guarding against the effects of 'careerism' among leaders;
4 the need to provide sufficient candidate autonomy to prevent party organization elites from reserving powers for themselves, but not so much as to reduce candidate dependence on members;
5 the need to provide research and other party resources to leaders in government, so as to provide a party input into policy-making, without at the same time generating patronage resources for these leaders;
6 the tendency to personalize election campaigns in regimes where there are strong populist traditions; and
7 the need to find a form of funding which provides adequate party resources, and which does not make parties overly dependent on private interests, but which also gives them an incentive to maximize the size of their memberships.

The obvious question we must now put is: Do the problems we have identified amount to an 'iron law of oligarchy', even if it is not quite the law formulated by Michels? There are reasons for believing it does not. Michels' argument was that there was an inevitable tendency to oligarchy, and in large measure the inevitability stemmed from alleged psychological predispositions of the masses, rather than from organizational considerations. But, in any case, what we have outlined are problems to be faced in democratizing organizations, rather than factors making democratic control impossible. For Michels, no organization could remain democratic; whereas we are suggesting that, at the very worst, we can identify important differences in the degree of elite control of parties. Where Michels' conclusion is similar to ours is that we recognize that full democracy is difficult to attain, unless structures, resources and procedures are finely balanced between competing objectives. Indeed, we recognize that in some circumstances, as when there are strong populist tendencies in a political culture, extensive democracy in party may prove impossible to realize. Nevertheless, while, in particular, the need to balance extensive party resources for policy-making purposes against the patronage opportunities this creates for elites makes developing democratic party structures difficult, it is not impossible to envisage how the difficulties might be overcome. For example, party rules prohibiting salaried party officials from becoming party candidates, appointment and reappointment of party officials and representatives on outside bodies being subject to veto by representatives of party members, and other similar devices, may help to reduce power centralization. The democrat is *not* fighting against an 'iron law'.

DEMOCRATIZING POLITICAL PARTIES

If, at the outset, attempts at democratization of parties involve highly complex issues, the prospects of success are not increased by the fact that conflict about democratization is usually intertwined with power struggles within a party. This results, quite obviously, in the protagonists seeking to impose on their parties procedures most beneficial to their faction, and in these procedures being defended in terms of 'democracy'. Not surprisingly, reform measures often reflect the balance of power in a party and the consequences of specific reforms may be quite indefensible in terms of democracy. We must expect to find considerably more failure than success in efforts at reform. Furthermore, because those groups which do well out of a given set of arrangements have little incentive to change them, major reform movements in parties are relatively uncommon. Only when there is a serious crisis in a party, or when a new party emerges, does the issue of how to promote democracy within parties actually arise. The upshot of this is that there are remarkably few instances where democratization of a party has been attempted and virtually all of these have produced only partial success at best. This contrasts with other areas of social life where greater democracy has been sought – such as in neighbourhoods or in industry, where the number of 'experiments' has been much greater. In this section we focus on the four main instances in the last twenty years where democratizing the party has become a major controversy: the British Labour party in the 1970s and early 1980s; the Democratic party in the United States in regard to presidential selection; the Parti Québécois; and the formation of the Greens in West Germany.

For our purposes here the British case is perhaps the least interesting. A movement for greater democracy in the party began in the 1960s against a background of right-of-centre control of the party – both at the national level, because of the relative independence of the parliamentary party and the power of the then largely right-wing controlled trade unions, and at the local level where many inner-city parties were dominated by small right-wing cliques. The powerlessness of the members seeking reform was transformed by major shifts in the leadership of large trade unions. While this meant that the issue of party reform was a serious item on the agenda by the mid-1970s, it also meant that the issue of party democracy was to be linked directly to the battle between left and right within the party. Generally, the right opposed any reform because this would weaken their position, while the left came to advocate proposals for reform most compatible with their strengths. This involved giving greater power to the constituency parties and their rapidly declining memberships. However, no proposal which weakened the trade unions' influence in the party would ever get past the bloc vote of the unions at the Annual Conference, so that the issue of what should be reformed came to reflect the interests of the left-of-centre constituency parties and their trade union allies. Consequently, the debate about reform centred on three issues: the compulsory re-selection of MPs; the procedures for selecting the leader; and control of the manifesto. In the event, control of the manifesto was not given solely to the National Executive Committee, but compulsory reselection of MPs was introduced, together with an electoral college for selecting the party leader. This second reform meant that now MPs and constituency parties each had thirty per cent of the vote, while the trade unions had forty per cent; in 1981 this system replaced the older procedure in which complete power rested with the parliamentarians. The net result was to increase the area of direct trade union influence to include the election of the leader, to remove the 'anomaly' of (in many cases) selecting an MP for life, and to give constituency parties some say in selecting a leader. While it generated enormous controversy within the party, and encouraged the formation of a splinter party (the SDP), the issues addressed were actually rather small ones in comparison with the undeniably undemocratic features of the party – its low and declining membership density, the power of trade unions in relation to individual members, and the almost complete lack of research resources with which to develop party policies that would mesh with the objectives of the members. But, of course, these wider ranging issues never really had a chance of being raised given the existing power structure in the party and the fact that democracy in the party was an issue tagged onto conflicts over substantive policy issues. Nor, in the foreseeable future, is there any prospect that there might be a debate over such issues. Because of its very small membership, the party has proved susceptible in some constituencies to being dominated by relatively small groups, first of the right and then of the left. Unless it can manage to increase vastly its membership, the party cannot afford to cede power to the members for fear that some group may be able to exercise power far exceeding its influence in the electorate.

In the United States the failure of party reform did not stem from a failure to address significant issues of control within a party, but rather from the inability of the national party to determine how state parties responded to reform. As we saw in chapter 5, the catalyst for reform was the contentious Democratic party National Convention in Chicago in 1968. Although the party regulars succeeded in nominating Hubert Humphrey that year, there was also narrow support for establishing two party Commissions – the one to examine party structure and delegate selection and the other to examine party rules. The two worked largely independently of each other and while the latter (the O'Hara Commission) produced relatively uncontroversial proposals, the former (the McGovern–Fraser Commission) made sweeping recommendations for change. The main thrust of the proposals was that at future conventions every state party would have to conform to various guidelines relating to procedures for participation in delegate selection and to the composition of state delegations. The states were no longer left discretion as to how their delegations would be chosen. Of course, in an obvious sense, this was a fairly limited reform because the national party could not even presume to advise state parties as to how they might organize other aspects of their affairs. But it was the first occasion when a national party had even claimed these powers and, with the separation of powers in the United States, the nomination of a presidential candidate is especially significant, far more important than the selection of a leader under a parliamentary system. The ethos behind the McGovern–Fraser proposals was that activists in presidential selection were similar to members in mass membership parties and therefore had similar rights relating to the representation of their views.

The proposals were accepted by the Democratic party, though not without a fierce controversy, but the actual outcome was not anticipated or desired by most of those who served on the Commission or who supported the proposals. Their main disadvantage was that they made selecting delegates from caucuses to conventions, and then from one level of convention to another, a complex business. State parties had to have written rules covering delegate selection guaranteeing uniform times and dates for meetings, they had to take 'affirmative steps' to include minority groups (a requirement that was interpreted in 1972 as implying a 'quota' system), and they had to try to give proportional representation to supporters of each candidate at every stage of the nomination process. Nor was this all – among the other procedures adopted was a quorum of forty people at delegate selection meetings. The package of proposals might have been relatively easy for a mass membership party to incorporate, but for parties with no tradition of party membership it seemed far too complex an enterprise. And there was an easy way to circumvent these requirements. By introducing a presidential primary, a party could more easily meet the McGovern–Fraser guidelines without the need for time-consuming planning sessions or extensive debates about, say, how to increase candidate A's delegation so it was in proportion to his or her support among those attending a caucus or convention, without decreasing the size of a particular minority in the delegation. Consequently, the number of presidential primaries increased dramatically, as did the proportion of total delegates chosen in primaries. This had an impact too on the Republican party, in which demands for intra-party democracy had not been very strong. Because many states were controlled by Democrats, and because primaries attracted far more media coverage than conventions, a combination of the 'stick and the carrot' led Republican parties to follow the Democratic lead. Within eight years (between 1968 and 1976) the use of the presidential primary doubled – by the latter date it was employed in thirty states. The main beneficiaries of the reforms, then, were not the activists but the candidates. Primaries made the candidates, who could appeal above the heads of party activitists to the electorate, the principal actors in the nomination process. In 1976 this development was epitomized by the capturing of the Democratic nomination by Jimmy Carter, an insignificant ex-governor of Georgia only a year earlier. Since then, further modifications to selection procedure, and more especially greater knowledge about how the system works among politicians, have made it less likely that outsiders like this can capture the nomination. But the nomination system remains one in which it is the candidates who organize their selection, rather than it being a real interaction between candidate and party.

However, it might be argued that the real hope for fully democratic parties cannot be expected to lie with older parties but with new alignments or 'breakaway' parties. Yet, just as the former have generally been successful in resisting protests about the non-democratic character of intra-party relations, so too have most of the latter resisted demands for mass control of party structures. Compromises with activists have usually worked to the advantage of party elites, so that participatory structures have been far less effective in practice than their proponents would have believed initially. This point is clearly demonstrated in the case of the Parti Québécois (PQ) which was founded in 1968. The party was a fusion of technocratic elites who had split away from the province's Liberal party, and a more radical group whose organizational blueprint for the party was derived partly from that of the Communist League of Yugoslavia.

> Its goal was to create a party of militants. The key to the plan was the creation of parallel structures in the party. On the one hand, there would be the traditional electoral structure composed of three committees: finance, organization, and publicity; on the other, a parallel 'political' structure contained in three other committees . . . These 'political' committees would have members at all levels of the party and would constitute the principal motor of the PQ.[36]

These committees would be controlled by members through an annual convention, and between conventions a national council was to oversee the application of the party programme and direct strategy. Fearful of being out-voted, the group surrounding the party leader, René Lévesque, agreed to the demands of the participationists. However, within a few years leadership control of electoral machinery and electoral strategy enabled them to circumvent the party structures imposed on them. This was reinforced when the party rather unexpectedly won the 1976 provincial election and took office. This provided a classic example of the point made above (see pages 167–8) that the occupation of office yields power to the leadership:

> a national council meeting December 18, 1976, contrasted sharply with similar meetings before the election, where party leaders often found themselves in a minority on crucial votes. The newly elected premier made it clear that he considered the party's role would be secondary from now on: 'The party must not take itself for the government and must not claim to force its will upon it.' Council members who, six months earlier, insisted on the party's tight control of a PQ government, applauded happily.[37]

Quite simply, the structures introduced by the radicals had been insufficient to prevent the party leadership from utilizing its advantages.

An even more radical attempt to provide for democratic control of a party has been made by the Greens in West Germany.[38] The Greens first put forward an 'alternative list' of candidates in 1977. They became a political party in 1980 and since then have won, and subsequently sustained, parliamentary representation at both federal and *Land* levels. A number of its founding members had been frustrated in their efforts to change the policies of the SPD and from the outset the Green party was designed to be very different from the bureaucratized SPD. However, as with the Parti Québécois, the search for an effective form of *democratic* control has proved elusive.

For our purposes, there are three principal respects in which the Greens aimed at creating a different kind of organization from the other parties in post-war Germany. First, they wanted greater participation in the party, with it being open to anyone who wished to exert influence in politics: party meetings were to be open to all interested persons or groups. Moreover, lower level meetings were not merely advisory bodies; rather their resolutions were supposed to bind the parliamentary leadership to act in accordance with the wishes of these meetings. Parliamentarians would thus become mandated agents – the kind of representation which Edmund Burke, for example, had denounced in England in the eighteenth century. In rejecting the view of the representative as a 'trustee', the Greens advocated *Basisdemokratie*, or democracy from below. Second, the party's founders wished to avoid the experience of the SPD in fostering the growth of a class of professional politicians within the party, and several devices were introduced to prevent embourgeoisement and careerism. Green members of the *Bundestag* and of the *Land* legislatures would not remain as parliamentarians for the duration of a parliament but instead would be 'rotated' every two years. In part, this would be made possible by the party-list system of voting which would permit the replacement of legislators without the risk of losing seats in by-elections. Another device was to forbid Green legislators from retaining more of their salary than a skilled worker in Germany would earn. The remaining portion of the salary was to be paid to the party. Again, multiple-office holding in the party, a common feature in West German politics, was forbidden, so that no individual party leader could consolidate his or her position through control of a number of institutions.

Finally, they wished to provide much greater representation for women in the party hierarchy than did other parties.

The significance of the Greens' experiment is that it went much further than the PQ in recognizing that devices for creating formal political control by members may well be insufficient to prevent party elites from dominating. Nevertheless, if the experiment as a whole marks an important departure in the democratization of parties, neither the Greens' objectives nor their proposed practices were highly innovative in character. In the nineteenth century many socialist parties, of course, had begun by espousing a 'mandate' view of democracy, only for this to be modified once they gained seats in national legislatures. The idea that parties should be open to interested persons and groups, and not just to those who were prepared to commit their loyalty to a party, has been a well-established strand of anti-partism in America. In the Progressive era it resulted in the nomination process of parties in some states being opened to all voters through the introduction of 'open' primary elections. Again, in both West Germany and the United States (among other countries) a system of elected public officials paying a portion of their salary into party coffers has long been practised. However, the Greens' version of this does differ in that its objective is to prevent embourgeoisement and careerism, rather than to raise money for the party. Moreover, the commitment to increasing the participation of women in the party had an antecedent in the United States, where 'affirmative action' programmes were introduced in the Democratic party a few years earlier.

As an electoral force the Greens made considerable progress – at the federal level they turned a 'two and a half' party system into a 'two and two halves' system, and they entered into a coalition government in Hesse. In decentralizing power, though, they have been rather less successful. The main achievement has been to create a party in which women are as well represented in the hierarchy as men; because it is a new party and the principle has been vigourously pursued, the Greens have far more women in senior positions than have the American Democrats. (In the state elections in Hamburg in 1986 the Greens had all-female party slate and were electorally successful with this slate.) However, although it may be possible that the policy of opening the party structures to all would-be participants may have mobilized some people who were not previously active in politics – and there are no data on this – a number of problems have been caused by this policy. Because membership was not a *sine qua non* for participating, there was little incentive for anyone actually to join the party. Consequently, and rather paradoxically for a party committed to democracy from below, the Greens, with only 25–30,000 members, have fewer members per voter than any other party in the country. Moreover, attendances at local meetings seem to have involved many 'irregulars', rather than being dominated by large groups of regular attenders. This has caused two problems for the party. It has made the principle of the mandate from below difficult to implement because subsequent meetings have sometimes overturned the decisions of earlier ones. This led to the abandonment of directives from the '*Basis*', and instead representatives in the Bundestag now follow the decisions of more central bodies, the Party Conference and the Federal Grand Committee. In fact, the latter seems to have been a rather ineffective organization in the making of policy and power has thereby accrued to the legislators. In addition, control of the party seems to have fallen into the hands of a relatively small number of functionaries. Just as American party reformers have been frustrated in the twentieth century, the German experience displays the difficulties of widening power in an organization when relatively few people are prepared, or are able, to devote the time for regular participation in it.

This weakness in the '*Basis*' made still more complex the Greens' efforts at preventing the emergence of an elite of professional politicians, but it was certainly not the only reason for limited success in this area. Another factor was the electoral system. While party-list voting gave the Greens legislative representation and permitted 'rotation' to be practised, it meant that there was no *real* '*Basis*' for any Green members of the *Bundestag* to be accountable to, because none of them represented geographically defined constituencies. Rotation itself was controversial. While rotation proceeded in some *Land* parliaments, a more flexible approach had to be adopted at the federal level, where the threat of resignations from the party could have cost the Greens their status as a party in the *Bundestag*. (There is a minimum number of seats a party must hold in the chamber to constitute a party there; this is important because only parties meeting this requirement are eligible to receive a vast array of resources from the state.) Some legislators initially resisted rotation and this led to the modification of the policy. A Green member of the *Bundestag* could avoid rotation if seventy per cent of the relevant *Basis* supported the proposal. However, by the end of 1986 only one prominent Green, the internationally known

Petra Kelly, had not been rotated. Those politicians who were rotated tended not to return to the 'ranks' of the party but found various niches at its highest levels. Again, while the policy of having successors employed by serving legislators (the *Nachrücker* system) provided for policy continuity, there were instances of tension between the individuals concerned. Consequently, in 1987 rotation was abandoned as unworkable and the newly elected parliament contained a number of Green members who had served previously. In addition, there was an emerging problem in the paying of part of a legislator's salary to the party. The party's one minister (in Hesse) indicated dissatisfaction with the agreement and potentially there is a serious flaw in the practice. West German politics has been plagued by the policy of interest groups making payments to politicians. Even public financing of parties did not prevent another major scandal, the 'Flick' scandal, developing in the early 1980s. If the Greens do increase their support, and enter more coalition governments, their problems in controlling venality will be that much greater because of the relatively low salaries their members receive – the temptation to receive gifts will be even greater than in the established parties. The Greens cannot expect that screening of their legislators, before they enter office, will be an adequate safeguard.

CONCLUDING REMARKS

From a comparative perspective, how difficult are parties to democratize? Compared with some other membership-based, co-operative bodies, they are perhaps not that difficult. With building societies, for example, where there are no local members' organizations and managers need members only to lend money and to take out mortgages, the problems of placing greater power in the hands of members seem that much greater. If, though, we compare parties with producers' co-operatives, where the number of members is much smaller, there are two obvious problems members face in controlling elites which are not present in the case of co-operatives. Co-operatives produce their goods all the time, while the activities of parties change when they enter government and require party elites to work with other elites; there is no equivalent in a co-operative to the party voters to whom appeals can be made above the heads of members. The purchasers of a product from a co-operative are a check on the co-operative in that if they no longer like the product they will not buy it; not only is information about their demand available all the time but also the consumers are not an element of the enterprise to whom 'appeals' can be made. With parties, the governing function and the electoral connection add to the difficulties of devising arrangements in which power can be shared in an organization. If we extend the range of comparison somewhat, an initial impression would be that parties might be easier to democratize than large economic enterprises, but prove rather more difficult than, say, introducing neighbourhood self-government. But beyond this level of generalization comparisons become complex partly because there have been so few efforts to democratize parties.

In the light of the fact that there are so few parties in the western world and the problem that issues of democratization are usually tied to power struggles in a party, it is not surprising that there have been both so few attempts at democratization and also rather limited success for those reforms which have been instituted. But this does not mean that failure is inevitable or that there is an 'iron law' of the kind Michels sought to identify. In this chapter we have examined a number of ways in which democratization involves the creation of a balance – for example, between the need for party research and other resources to provide a party input into government and the need to restrict the opportunities for leadership patronage. Such balances are difficult to find, and we should not be surprised that so many 'experiments' end in failure. The difficulty with parties is that their small number mean that there are so few instances from which to learn – again in comparison with, say, the information available about producer co-operatives or about industrial democracy. Yet there are reasons for believing that the pressure for greater democracy, at least in some parties, will increase: as we noted earlier there is a growing middle class which is oriented towards participation. The West German Greens are merely one manifestation of this.

7

CONTROL EXERCISED BY POLITICAL PARTIES

In the last chapter we examined the relationship between elites and members in political parties and considered the problems the latter face in wresting control of a party from the former. But, of course, parties themselves, and those that run them, may exercise power over a much larger body of people. Most clearly this occurs when the party forms a government or is a member of a coalition which does so: at least in theory, control of the state gives a party some control over the members of that state. However, parties can 'penetrate' a society even when they are not in government or in ways which are really an adjunct of their leaders' occupation of offices of the state. In this chapter we are concerned with how parties control larger political environments – both their own social bases and wider publics. We begin by examining the idea of party government; we move on to consider the varying degrees to which parties in liberal democracies penetrate the institutions of the state; we then see that party penetration of society itself differs in these democracies – from the high degree of penetration found in consociational democracies, to the small role they play in Anglo-American democracies; finally we look at the much publicized debate about whether 'politics matters' – that is, whether it makes any difference to the policy output of the state as to which parties are in government.

PARTY GOVERNMENT

In chapter 3 we noted that in Britain in the twentieth century the idea of the government having a mandate from the electorate to carry out a particular policy programme became a popular one. With this acceptance of the notion of the mandate, the last element necessary for the practice of *party government* was in place. While the first mass parties had developed in the United States, and while the model for the mass membership party came from Germany, Britain is usually regarded as providing the first exemplar of party government and it is with this that most other instances of state–party relations are compared. Why is this? By the end of the nineteenth century there were several features in Britain which, taken together, seemed to yield a coherent model of parties in the modern state which was compatible with the requirements of democracy:

1   There was competition between parties in elections with the winning party then proceeding to form a government. That there were only two major parties meant that there was a direct link between election result and government formation – there was not the complicating factor of multi-partism; as W. S. Gilbert had announced in the operetta *Iolanthe*, every little boy and girl born alive was either a little Liberal or a little Conservative. In fact, this two-party model of British politics was already inapplicable after the split over the Home Rule bill in 1886. From then until 1931 British party politics ranged from being a 'two and a half' party system, through a 'two and two halves' system to a three-party system. The illusion of the two-party state remained, though, because, even when the largest party had not secured a parliamentary majority, it was not coalition government which resulted but minority governments kept in office by the acquiescence of third parties.

2   At least in theory, there were no constitutional restrictions on what a party in government could do, providing it followed the relevant conventions and procedures in enacting its policies. Unlike Germany, at that time, the state became the servant of the governing party.

3   The parties were sufficiently cohesive at the parliamentary level that a government could be sure of getting its measures enacted into law. In this respect British parties were noticeably different from American parties; Woodrow Wilson, writing in the 1880s, was the first of many American commentators to point to this inadequacy of their parties.[1]

4   The two main British parties did not 'penetrate' society deeply, in that they did not structure and organize most aspects of people's lives. Many of their leaders wanted a greater role for party, but, for a variety of reasons, this did not develop in Britain. They remained 'skeletal' organizations, and because

of this the idea that voters were choosers, in much the same way as actors in an economic market, could take hold. It was important for the notion of party government which involved party control of the state but not party control of society.

The idea of party government was a powerful one: the British case (as it was understood) came to be seen as normal, while other kinds of relations between party, state and society were deviant. This was reflected, for example, in the early analyses of party systems where the main line of division was thought to be between two-party and multi-party systems. In America it was to the British model that would-be reformers of American parties turned, up to and including the APSA Committee Report of 1950.[2] Moreover, because of their colonial empire, the British were successful in exporting the British version of party government to newly independent colonies – at least they did so to their former white colonies; the transplanting of this model to other cultures usually met with failure or with considerable modification to it. Because of this tendency to identify party government with British practice, it was not until comparatively recently that the concept itself has been subjected to more rigorous analysis. One consequence of this was that it became both easy and common to set up 'party government' as a straw-man which could be demonstrated to be incapable of realization in whichever non-British state was under discussion. Richard Rose, however, has attempted to identify the conditions which would have to be met if a party was to influence government in the way suggested by proponents of party government. These are:

1 Partisans must formulate policy intentions for enactment once in office . . .
2 A party's intentions must be supported by statements of 'not unworkable' means to desired ends . . .
3 At least one party must exist and, after some form of contest, become the government . . .
4 Nominees of the party occupy the most important positions in a regime . . .
5 The number of partisans nominated for office should be large enough to permit partisans to become involved in many aspects of government . . .
6 Partisans in office must have skills necessary to control large bureaucratic organizations . . .

7 Partisans in office must give high priority to carrying out party
   policies . . .
8 Party policies must be put into practice by the administration
   of government . . .[3]

The significance of this set of conditions is two-fold. On the one
hand, Rose is explicitly separating party *government* from the idea
of electoral choice. His third condition means that party
government could still be practised by a party coming to power
through a non-electoral contest, such as a civil war. Equally,
although Rose does not discuss this, another theoretical possibility
is that only one party might be allowed to exist but independent
candidates might contest elections; if the party candidates won
enough seats to form a government, then there would be party
government providing all the other conditions were met.
Moreover, although the way he has formulated the condition is
ambiguous on the point, it is clear from his later discussion that
Rose does not believe that party government must be single party,
rather than coalition, government. He argues that 'Coalition
government is not a denial of party politics, but rather party
politics in another form', and he goes on to indicate the
circumstances in which 'a coalition government would tend to
produce a substantial number of partisan achievements – but they
would be drawn from two parties rather than one'.[4] In other
words, Rose is not committed to the view that single-party
government of the British type is a superior kind of party
government; his emphasis is on what parties *do* in government,
rather on how they are 'chosen' or on whether the whole
programme of any single party can command majority support in
the legislature. It is possible, then, that Italian multi-partism, say,
might yield a clearer exemplar of party government that Britain.
On the other hand, Rose's fifth and sixth conditions draw
attention to a possible flaw in the British version of party
government – that, while parties may have the right to control the
state, they may lack the resources to be effective in enacting party
programmes. Again, other countries might yield far better
examples of parties having an input into state policy.
    By detaching the concept of party government from its
historical roots, Rose has focused attention on substantive issues
for political scientists and away from the uninteresting issue of
comparing an idealized version of state–party relations in Britain
with the rest of the world. We have already considered the
possibility of there being democracy without party competition in

chapter 2, and here we consider how party government might be possible under multi-partism in connection with the 'does politics matter' debate in pages 203–13. The other important issue raised by Rose, the penetration of the state by parties, is the one to which we now turn.

PARTY PENETRATION OF THE STATE

As we have just seen, two of Rose's conditions for party government are the occupation of important offices by party nominees, and a large enough number of such nominees so that many aspects of government can involve partisans. While, of course, no one has ever suggested that parties could, or should, provide an entire state bureaucracy from within their own ranks on assuming office, one of the main obstacles to party government has been the absence of enough positions to be filled by partisans. One explanation of this is to point to the skeletal nature of parties themselves and then to argue that the issue of much greater party penetration of the state has never arisen because parties have never had the kind of expertise necessary for replacing whole layers of state administration. But another way of looking at this is to argue that the state itself helped to set the boundaries within which parties could develop, and in many countries the tradition of a non-partisan bureaucracy was well-established by the time liberal democracy emerged. In much of Europe the idea of the state, and of its officers whose prime responsibility was to serve it and to be loyal to it, formed the background against which parties had to seek to run that state. As Dyson has said of Germany: 'Identification of state and bureaucracy has traditionally been at the expense of the authority of the parties.'[5] In England a supposedly politically neutral civil service had developed by the end of the nineteenth century, but from very different origins. There was no tradition of the state in England, rather the monarch had his or her army, navy and ministers. But the departments managed by the ministers were not the monarch's, but 'largely the private establishments' of these ministers.[6] In many respects this system had the potential for party patronage to replace private patronage, and indeed in the eighteenth century patronage was used extensively to manage the House of Commons. That parties in the late nineteenth century did not inherit a bureaucracy run on party lines can be attributed mainly to two factors. The inefficiency and cost of British bureaucracy was such that there was pressure, from the eighteenth century onwards, to reform various aspects of it. Beginning with the exclusion of government contractors from parliament in 1782, through reforms of the budgeting procedures to the implementation of the Northcote–Trevelyan reforms in 1855, there were demands to remove the excesses of the system. In addition, one feature of this system militated against even parliamentary parties from using the patronage to bring in their own people when taking office. The Crown did not own the posts – specific individuals did – so that persons could not be removed from them except with compensation. As Finer says, the 'very vices of the British system created a bulwark against the rotation of office'.[7] Consequently, the British version of party government came to be identified with an impartial civil service having only a tiny layer of political masters above it. From the 1960s onwards this very limited penetration of the administration by parties was to lead several writers to question whether Rose's fifth condition was met in the British case. At the popular level this led to the *Yes Minister* view of party control of the state mentioned in the last chapter.

In the United States a very different set of party–state relations was to develop, even though the ex-colonies inherited from Britain a 'state-less' conception of the state and appointments in the new federal administration were made, as in Britain, on personal recommendation. In the first thirty years of the nineteenth century the American system was widely admired in Britain because it seemed to lack the obvious defects of a system of administration which had added new positions, but subtracted hardly any, for nearly 900 years. But after the accession of Andrew Jackson to the presidency in 1828, federal patronage came to be used extensively as a means of rewarding political supporters. At the outset this differed little from what had happened when Jefferson came to office in 1801 or indeed from parliamentary management in eighteenth-century Britain. But the system was transformed by the advent of two-party competition which produced frequent changes of power in Washington between the 1830s and the 1850s. This point is made by Finer, who argues that 'The succession of purges and counterpurges established the spoils' system formally as an institution of American Government at precisely the time when the order in council of 1855 was beginning to take the British Civil Service out of politics.'[8] Thus, at the federal level of politics parties were doing just what they did at the local levels – putting their own supporters into office. While national politicians were not engaged in such overtly criminal activities as those of many city bosses in the 1870s and 1880s, party domination of administration was very much the same.

Have we found, then, a good exemplar of party government? While Rose's fifth condition would seem to have been met, the sixth and seventh were almost certainly not. The system was, as Finer said, a spoils' system, so that the faithful and the financial contributors were rewarded with office, and not those who might have the skills necessary to run bureaucratic bodies. Nowhere is this better illustrated than by the American Post Office which remained a source of presidential patronage until well after the Second World War. Yet even now the Post Office is almost a synonym for incompetence and bureaucratic inefficiency; the American public's perception of this institution is not paralleled by similarly negative views of other government organizations. Not only did spoils have to be distributed to satisfy party supporters, but there were not the relevant party bureaucracies or party-owned enterprises to serve as a training or testing ground for those who would be brought into government. Furthermore, there were not the party policies to which partisans could give priority in office (condition seven). The decentralized American parties were not programmatic. While issues did (rather broadly) divide the parties, a point often ignored by those who see them as merely being 'Tweedledum and Tweedledee', there was not the institutional structure to provide the incentive for them to become more programmatic. Party penetration of the state in the nineteenth century could not be transformed into party government in the twentieth century.

Indeed, during this century the interaction of three factors has led to an extraordinary decline in party involvement in the American state. Beginning with the reforms in the Progressive era, a series of measures at local, state and federal levels has greatly reduced the number of positions which could be held by political appointees. Many areas of administration and regulation have been granted to, or been handed over to, independent or semi-independent agencies – a change which, as we suggested in chapter 5, has benefited (and perhaps even encouraged the growth of) professions and 'professionals'. Again, the introduction of so-called civil service rules of appointment and promotion in governments, together with measures like the Hatch Act limiting the political activity of federal employees, has increased the size of the non-political sector of government. In some cases these changes did not occur until well into this century; in Denver, for example, all city employees served at the pleasure of the mayor until the defeat of the quasi-party machine there in 1947. Some highly visible patronage positions remain, of which ambassadorships are the most apparent, but these are trivial when compared with the scale of patronage appointments available in the nineteenth century. The decline of party and the rise of the individual candidate has also produced a pronounced tendency for the remaining political positions to be granted to those who have personal loyalty to the victor. Indeed, Brown has concluded that

> The evidence of the five most recent administrations indicates that extensive use of scarce presidential appointments to reward party stalwarts or to bolster party organizations is no longer viewed by the White House as a profitable exercise. That is not to say, however, that patronage no longer exists nor that presidential appointments are now nonpartisan. Alternate reasons and mechanisms for the distribution of presidential plums have arisen, including the emergence in the White House of the public liaison operation, the Office of Congressional Relations, and personal advisory systems much less reliant on the party organizations.[9]

Brown sees the Kennedy administration as being the major break with the past, and it was, for example, Kennedy who finally took the American Post Office out of politics. Finally, the expansion of government activity and the growing complexity of the programmes for which governments have responsibility has placed a much greater premium on the hiring of those with relevant expertise. But since there are not party structures in which such expertise could be nurtured, the American policy-making universe has become populated by a relatively new breed of political actor:

> Instead of party politicians, today's political executives tend to be policy politicians, able to move among the various networks, recognized as knowledgeable about the substance of issues concerning these networks, but not irretrievably identified with highly controversial positions. Their reputations among those 'in the know' makes them available for presidential appointments. Their mushiness on most sensitive issues makes them acceptable.[10]

The American experience of reducing party penetration of the state is, in fact, highly unusual. The more common development has been for parties to expand their involvement with state institutions. This is not to say, though, that they have always become wholly dominant elements. For example, in Austria the *Proporz* system meant that parties have their supporters in positions in government administration and in public sector enterprises. Yet at the same time the parties themselves are penetrated by interest organizations which are also co-opted into government decision-making. The result is not so much party government as what many commentators have regarded as the most highly developed example of 'neo-' or 'liberal' corporatism. Smith describes this Austrian system of policy-making as follows: 'Separate and *statutory* representation is provided in . . . "chambers" each reflecting a particular aspect of economic activity. These bodies articulate particular interests and are the basis of the "social partnership" between the government, organised labour and business interests.'[11] There are a number of 'chambers', some relating to the professions, but only three are really important: Labour, Commerce and Agriculture. The role parties have played in the post-war Austrian state is directly connected with the problems the state faced in the inter-war years. The state created by the Treaty of Versailles in 1919 was an artificial creation with virtually no legitimacy. Hence, if a party 'won' an election, it was regarded as being the state, and politics in inter-war Austria featured exceptionally intense conflict between the major parties which led to the breakdown of the polity. In the post-war reconstruction of the regime this tradition of strong parties was linked to a corporatist tradition with origins in the Hapsburg empire. This did not lead to parties being marginalized in the new regime; far from it – Austria has the highest rate of party membership in the western world, with about forty per cent of the adult population being members of parties. But, for the parties, the cost of being so highly integrated into the state was sharing power with organized interests. This 'partnership' is very different from the position in the United States. There, too, interest groups play a central role in policy-making, and in some models of the process (including the well-known 'iron triangles') they have developed a symbiotic relationship with institutions of the state.[12] But in the United States neither the parties nor the groups are formally represented in the state: there is no 'social partnership' and, as in the rational–efficient model of parties, party 'is "downgraded" to be only one of a variety of competing political actors including interest groups and the like'.[13]

The relation between party and state is rather different in West Germany, which lacks the fully corporatist structure found in Austria, but here too the Second World War was instrumental in changing the role of parties. Before 1933 parties did not have responsibility for the state. They emerged from the war 'undisputably as the most "reliable" institutions with the full support of the Allies'.[14] The recognition that parties were a cornerstone of democracy has led to the growing acceptance of

Germany since 1949 as a *Parteienstaat* (a party state). One consequence of this has been that the parties have been able to permeate the state bureaucracy. There has been an increased use of *politische Beamte* – 'political' officials, amongst whom 'There is emerging a new type of politically conscious official who is less detached and procedure-oriented and more problem-and-program oriented, more open and flexible for new problem-solving strategies.'[15] However, there are three important qualifications to consider when using the German case as an example of how parties have extended their influence over the state. First, of course, the history of German state bureaucracy continues to exert an influence over the present, so that the transformation to a polity in which party dominates the administration is far from complete. Second, the opening up of the bureaucracy may provide for more politically aware officials, but it also increases the incentive for 'careerists' to espouse political values and for party and state career structures to become more entwined. That is, one cost of party penetration of the state is that it encourages participation in the party by those who have a stake in modifying its goals; this appears to have been the case in the SPD.[16] Third, while they have permeated the state, the governing parties in Germany have not acted in the *Bundestag* in accordance with the party government model. In comparing Germany with Britain and France, King has argued that it displays a cross-party mode of executive–legislative relations. Parties which are not in the governing coalition, together with civil servants, play a far more important role in committees, and the committees are the central part of the work of the *Bundestag*.[17]

In Britain too the parties have tried to increase their influence over the 'neutral' civil service. In 1974 the Labour government introduced a few temporary political appointees into many of the government departments, but this attempt at providing political 'input' was widely regarded as a failure. The appointees were too few in number, too junior and found senior civil servants suspicious of their activities. A far more radical approach has been tried by the succeeding Conservative government. The advisor system was retained but the main thrust of the policy was to place in key positions in the civil service, and in other bodies. people who were known to be sympathetic to the policy objectives of the government. The most obvious break with tradition was in appointments within the senior civil service where, in some cases, relatively junior persons were promoted to senior posts. In appointments to health authorities and to the nationalized

industries, the Conservative government made political considerations even more explicit than they had been. The purpose
was not to generate patronage but to make it more possible
for policies to be implemented in the manner intended by
the government. (A parallel development in France in 1986 was the
Chirac government's dismissal of the heads of twelve of the
twenty-five nationalized enterprises it planned to privatize; they
were replaced by individuals who were to prepare the enterprises
for privatization.) Clearly, this policy will have an impact on
future governments. It is quite possible that when other parties
come to power they may simply remove (or shift sideways to
unimportant posts) many of those who are recognized as
sympathisers with Conservative policies. It is not hard to envisage
that, if parties are defeated at elections as regularly as they were in
the period 1959–79, 'rotation' in the administration may become a
feature of British government.

One constraint on the growth of party penetration of the state
has been the possibility of electoral defeat and consequent ejection
from office. A large politicized element in an administration poses
problems when governments change: the possible disruption to
programmes caused by the loss of officials and the difficulty of
attracting suitable staff when tenure is uncertain, being the most
obvious. However, when a party can remain in government for a
very long period, the patronage value of positions in the state
administration becomes an important incentive available to
parties. They can consolidate their position in the electorate, as
well as having sympathetic personnel in office. The classic example
of this has been Italy, where the Christian Democrats have been in
every coalition government since the war. Of the DC, Leonardi
has argued:

> the Christian Democratic party seems to have been able to
> transform its dominant role in the Italian political system into a
> lever to gain access to the top as well to intermediate and lower
> positions in the public sector. This access privilege has been
> transformed into a vehicle for placing party leaders in jobs in the
> public sector, thereby decreasing the economic burden on the party
> organization. Through such a placement, the party is able to call
> upon the services of an activist whose economic condition depends
> on his relationship with the party, but it also provides the party
> with a direct link with the public sector. The party activist
> employed in the public sector is expected to perform two roles: as a
> part-time party worker and as a conduit for party policies and
> preferences in the administrative apparatus of the state.[18]

Of course, to argue that domination by one party provides an incentive to penetrate the state does not mean that it will take advantage of this; the party's dominance may be so secure that it is unnecessary, as in India. Or there may be widespread rejection of certain forms of patronage, which limit a party's opportunities, as in the Scandinavian countries where social democratic parties were dominant until the 1970s. But even here we saw, in chapter 5, that social democrats have utilized liberal corporatist tendencies to reinforce their electoral dominance. Yet, there can be little doubt that periodic ejection from office does constitute some form of restriction on modern parties using state offices in the way that the British 'court party' did in the eighteenth century.

At the risk of considerable oversimplification, it may be suggested that the extent of party penetration of the state is influenced by four factors: the tradition of a strong state inherited from the pre-liberal-democratic era; long periods of single-party dominance under liberal democracy; the relatively early replacement of local elites by national party organizations in the organizing of elections; and, in the case of liberal democracies that collapsed in the twentieth century, the absence of legitimate rival organizations that could challenge parties when liberal democracy was restored. As can be seen in table 7.1 (which cites several democracies to illustrate the point), party penetration of the state ranges from the United States, where there are no factors present to promote it, to Austria, where all four factors are present.

What has become apparent in this section is that party penetration of the state varies enormously from one regime to another. Moreover, even when parties are deeply involved in state administration, this does not necessarily mean that they are all-powerful. Penetrating the state can lead to their being weakened as partisans. Yet, whatever the influence of the American model in relation, say, to the campaign styles of parties elsewhere, the experience there of parties becoming detached from the state in the twentieth century is probably unique. Indeed, of all the respects in which American parties are claimed to be 'exceptional', this is probably the most significant. While in other liberal democracies there seem to be various forces moving parties towards a greater integration with the state, in the United States the very opposite tendencies have been observed.

PARTY PENETRATION OF SOCIETY

Just as the liberal democracies vary in respect of the degree to which parties can 'colonize' the state, so they also differ in the parties' penetration of society. By penetration of society we mean that there are party ties to other organizations that enable parties to influence mass opinion and behaviour in a variety of ways. In some cases, as with the PCI, the party itself creates these organizations, but more commonly, perhaps, the party and the organizations have both grown out of broader social movements. But it is not the origin of the relationship that is important for party penetration of society, but the fact that there is influence downwards from the party as well as influence 'from below'. Consequently, we need to distinguish societal penetration by parties from instances of parties simply responding to and reflecting the power of other organizations in society. For example, in Ireland the power of the Catholic Church affects all parties, including the Labour party, but this is not a case of party penetration. Not only are all parties similarly influenced by the same organization but the parties can exercise little control over mass publics through the intermediation of the church; the relationship is uni-directional. Conversely, of course, if parties were so powerful that the related organizations had little influence over them, we might suspect that democracy itself could be undermined. To return to a theme discussed in chapter 2, broader social organizations constitute a significant potential check on the power of political elites; if too many organizations are tied into and dominated by the party system, an important checking device in any democracy may be undermined.

In some states parties have only relatively weak links with other kinds of organization, while in others there are very close connections. Obviously, there is a relation between party penetration of the state and of society. Devices like a *Proporz* system serve to encourage people to join or be associated with a party, while an extensive complex of institutions provides a party with personnel to fill state offices and also structures through which some of the activities and services of the state may be channelled. In the United States not only do we find that party nominees occupy only a relatively small number of the important positions in the regime (compare Rose's fourth condition), but parties have few direct links with other kinds of organization. For example, while the New Deal did result in the labour unions entering an informal alliance with the Democratic party, it was no more than this. The unions were active participants in many local parties and in the Democratic party nationally, but no *formal* provision was made for the representation of unions or their delegates. Indeed, they could withdraw support for a Democratic

Table 7.1. Factors influencing party penetration of the state and their distribution among selected liberal democracies

	Tradition of strong state	Long periods of single-party dominance	Relative early development of national party organizations to replace local elites	Absence of legitimate rival organizations following breakdown of liberal democracy in 20th century
US			×	
UK, Australia, Canada, New Zealand				
India				
France	×	× not before 1958		
Japan		×		
Ireland		×	×	
Netherlands	×		×	
Italy	×	×	×	×
Germany	×		×	×
Sweden		×	×	
Austria	×	×	×	×

candidate and openly endorse a Republican – though at the national level the biggest breach, in 1972, led only to the non-endorsement of the Democrat, George McGovern, by the AFL–CIO. Furthermore, neither the Democrats nor the Republicans have social organizations, churches or other bodies linked to them in ways which would make 'parties the life and soul of the people'. Some parties in Europe, especially caucus–cadre ones, have also been narrowly political bodies with no links to other organizations, of which the non-Gaullist right and centre-right parties in France were amongst the best examples. But, of course, some conservative parties have actually had very strong linkages of an informal kind with other structures, so that formal ties were not needed. Before 1974, Conservatives in the English 'shire' counties often allowed 'independents' to run county government; this did not reflect an inability to organize in these counties – on the contrary, conservatism overlapped with so many other kinds of organization and activity that party politics in local government was unnecessary.

Most European parties lie somewhere between the highly isolated American parties and the 'pillar' system found in the Netherlands, especially during the era of consociational democracy, 1917 to 1967. The Dutch parties were unusual in that they were at the apex of a whole series of organizations, in the 'pillars' (such as unions, social organizations and so on), which catered exclusively to the members of particular pillars. As Houska remarks:

> A typical Dutch Catholic, for example, might be a member of a Catholic trade union, the Catholic political party, the parish men's club, and the local Catholic football association . . . The family would subscribe to a Catholic television guide, watch the Catholic television network, listen to the Catholic radio, and read a Catholic daily newspaper. On vacation they would travel with a Catholic travel association.[19]

While both the Netherlands and Austria have been regarded as two of the main exemplars of consociational democracy, there are important differences between them. For our purposes the most significant is that in Austria it was the role given to the parties in the working of the state after 1945 which placed them at the centre of a series of networks; in the Netherland it was the growth in the parties' related organizations which permitted the consociational approach to government to be used from 1917 onwards.[20] As Pappalardo notes, 'by 1917 the development of the segmented structures had greatly stiffened the boundaries between the blocs'.[21] The consociational approach involved political elites co-operating in a 'grand coalition' in government, with a willingness to compromise surmounting all other considerations. At the electoral level this meant that the parties did not act as 'catch-all' parties in trying to maximize their votes, but rather kept their appeals to their own group – socialist, Catholic, or Protestant. Nevertheless,

> electoral campaigns were more or less imbued with dramatic tones and ideological appeals to the masses, contrasting with the pragmatism and moderation peculiar to the relationships among the elites. The contradiction, however, is more apparent than real: behind these tones and appeals lay an awareness that in segmented societies floating votes are few and catchall strategies unprofitable. Given this awareness, it goes without saying that parties had to strive to mobilize the faithful as effectively as possible if they wished to maximize gains and avoid losses. And the faithful are obviously more sensitive to a language like that of the Dutch elites, which was highly ideological.[22]

The ideology helped to preserve segmentation, while the segmented institutions put pressure on the elites to maintain accommodationist politics, which, in turn, demanded an ideological electoral strategy in relation to the party faithful.

Holland and Austria are not the only states to have practised consociational democracy. Belgium is the third of the 'clear-cut' cases; there too parties are closely linked with associated groups, although the geographical separation of the two linguistic communities perhaps made party penetration of society a less obvious feature of society than in the Dutch case. However, in Belgium in the 1950s and in the Netherlands in the 1960s the consociational approach came under pressure. In Belgium a significant factor in this was one which was absent in the Netherlands. The political elites found it increasingly difficult to contain mass-level conflicts on the language issue; the increased difficulty of managing their own supporters was compounded by the emergence of new splinter parties competing for the votes of party loyalists. Deprived of their electoral monopolies, electoral strategies became more complex although only one party (the Liberals) is really a catch-all party at the moment. But in both Belgium and the Netherlands there was another consideration inclining the parties to a catch-all approach. Changing social structures and relations were creating new kinds of voters for whom both the associated organizations and the secretive elitist politics had little attraction. There was an incentive for the parties to attract such voters and, in some cases, they were 'pushed' to do so by these new groups becoming active members in the party. A survey of the Dutch Labour party in 1978, for example, found that a huge membership turnover was occurring – only sixty per cent of members had been in the party for more than five years and only a third had been there for more than twelve.[23] Once again, we see a manifestation of something to which we alluded earlier. In the late twentieth century parties are finding it far more difficult to provide facilities and services wanted by their members or voters; they face more competition for the attention, time and partici- pation of people and so party penetration of society is that much more difficult. Before we turn to consider this problem more generally, though, we must first point out that party penetration of society does not necessarily lead to accommodationist politics. It can lead to the very opposite and perhaps the best example of this is the Nationalist party in South Africa.

One of the more interesting features of this party is that, while it is closely associated with political repression, it is a party which is rather democratic internally and which has succeeded in penetrating Afrikaner society in a way to which many European socialist parties would aspire. Hodder-Williams has written of it:

> The democratic nature of the autonomous provincial parties, taken with the initial lack of complete Afrikaner unity . . . required either formal structures or informal arrangements to bring together and keep consolidated a potentially divided Afrikanerdom. The professional and cultural organizations, reaching down to the youth organization, the Vortrekkers, and the Afrikaans-medium primary schools laid good foundations. The Dutch Reformed Churches, in which any aspiring Afrikaans public figure will be an active member, lent not only social solidarity but also Christian justification for government policies . . . But by far the most important vehicle for holding Afrikanerdom together was the *Afrikaner Broederbond* . . .[24]

The Broederbond not only helped to bring about exclusively Afrikaner economic enterprises, an area in which the British had dominated, but it was responsible for developing an Afrikaner ideology. The party is at the apex of a wide range of organizations, all of which are devoted to the pursuit of particular socio-political goals. Here is an example of a party which is not just a narrowly defined political organization but which is also an integral part of a wider political movement. Unlike many European socialist parties, though, the Nationalists have not only developed the supporting organizations but have also, until quite recently, managed to prevent them from generating goals and identities independently of the movement. There was not the sort of breach, for example, that was seen in the British Labour movement between party and unions after the mid-1960s. This South African example provides further evidence against a view of party development which became widespread among American political scientists in the 1950s and 1960s.

This was the argument that parties were, in essence, narrowly political organizations and that only the intrusion of socialist parties, and the responses this induced in other parties, brought about parties with deep organizational roots in their societies. (Partly, this view had its origins in the reaction to the claims of Duverger that socialist parties were really responsible for what he regarded as the dominant organizational form.) There can be little doubt – and we have argued the point in this book – that the European socialist parties did force many bourgeois and conservative parties to change the way they 'linked' with their electorates. But, while it might be possible to argue that a major socialist movement was a sufficient condition for such a development (though we saw in chapter 5 that, contrary to this argument, the Swedish and Finnish Conservatives took decades to form a mass organizational base), it is certainly not a necessary condition. As in inter-war South Africa, there are parties which have deeply penetrated their societies but which are not socialist or essentially a response to socialist organization. More pertinently, perhaps, there are also examples in liberal democracies where such parties have not led to the politics of Dutch-style elite accommodation; Italy is one instance. Like parties in West Germany and Austria, those in Italy became powerful in the years after 1945 because there were no other credible institutions which could exercise power:

> Many interest groups were in effect captured by either the Christian Democrats (DC) or Communists, and subordinated to the interest of their political controllers. For the Communist party (PCI), which in 1947 was expelled from government, this widespread network of social control enabled it to dominate the opposition, and gradually expand its electoral, parliamentary, and eventually industrial influence. For the Christian Democrats a similar if less robust party machine was supplemented both by the Catholic world, and by the expanding resources of the state . . . .[25]

Just as the 'cradle to grave' approach had worked in the Netherlands, so in Italy did the main parties attempt organizational encapsulation – having their voters live in an environment where the party was involved in some way in most aspects of their lives. The interesting point about the Italian case is that it could develop so late into the twentieth century, at a time when, in Britain for example, the parties' organizational penetration of society was close to passing its peak.

Nevertheless, by the second half of the century there were mounting pressures on parties which had succeeded in sinking deep social roots. For religious parties, the secularization of society, especially with the continuing decline of rural populations, eroded the electoral base. Correspondingly, working-class parties found that the industrial sector of most western economies was growing much more slowly than the less-unionized service sectors. Moreover, changes in communications made it less easy for parties to keep unwanted information and values from their loyal electorates – the Italian Communist voter who would not dream of buying a Catholic newspaper might well watch television programmes in which DC opinions were expressed. Although parties may not have had quite the control over their electorates in the past that they were once thought to – and this point has certainly been argued with respect to Italy – there can be little doubt that many of the resources for control have declined.[26] But what follows from this? On the one hand, it would be incorrect to argue that parties no longer need to try to penetrate society, or that they can adopt other means of winning elections. Setting the climate of debate at the local level still counts, as the CDU experience in the 1970s suggests.[27] On the other hand, if a party can place itself at the centre of networks involving the state and interest associations, then it can prevent itself from becoming like an American party – that is just one of a number of political actors. Yet, as we have seen, there is a cost to this in terms of the party itself being open to influence and penetration by these interests

If the general trend in liberal democracies has been towards a weakening of parties' ability to penetrate society, there are two qualifications to be made to this conclusion. The first is that there are a few instances of parties generating more loyalty from their voters in the last twenty or thirty years. The most notable example of this is France, where identification with particular political parties was found among fifty per cent of the electorate at the end of the 1950s, whereas now eighty-five per cent are identifiers.[28] The French case is very unusual, though, in that organized modern parties were so slow to develop there. The second qualification is that the breaking down of organizational penetration of society, and the decline of voter loyalty, is occurring comparatively slowly in most cases. As we have noted before, the partisan dealignment seen in Britain and the highly volatile voting behaviour now seen there is not typical; nor is the speed with which party organizations in the United States collapsed and party identification weakened from the 1960s onwards. As I have argued elsewhere, a combination of several factors were responsible for the hasty demise of what remained of American local parties.[29] Furthermore, while interest organizations have helped in this destruction (funding by PACs has contributed to the dominance of individual candidates), they do not necessarily play such a role elsewhere. This point can be made, not with respect to the obvious example of parties channelling interest group politics (Austria), but with an example where we might expect parties to suffer a similar fate to the American parties: Japan. Japanese politics is dominated by one party, which is heavily factionalized, and individual candidates have their own organizations; interest groups are also highly involved (in financial and other ways) in Japanese politics. These are precisely the sorts of conditions in which we might expect the dismantling of party structures – in India under Indira Gandhi the structures of the dominant party were dismantled by her.[30] But in Japan the pre-eminence of business elites did not lead to the de-institutionalization of the Liberal Democratic party, although their penetration of the party has been extensive. Thus, although there are important instances of party ties with the electorate being greatly weakened and of parties losing their resources to sustain such ties because of de-institutionalization, they do not seem to represent a general trend.

DO PARTIES MATTER?

However, if we accept that there is no evidence of a general drift towards the marginalization of parties in terms of controlling the state and as influences in society, there remains the question of whether parties can, in fact, make a difference in terms of the policy output of the state. This issue became a major area of controversy from the mid-1970s onwards, with some studies claiming to show that it did not matter much which party was in government while others contended that parties did make a difference. This debate is highly significant, of course, in any discussion of democratization. If parties really did not 'matter', then arguments about voter choice, about the political education parties can provide and about the means of providing democratic control over parties become rather secondary issues for students of politics. Certainly, a number of the arguments developed in this book would lose much of their interest. It is important, therefore, to disentangle an argument that has become rather complex.

The obvious starting place is to note that the informed layperson would take the view that parties certainly do matter. After all, with the possible exception of the Netherlands, the three countries which have had the most extensive systems of public welfare are Denmark, Norway and Sweden, and they also happen to be the three states where social democratic parties enjoyed the greatest electoral success in the twentieth century. Surely this can be no coincidence. This argument from common sense underlies a forceful, if methodologically suspect, analysis of the difference parties make by Castles and McKinlay, although they regard *the absence of strong right-wing parties* as being a key element in the explanation of differences in welfare provision.[31] Why, then, should so much debate have been engendered by such an apparently clear-cut issue? There are several different aspects in accounting for this. In part, it simply reflected the dominance of the sociological approach to politics in the 1970s. Again, actually measuring welfare provision is a complex matter, and this makes it possible for seemingly counter-intuitive explanations of differences in policy outputs between the states to be propounded and justified. More substantively, though, parties are certainly not the only factors affecting levels of welfare provision, so that we should not expect to find a simple relation between party control and policy output. Then again, once policy areas other than those relating to welfare provision came to be included in comparative studies between states, it was not surprising that differences relating to party control became less distinct, because it was less clear what the differences should, in theory, be. Having made these initial observations, we can now begin to understand some of the important issues relevant to understanding this debate.

One point to note is that we must be careful in comparing the policy output of different regimes, or in imputing objectives to parties which may be over-simplifications of their real objectives. For example, as Castles and McKinlay emphasized, regimes at different stages of economic development face different constraints in terms of the services governments can provide. It is not surprising, then, that some studies of policies in the American states concluded that the kinds of public policies enacted closely correlated with the level of economic development in the various states.[32] That some of these studies also revealed that political factors seemed to explain relatively little of the difference between the states is also unsurprising, because the kind of federalism practised in the United States would make it difficult for states to depart *too* radically from those of their neighbours. In making comparisons we have to ensure that these are between regimes at relatively similar levels of economic development, and in the light of the institutional constraints parties face in effecting policies when in government. This latter consideration is also relevant when considering the objectives parties have. Their inability to implement the policies they would really want may lead them to pursue overtly very different policies. Consider Fried's findings on the policies of Communist administrations in Italian cities: 'To predict budgetary variables in Italian Communist cities the doctrines of Marxist socialism seem a good deal less helpful than those of "fiscal responsibility".'[33] Yet, as he argues, this reflects a deliberate strategy by the party in wanting to appear to provide efficient administration, as a way of attracting middle-class supporters.[34] Given that the independence of Italian city governments is circumscribed by state powers, this policy made sense in terms of building long-term political support. However, this is precisely the sort of case which would undermine efforts to test the influence of party on government budgets, if it were assumed that left-wing parties always wanted to maximize government expenditures.

Another consideration is that the external constraints on governments have probably increased, so that currently parties have less scope for radical change in policies than they would have had fifty years ago. There are several forces at work here. One is the much greater international penetration of national economies. More than forty years of liberal international trade, combined with the growth of trans-national institutions and enterprises, has made it more difficult for states to introduce macro-economic strategies which diverge from those of other states. In 1981 the French Socialist government attempted to introduce a new strategy of economic expansion on its accession to power. Within eighteen months the policy had collapsed. It has been predicated on the assumption of much greater growth in the American economy, and when this failed to materialize French unemployment did not fall as much as had been expected. Instead, other countries, most notably West Germany, were among the beneficiaries of French expansionism which created foreign-exchange difficulties for the

French. These spillover effects of the policy could not be corrected because, as a member of the EEC, France was not able to use the threat of protectionism as a device to keep the principal impact of its policies within the domestic economy. Another, and sometimes related, force has been the system of international alliances which has dominated foreign policy since 1945. This has had an impact also on the smaller number of liberal democracies which are not formally part of these alliances. While foreign policy always was more influenced by long-term considerations, placing it more outside party control, the static system of alliances of the post-1945 period has made it even more difficult for parties to enact very different policies from their predecessors in government. This has been reinforced by the fact that the alliances have, on both sides, been dominated by one state rather than power being split between a number of similarly sized states. The best example of this problem of pursuing policies which fall outside the consensus is that of the policy of the Labour government in New Zealand in no longer permitting vessels carrying nuclear weapons to call at New Zealand ports. The United States, which dominates the ANZUS organization in the way that it dominates NATO, refused to compromise on the issue and effectively put the ANZUS treaty 'on ice', and has deprived the New Zealand government of intelligence information. In the case of a NATO member, which had, say, implemented a non-nuclear policy on its own territory, such action would have very serious effects on the state's defence capability and possibly lead to the modification of the policy. In the New Zealand example, the ability of the government to maintain its policy lies in the fact that there is no forseeable external threat to New Zealand.

New Zealand also provides a further example of how growth in economic interdependence can affect foreign policy, although in this case it is not one which would have likely divided the two parties. In 1986 the government came to an agreement to hand over to France two agents of the French secret service who had been convicted of blowing up a ship, owned by the Greenpeace organization, in a New Zealand harbour. The main pressure on the government to come to an agreement was possible French opposition to EEC countries importing New Zealand agricultural products. Twenty years before this would have been a far less effective weapon because Britain, New Zealand's main trading partner in Europe, was not then a member of the EEC. But we should not assume that defence and trade treaties, or the system of liberal international trade, will necessarily be preserved in their present forms. In the very long term these constraints on parties may be much less than they are now.

Yet another factor which has increased the constraints on governments is one relevant to sub-national government. As the demand for services has increased, so their tax bases have often been insufficient to meet it, and they have either been unable to respond to this demand or central government has had to increase its financial support to these governments. Financial dependence does not, of course, entail the governments having to accept directives from the centre, and many commentators on inter-government relations in the United States now stress the vitality of state government, rather than the subservience many feared would result from the vast expansion of the grants-in-aid programmes in the 1960s. However, the American state governments were well protected by constitutional and political barriers against undue federal government intrusion. The greater problem is that of local governments in unitary systems. The British example in the period after 1979 is the outstanding one in this respect. Faced by (primarily) Labour councils which had very different expenditure policies and priorities than those of the Conservative central government, the latter used a series of measures to prevent expenditures which exceeded its targets. One of the principal measures was cuts in grants to those authorities which did 'overspend'. Obviously, such measures reduce the difference between the expenditure patterns of Conservative and Labour councils.

A further consideration, relevant in understanding the 'does politics matter?' question, is that under some standard Downsian assumptions about party competition, there is an incentive for parties to converge on the centre of the political spectrum, wherever that may be.[35] The parties may not 'make a difference' because the logic of the electoral market *forces them not to be very different from their competitors.* Parties would matter more if the configuration of voters was different. It is often said of British politics in the quarter century after 1945 that there was a consensus which both major parties sought to exploit electorally. If the argument about convergence on the centre is correct, then we must be careful to separate those societies in which parties are forced to converge from those where they are not and apply the principal tests about the relevance of parties to the latter. In fact, as we suggested when discussing the role of parties as vehicles for choice in chapter 3, the connection between voter opinions and party policies is far more complex than Downsian analysis would allow.

Nevertheless, it is more important to distinguish the electoral constraints which reduce party difference from the factors which may prevent or hamper parties from putting different policies into effect.

Then again there is the problem of governments which lack the necessary legislative majorities to implement wholly, or indeed at all, their main policies, so that existing policies are likely to continue. Party differences here may well be quite small but for reasons which have nothing to do with a supposed 'natural' expansion of state services. There are three main ways in which this inability to control a legislative programme may come about.

1　In presidential systems different parties may control the legislature and the executive. Until recently the main examples of this were in the United States. However, the 1986 parliamentary elections in France brought a majority for the two mainstream parties of the right, although the Socialist president still had a further two years of his term to serve. There began an experimental period of *cohabitation*. In the United States divided control has been a common feature of government at both the federal and state levels. Between 1930 and 1988 the same party controlled the presidency and both houses of the legislature for only thirty-four years, and twenty-two of the years of divided control occurred between 1954 and 1988. A similar pattern is evident at the state level where different periods of office can produce a hostile legislature half-way through a governor's term. In the years up to the mid-1960s electoral malapportionment also increased the frequency of divided control. The effects of this were reduced by Supreme Court interventions, but a greater willingness of voters to 'split their tickets' led to divided control being just as common in the two-party competitive states in the mid-1970s as it was in the mid-1950s.[36]

2　Parties in non-presidential systems may fail to secure an overall majority in the legislature, or only a very small and 'unworkable' one, so that they are forced to restrict their introduction of controversial proposals. In Britain parties were, in theory, 'handicapped' in this way for eleven years in the period 1900–45 (1910–18, 1923–4 and 1929–31) and for eight years in the period 1945–86 (1950–1, 1964–6 and 1974–9). However, the growing strength of other parties (the Liberals, nationalist parties and later the SDP) has led many to predict that the incidence of minority governments will increase. Of the ex-British colonies, Canada is the one in which minority governments are most common; they were in power for ten years in the period 1945–86. In western Europe minority governments are even more common – some of them, as often in Italy, being coalition governments which have failed to find sufficient coalition partners to form an overall majority. They have been especially common in states where there is one party larger than the others but which often cannot obtain sufficient electoral support to obtain a majority – Sweden, Norway, Denmark and Ireland are examples of this. In Sweden there were minority governments for nearly two-thirds of the period 1945–83.[37] It should be noted, though, that in Norway and Denmark the dominance of the social democratic parties there has been eroded in the last two decades.

3   There is the issue (mentioned in chapter 3), when discussing the choice exercised by voters, of the element of party policy which enters into the programmes of coalition governments. At that stage we were concerned with the question of whether voter choice could be exercised in such circumstances. We are interested in this question here but in the context of whether it makes 'a difference' to government policy as to which parties form the coalition government in a given country. The answer to this question depends on two, quite possibly related, assumptions we make about coalition formation. One involves the objectives we attribute to the parties (and especially to their leaders) in the negotiations over coalition formation. How concerned about the policy of possible coalitions are they compared with maximizing the number of governments posts (or some other non-policy objective) for their party in the coalition? The other assumption (or, rather, set of assumptions) concerns the factors which allocate power within the coalition formation process? For example, will parties only form coalitions with those parties closest to them on the ideological spectrum? If so, is the participation of certain parties thereby essential to the formation of any government, and do they exercise this power to get most of their own policies onto the coalition agenda? If a number of possible coalitions are possible, given the distribution of power among the various parties, of how much value do the parties give to the continuation of a government? Not surprisingly, comparisons between states on party input to public policy become difficult, but a study by Schofield and Laver has reached a tentative conclusion about the relative importance of ideology and government portfolios in party bargaining in different European countries. They argue that

in Austria, Germany, Ireland, Luxembourg and Norway, coalition formation is based on bargaining on policies which are capable of being placed on a single political dimension (or spectrum).

> With the assumption that parties have preferred policy positions on this single dimension, then it can be shown that an 'equilibrium' associated with the median party will always exist . . . coalition governments in such systems will tend to be relatively stable.
>
> In the second group of countries (Belgium, Denmark, Finland, Iceland and Sweden) on the contrary we suggest that distributional aspects of political bargaining are more important. One reason might very well be that the natural policy space in these systems is of two or more dimensions. In this case there will tend to be no equilibrium. As a consequence we expect relatively short-lived coalition governments. Because of this inherent instability, parties might well focus on obtaining direct access to policy areas, and thus attempt to maximize the number of cabinet posts they control.[38]

If this conjecture is correct, then we would expect the first group of countries to reveal a much greater party input into legislative programmes than the second. But, overall, this would result in parties making 'more difference' only if control of the legislative agenda is relatively more important in these political systems than is direct executive action. Whether this is likely to be true involves issues which are too complex to discuss here.

A final, but crucial, consideration when evaluating the 'does politics matter?' debate is that as important as the policies parties bring onto the agenda are the ones they keep off it. As Schattschneider has observed, 'the definition of the alternatives is the supreme instrument of power',[39] and having one kind of party as a major party will preclude certain kinds of issues getting onto the agenda because they do not divide that party from its competitors. Another kind of party might well be able to make that issue a central one, but it cannot break into the party system because the other issues around which it would hope to mobilize have been embraced already by major parties. In the case of British politics there are three issues which, it might be argued, were largely kept off the agenda by a consensus between the major parties in the 1950s, 1960s and 1970s. By many conservatives, the issue of race relations is seen as one which the parties chose to handle as a consensus matter; those, like Enoch Powell, who chose to explore alternatives to this consensus were excluded from power. Correspondingly, on the left, nuclear defence was treated in the same way until the late 1970s – the unilateralist approach to nuclear disarmament was little-represented among the influential members of the 1964–70 and 1974–9 Labour governments. The third issue is Northern Ireland where again the major parties have sought to preserve a consensus approach. Again, in the United States we can find examples of how parties removed some issues from the centre of public debate. The administrations of Franklin Roosevelt continued the tradition of the federal government not becoming involved in the issue of civil rights for blacks; this helped to preserve his political coalition, and it was not until 1948 that a commitment to federal government action on civil rights became part of the Democratic party platform. Again, one product of the McCarthy era was that a consensus approach to foreign and defence matters emerged in the United States – Democratic liberals who had been worried by the apparent success of the anti-Communism message in the early 1950s were determined not to be seen thereafter as 'soft on Communism'. John Kennedy, for example, adopted as a major plank in his 1960 election campaign the claim that the Eisenhower administration had allowed 'a missile gap' to develop in the arms race. It was not until later that decade, with the growing entanglement in Vietnam, that this consensual approach began to erode and liberals came to believe that alternative approaches to defence policy would not be disastrous electorally.

What emerges from this discussion is that simple comparisons of the policies of different governing parties may well be insufficient in revealing whether 'politics matters'. There may be considerable differences between parties even though on many major policy areas there are powerful external constraints to moving outside the existing consensus; we cannot always impute party objectives from the party's overall ideology in given governing situations; parties may want to be different but be constrained by the electoral market; they may lack the legislative majorities necessary to implement their policies; and their most important contribution to the policy agenda might be the items they keep off it. What, then, of the evidence of the studies which have been conducted? Several of the most important ones, including Rose's analysis of Britain, have emphasized the external constraints facing parties and the relatively small difference politics seem to make. Even in the book's second edition, which takes account of the first Thatcher administration, Rose does not change his general conclusion.[40] Yet, just as it might be argued that in laying out the conditions for party government he made the conditions very severe, so that in most states parties are going to look incapable of providing true party government, so here it can be argued that he has focused mainly on the areas where the parties could be least expected to make a difference in the short term. We would not expect them to differ that much in managing the economy, say; British parties simply lack the resources to develop alternative economic strategies in opposition, whatever they may claim. Rose is right to point out that government expenditure has continued to grow irrespective of which party is in power, and, of course, past commitments usually get carried forward so that, overall, it is often difficult to transform radically the pattern of public expenditure within a four-year administration.

Yet, having accepted these points, we must not lose sight of the obvious. The high levels of public welfare in Scandinavia cannot be explained away as a rather complex response to being some of the most advanced industrial economies. If it were, we might expect that post-war Japan would not have remained one of the liberal democracies with the least well developed systems of public welfare provision. And parties do make a difference in terms of who benefits relatively from government expenditure or from changes in government tax policy. The well-documented appearance of a relatively large group of the very wealthy in south-eastern England in the 1980s, for example, can be related directly to major changes made by the Conservative government in income tax policy. Indeed, the evidence of the vast number of studies which have probed different aspects of the 'does politics matter?' debate is that, *where it might be expected parties could make a difference, they do.* The more 'left-wing' parties do tend to spend more on welfare policies and be more responsive to increases in unemployment than to increases in inflation.[41] But this is not to deny that the factors we have identified which limit the scope of parties to change policies are strong in particular areas of policy or in particular electoral or legislative situations. Obviously, one of the main challenges facing radical parties is to devise ways of overcoming, or circumventing, these barriers. The approach of the most radical Conservative administration in Britain since 1945 was to try to change attitudes towards and expectations of the state, so that in the longer term domestic government programmes could be reduced. That this has not shown up in a complete reversal of the trend towards greater government expenditure can be attributed to three factors. First, the aim was to make possible changes in the role of the British state in the longer term. Second, a policy directed towards minimizing inflation increased unemployment even further and this made it politically difficult at the same time for the government to reduce drastically high expenditure programmes, such as unemployment and related benefits. Third, while it wanted to reduce domestic expenditures, the Conservative government also favoured increasing expenditure on defence. For these reasons the proportion of GDP taken up by public expenditure fell by only 0.3 per cent in the period 1979–82 compared with the period 1974–79, while it remained more than 4 per cent greater than in the period 1970–4.[42] But this sort of data necessarily understates the difference that the Conservative government has made.

To return to the conditions for party government which we discussed at the beginning of this chapter. Rose's eighth condition (that party policies must be put into practice by the administration of government) begins to look an especially severe one, if it is interpreted to mean that parties can actually implement what they choose to implement. They cannot affect in the short term (and in some cases, in the longer term too) a number of facets of both state and society which they would want to. Rose and the other sceptics about the power of parties are correct – there are important external constraints on them. But once we control for this, the ability of parties to make a difference begins to look impressive, both in terms of policies (especially welfare policies) and in terms of what they organize out of politics. But we must remember to examine differences in policy output in relation to parties' actual policy objectives. For example, Rose and Peters found that in the period 1951–76 the largest percentage increase in government expenditure in western Europe was in Italy.[43] While the Christian Democrats have been the main party in all the post-war governments, it is highly misleading to regard this as a conventional party of the right. Faced by a strong Communist party, they have (in Hine's words) 'expanded welfare spending in a way uncharacteristic of parties of the right'.[44] In other words, the Italian case would fit well into an account of the difference parties make – because it shows how a party has had to respond in terms of its policies to the electoral challenge of its competitors.[45] While it does not meet fully all of the conditions for party government, Italy clearly does practice a form of party government. In this respect it is like many other liberal democracies.

CONCLUDING REMARKS

Viewed from the perspective of the late twentieth century, the achievements of parties in penetrating the state, in shaping opinions and attitudes in society and in implementing their programmes and policies may seem rather limited. In many cases they have not been able to establish more than superficial control of the state, their ability to control electorates is somewhat restricted and may be getting weaker, and, particularly among parties on the left, there has often been a sense of failure in terms of the enactment of policies. Only in Sweden, where a social democratic party was in power continuously for more than forty years, have recriminations and guilt about performance in office not been a significant feature of socialist parties. But to take this view is to ignore the very great difficulties most parties have had to face in building up mechanisms for exercising state power, in creating resources with which to 'reach' their voters, and in overcoming the external factors which gives 'a life of its own' to the policy-making process. Indeed, what is remarkable about parties is not that they have achieved so little but that they have achieved so much. Except in the United States, parties have not disintegrated and have not become secondary actors in a political universe dominated by interest groups. They are continuing to experiment with ways to make state bureaucracies more amenable to party influence, although few parties have had the advantages of those in Austria in having a new constitution in which parties were permitted to play a central role. They have not lost their influence completely in opinion formation which social change and technological innovation might well have brought about. Furthermore, when allowance is made for the various ways in which parties could not be expected to make a difference in terms of the policy output of a state, the evidence suggests that parties do play a major part in determining policy. As von Beyme has argued:

> The thesis that it is only of secondary importance which party is in power is generally propounded by those who see oppositional Socialism as it was when the Socialists had very little political influence anywhere, or certainly far less than the trade unions on which they so much depended and which were in a much better position to fight . . .[46]

Parties may not have transformed societies, but they have shaped how they have developed, and with greater experience in controlling the state and in influencing mass publics, there is no reason to suppose that they cannot be at least as great an influence in the future.

8

THE FUTURE OF PARTIES AS AGENTS
OF DEMOCRACY

In chapter 1 we identified three elements of democracy: interest optimalization; the exercise of control; and civic orientation. From the discussion in chapter 3, it is apparent that party competition is a very imperfect mechanism for bringing about the optimal aggregation of interests. Leaving aside the problems of voting cycles, voting paradoxes and so on, it is clear that the way parties actually compete against each other in many political systems makes it unlikely that interest aggregation based on political equality will occur. Parties collude, though only in Switzerland is this overt; they partly determine the dominant interests and cleavages within the state; and because of the need for coalition governments in many states, the link between party programmes (where they exist) and government is often (at best) indirect. In short, if interest optimalization were the only element of democracy, we would be forced to conclude that the ability of parties to advance democracy is rather limited. With regard to civic orientation, parties have made one important contribution: they have helped direct mass political acitivity towards normal political channels. But beyond this their role in developing public-regardingness has been restricted. Few parties have developed the kinds of forums for participation that might result in a weakening of the politics of self-interest. Even in states where party structures have been extensive, as in Austria, parties have been linked to interest group systems that have tended to encourage some aspects of private-regarding politics, even though they have also helped to foster an ethos of compromise.

The main focus of the book, then, has been on how parties have enabled citizens to exercise greater control over their lives. And the main theme running through this book has been that, as agents of this element of democracy, parties in the twentieth century have largely been exemplars of unfulfilled potential. Parties have contributed to the extension of popular control in liberal democracies, but the extent of democracy in these regimes is still rather limited. Equally, parties in these regimes have been, at most, only partly democratized themselves. We have identified five aspects to this incomplete success: First, in competing against each other, parties do permit some form of choice to be presented to voters; elections are not wholly 'issueless' and, although many electoral systems partly obscure the alternatives presented to electorates by parties, there is in most cases some link between electoral competition and the objectives subsequently pursued by the state. Second, competition between parties does, even if only in a very restricted way, help to inform and educate citizens about the nature of political division in their society, and of some of the means of resolving this. Nevertheless, in many liberal democracies much electoral campaigning is not directed towards this but to other means of mobilizing voters such as by emphasis on leadership personalities – a development further encouraged by modern campaign techniques. Third, as a forum for political participation, many parties have failed to provide much scope for mass involvement in the nomination of candidates, in the choice of party objectives and policies and, increasingly perhaps, in the conduct of campaigns themselves. Fourth, democracy within parties has been an elusive objective; there are a number of problems to be overcome in constructing internal arrangements that maximize member or activist influence, and even those parties that have committed themselves to this objective have not done so. Fifth, parties have generally failed to find the appropriate balance between party penetration of state and society (which permits party policies to be carried out and parties to be a major force in society) and the need for limits to this penetration so as to restrict the resources available to party elites. (In addition, of course, if party penetration were very extensive, there is the danger that only party opinions would find full expression in the media.) As we have seen, party penetration of both state and society has been very variable; in some cases parties have been no match for the state and its bureaucracy, while in others parties have become so enmeshed with interest groups and with the state itself that it becomes more difficult for the parties to act as a separate force within society.

But, in admitting the failures of parties as institutions promoting democracy, it is important at the same time to reject the idea that parties are antithetical to democracy. As we noted in chapter 1, one strain of antipartism has always been found among some radical democrats; these are democrats who reject the idea that the state can be democratized at all. For them, it is absurd to think of democratic institutions controlling the state and of leaders using this control to democratize it; democracy can only exist in relatively small units of interaction – on the factory floor, or in neighbourhood councils, for example. Such views are not necessarily anarchistic – their proponents could believe that the emergence of some kind of state was inevitable and they may recognize that it should be more than a 'minimal state' in terms of the services it provides, but they may still deny that the state itself is open to democratic influence, or that it can be democratized. For them, democracy can be practised only at levels below that of the state, and the object of the democrat is to create forums for this. There are two objections to this view. How the state is controlled is, almost certainly, going to have some bearing on the extent of democracy in the lower level units; it requires state action for many of these units to be created and it is only be controlling the state that a democrat can hope to extend democracy. Few business firms have recognized the advantages of industrial democracy; many of the originally small co-operative ventures (such as retail co-operatives, or the British building societies) have now become large economic enterprises in which democracy varies but is usually not very extensive; and neighbourhood self-government requires state action to create the powers necessary for these bodies to be able to achieve anything. For the most part, then, it is only by controlling the state that democrats can exert the power necessary to open arenas for democracy. Moreover, because democratization works against the interests of some individuals or groups, it cannot be expected that, once it has been established at these lower levels, it will necessarily be allowed to continue. For this reason, those who advocate democratization may expect to have to persist in seeking power at the state level to prevent the possible erosion of earlier achievements and to provide an exemplar for democratization at other levels. An additional objection to this anti-state view of democracy is that parties may be disappointing agents of democracy, but they have not failed altogether. Claims that parties do not matter, or that parties are relatively minor actors in society, or as electoral intermediaries, or in organizing government, are not convincing, even though parties are probably not as influential as political scientists a generation or more ago seemed to think.

This brings us back to a subject we touched on in chapter 1 – the important role of 'fashion' in political science. One of the features of political science, as with many areas of human activity, is that it is much affected by fashion – some views become fashionable and replace earlier widely accepted views. Obviously, this is a complex process, but one of the reasons for it is that a scholar who tries to turn an accepted argument 'on its head' gets far more attention than one who merely tries to modify a conventional wisdom. The result is that we can point to a number of subjects in political science where over a relatively short period there has been a transformation in what people believed, and hence on the research in which they engaged. The decline of interest, in the 1950s, in the impact of constitutions on political systems is an obvious case. In relation to parties the turning point was the second half of 1960s and it is from then that we can date the quickly growing scepticism about the impact of parties.

Several factors helped to hasten the demise of the older view that parties were the central element in politics in the western democracies. In parts of continental Europe there were forces prompting a rising interest in neo-Marxism. Again, the first generation of behavioural studies on parties had extended our knowledge of parties rather less than might have been imagined. Eldersveld's much cited *Political Parties: A Behavioral Analysis*, for instance, is an interesting study but scarcely one that much changed our views of how American parties operated.[1] In a sense, political scientists were just growing tired of parties. At the same time, though, there was growing disillusionment in both Britain and the United States about the policies associated with parties and leaders that had supposedly represented a break with the past. The Labour government elected in Britain in 1964 was associated not now so much with a new economic policy, to replace the policies of 'stop–go' practised for thirteen years by the Conservatives, but with a continuation of such policies. Equally, the enthusiasm that had greeted the presidency of the Democrat Kennedy in 1960 had been replaced by division over Vietnam and controversy over the unintended effects of many of the Great Society programmes. This helped to spur the growth of the view that parties might be less significant than political scientists had proclaimed earlier in the 1950s. Moreover, the British and American experiences loomed much larger then than they do in political science today. With the possible exception of France, the west European states were not well known by the majority of Anglo-American political scientists. Lijphart's *The Politics of Accommodation* which in drawing attention to the politics of elite control in the Netherlands did much to inform the Anglo-American world that 'continental' multi-partism was not all some variant of the French Fourth Republic or post-war Italy, was not published until 1968.[2] Again, the European Consortium for Political Research, which helped to destroy the provincialism of British (if not American) political science was not fully operative until the early 1970s. In the meantime, scepticism about parties in Britain and America was growing, as it was in a number of other countries, including France and Italy, and by the mid-1970s it was becoming rampant. It is significant, then, that the first major comparative study to question this scepticism should have been written by a German, von Beyme. As we have seen, parties are far from moribund in West Germany, and the experience of Germany, where there is not a long tradition of party government, suggests that we need to modify the thesis that parties do not matter. But, of course, it would be foolish to use such models to propel political science back to asserting some of the extravagant claims made for parties in earlier decades.

However, if we can recognize that parties have continued to be, at least, somewhat effective as intermediaries in the liberal democratic state, there remains the important question of whether they can still be expected to operate as agents of democracy. In the longer term, are there developments likely to undermine their contribution to democracy or, conversely, can we identify possible changes in liberal democratic states that could enable parties to advance democratization more than they have in the twentieth century? In the remaining sections of the book we examine a number of factors which may well have an impact on parties in the future and assess their potential for either weakening or strengthening parties as agents of democracy. Many, though not all, of these factors involve arguments we have considered already in this book, and the point of the discussion here is to bring together a number of different arguments already presented.

SOCIAL CHANGE AND PARTIES' ELECTORAL AND ORGANIZATIONAL BASES

Parties are not simply sociologically determined epiphenomena. They do have their own interests and ways of operating which affects not only the distribution of values in a society but also can affect the preferences that are expressed by individuals and groups in it. Having acknowledged this, though, we cannot ignore the fact that social structure and division does have an important influence on how parties operate and the objectives they pursue. Major changes in class structure, in religious affiliations, in the ethnic

composition of a state, can all bring about important trans-
formations in parties and party systems. For example, anyone
examining party politics in Israel since 1947 would pay
considerable attention to the effect that the large influx of non-
European Jews since the 1960s has had on the parties and on the
issue agenda. Of course, most liberal democracies have not
experienced such a dramatic change in the electoral base and in
most it is religion and class that have been the main factors which,
at least in the past, have defined party politics. Continuing
secularization of western societies has tended to weaken specifically
religious parties, though the ability to combine appeals to the
religious with those attractive to non-practising Catholics and non-
Catholics has made the Christian Democratic parties in western
Europe among the most successful parties. Again, changes in
western economies, and particularly the declining relative
importance of manufacturing industry, have produced new social
groups that lack the traditional ties to class-based parties. As well
as fewer peasants now, compared with fifty years ago, there
are relatively fewer manual workers, small shopkeepers and
manufacturers. Correspondingly, there are more people employed
by governments, or dependent on government funding, and more
people employed in the service sectors. But what effect is the
continuation of these trends likely to have on parties in the future?

One argument is that these new social groups lack firm
attachments to the older parties and, because parties now loom
less large in social and political life than they did, these groups will
not develop strong loyalties to new parties either. Consequently,
maintaining large memberships will be more difficult for parties,
and they must now engage in overtly catch-all electoral strategies
because they cannot depend on the bedrock of support that they
once could. Those who accept this argument can point to the
decline of identification with parties in the United States, high
levels of electoral volatility in Britain and the United States, and
the rise of 'flash' protest parties (as in Denmark) as evidence of
what might occur more generally. However, there are a number of
objections to this line of argument.

For one thing, as we have just noted, the Christian Democrats
(operating in those parts of Europe where Catholics are more than
a small minority) have been remarkably successful in drawing
much wider support than that of *practising* Catholics. Parties have
adapted well to secularization. Moreover, there are some grounds
for arguing that the limits of secularization in some western
societies may be approaching. In making this argument, and in

drawing attention to the American experience, we must recognize that the American case is a peculiar one, although the causes are not unique to that country. By all measures, the United States has the largest proportion of believers and practitioners of religion of any western democracy.[3] There is also growing evidence of the clergy being increasingly involved in party politics in that country. In part, a spur for this was provided by the enforcement of voting rights for blacks from the 1960s onwards. The greater involvement of blacks in electoral politics brought even greater prominence than previously to black clergymen, who had always played a far more central role in the leadership of their communities than did the white clergy in theirs. (There are some parallels to this in experience of ethnic minorities in parts of central and eastern Europe, where the church was the only 'elite' career open to minorities). It is not surprising, then, that we find clergymen like Adam Clayton Powell in the 1940s among the first black congressmen – at least since the era of Reconstruction in the South. That the black clergy were willing to engage in partisan, as well as non-party, political activity was further revealed in the bid by the Reverend Jesse Jackson for the Democratic nomination for the presidency in 1984. The other recent development has been the involvement of right-wing fundamentalists. In the 1980 elections they supported efforts to defeat several prominent liberal Democrats in the American Senate, and in 1986 one of the best known of the right-wing clergymen, Pat Robertson, announced that he was considering a bid for the Republican presidential nomination in 1988. In the 1980s, then, religious organizations and leaders seemed to have become far more active in party politics.

But, for our purpose, the important issue is not so much this as the continuing high levels of religious observance in the United States and its possible significance for other western democracies, and most especially those, such as Australia and Canada, where there are still relatively high levels of immigration. One of the main explanations for the apparent paradox, that the most successful economy in meeting material needs should also be the most religious society in the west, is connected with the weak sense of belonging and identity among Americans. With the breaking-up of ethnic ghettos, many Americans lack a sense of any deep-rooted ties to a particular area or community. Rather than increasing secular tendencies, suburbanization arguably increases religious observance because it can help to provide some sense that a person 'belongs somewhere': the church makes up for lack of ties to a geographically defined community. It can be argued that changes in the industrial structure of other western states too may well produce sufficient mobility within the workforce to encourage religious observance among the uprooted. Obviously, this may do no more than offset pressures for secularization, but it does suggest that religion may not always be an ever-weakening bond that ties people to particular parties.

Another reason for arguing that socio-economic change may not make parties more marginal political institutions is that, as we noted in an earlier chapter, the lack of commitment to parties found in Britain and the United States is not universal. In some other countries, declining support for one party leads directly to support for a new party or for the smaller parties. On this argument, the 'flash' parties (like the Danish Progress party), are not typical of the newer or the smaller parties, in that the latter do not attract predominantly fickle voters. Again, in many western states there is little evidence of *highly* volatile shifts in support from one established party to another, compared with voting patterns in the past. To the contrary, there is some evidence for countries like Italy that the stability of voting patterns in *earlier* decades may have been exaggerated.[4] Furthermore, it can be argued that some reduction in the ties of segments of the electorate to particular parties actually makes it more likely that parties can aid democratization. On the one hand, strong ties provide less incentive for a party to seek to address new issues in its quest for votes, while on the other, if strong voter loyalty goes hand in hand with longevity in party office by members, a party elite may be able to exercise far greater control over internal affairs. Some degree of turnover in a party bureaucracy is necessary if the party's representatives are actually to be held accountable to the membership.

But there is a yet more compelling reason for believing that parties may be able to play a more central role in democratization in the future than they have thus far. One of the most obvious features of the late twentieth-century western politics is that it is far from the 'end of ideology' predicted twenty to thirty years ago. While traditional class divisions may have become less important because of the decline of the working class, political conflict has not become more muted: ethnic divisions in states like Belgium have become rather more difficult for political elites to manage; for a while in the 1970s there were a number of instances of significant 'peripheral nationalist' movements; and, perhaps, most importantly the decline of the working class has been accompanied by intense divisions within the middle class on both directly economic and non-economic issues. One line of division observed in a number of states has been that between those dependent for their livelihood on the state (in some form or another) and those dependent wholly on the private sector economy. But equally intense conflict has developed on non-economic issues – such as on nuclear defence, nuclear power and on moral (or lifestyle) issues such as abortion. For parties this means that political campaigning cannot be reduced to matters of personality or style – questions about objectives and policies arise giving parties the opportunity to present alternative programmes and goals before the electorate. It becomes possible for citizens to attempt to make choices, even though in some cases rather paradoxical results (in terms of the structure of preferences) may be generated. It will be more difficult, then, for parties to campaign, both in elections and indirectly between elections, on matters peripheral to social objectives.

But what of the emergence of new groups demanding more participatory structures? There are a number of points worth making about this. The first is that increasing education levels, combined with the breakdown of traditional moral codes, has been creating the potential for more participatory societies in the future. In a study conducted in the 1970s Inglehart compared the attitudes and activism of different age cohorts in nine western states. He concluded that 'feelings of efficacy and a general social activism are significantly higher among the young than the old in all nine nations'.[5] But as he noted, this might seem at odds with the well-known evidence that the young are among the least likely to vote, and that voting levels have either remained stable or declined. His solution to the apparent paradox lay in the role played by organizations in stimulating participation:

> This apparent paradox may be partially resolved when we recall that voting is the easiest and least discriminating form of political activism . . . it is an activity which established organizations are particularly well-equipped to stimulate. The young have relatively weak ties with political party machines, labor unions, and the church. Hence they are less readily mobilized via conventional organizational channels . . . But the young seem more likely than the old to engage in elite-challenging forms of political participation.[6]

There is, then, evidence that *potentially* future generations could be more participation-oriented than earlier generations.

Another point is that the growth of new organizational forms does put pressure on what Inglehart calls 'conventional organizational channels' to alter their practices. One of the best examples of this in relation to parties concerns one effect that the Greens have already had on the SPD in Germany. Faced with a party that had radically changed the representation of women in German political parties, the SPD responded by shifting its own commitment on the issue. In 1986, just six years after the formation of the Greens as a party, the SPD accepted that in future at least forty per cent of all parliamentary candidates must be women. Again, to reiterate a theme developed earlier, we should not expect all parties to respond to changing practices in parties and other organizations, but it is clear that some parties will have to respond.

This particular example alerts us to the need to move from talking generally about changing social attitudes towards hierarchy and participation to specific groups that might prompt such change. The women's movement is one example of how the mobilization of society can produce demands for participation in other organizations. Another group, partially cross-cutting this, of course, are those working in industries of the new technologies. Here we find the interaction of educational factors (many of the workers are highly educated) with that of organizational structure (many of these industries are less formally hierarchical than older manufacturing industries) combining to produce a culture in which involvement in decision-making is valued. Even if, as is likely, this does not produce economic democracy, we may expect that it will lead to demands for greater participation in other institutions in which such workers are involved. Then again, there are those dependent on the state for their livelihood who, in the 1980s, have discovered that dependence does not produce security, and who have demanded greater control both within their trade unions and over the decisions made by government that affect them. Finally, there are the professions and those occupations aspiring to professional status. For much of this century they have tended to be a conservatizing influence on demands for participation, as recognition *as* a profession and growing influence on government, have provided their members with acceptable material rewards. More recently, they have been threatened from a variety of sources. In the most direct form, this has stemmed from governmental action to break up monopolistic practices, but the expansion of state services, which brought in professionals to help supply them, has created an interest that is affected badly by the 'rolling back of the state'. The medical profession was antagonistic to the setting up of the National Health Service in Britain, just as the AMA opposed Medicare and Medicaid in the United States. But the very dependence of large numbers of doctors on these state programmes means that there is a ready source of opposition when there are proposals for their reduction. The important points about professionals are that individual control over decisions is highly valued in the practice of a profession, they are well educated and their demand for participatory structures in institutions through which they practice their profession, may extend to other organizations in which they are involved.

This list of social groups from which pressure for participatory organizational forms may emanate is not intended to be exhaustive. It is merely intended to illustrate how new socio-economic groups, and other groups that have become more active in recent decades, can become forces of change in organizations like parties. Obviously, given that their main focus of operation is likely to be organizations other than parties, the main effects will probably be indirect; but this does not mean that in the longer term they may not lead to significant changes in the way that some parties conduct their affairs.

THE DISMANTLING OF THE STATE

One of the main features of politics in the 1980s in Britain and the United States, and in a number of other western states as well, has been the attempt by conservative administrations to reduce the role of the state. This has taken two forms. There have been attempts to induce the belief among mass publics that the state cannot be as interventionist over a range of issue areas as was commonly believed in the immediate post-war years. There have also been efforts to remove the provision of some services from the state itself to 'third-party' agencies which the state may pay (at least in part) to do so. This has taken the form of 'privatization', in that private companies contract with the state to provide, for example, cleaning of state hospitals, and it has also been apparent in the state attempting to get some non-commercial organizations to take over part of the state's activities. In Britain this is evident, for example, in the government's reduction of funding for medical research, and its much greater reliance on charities to provide finance for this. If we were to assume that these efforts continue in the longer term, it might be argued that this will weaken parties in several ways. It will weaken public sector trade unions and hence those parties that have links to these unions; it will remove from public debate a range of issues that have long been at the centre of political conflict; and, most importantly, it will reduce the areas of social activity over which parties can have direct influence. The state which a party can penetrate will be that much smaller. Party competition will come to resemble much more the Schumpeterian ideal of conflict over the administrative competence of one elite 'team' (the one in government) rather than involving conflict over the *ends* of government.

Clearly, some critics of this argument might take issue with the claim that the efforts of the Reagan and Thatcher administrations, and more recently possibly of the Chirac government in France, will be effective in the longer term in dismantling the state. They might argue that this represents no more than a short-term departure from more general tendencies towards an expanded state role. Others might question whether privatizing service provision is primarily, though not exclusively, an Anglo-American phenomenon – one made possible by the weak tradition of the 'state' in the two countries. Where there is a more coherent idea of the state, it might be contended, 'hiving off' activities to other bodies poses greater problems of responsibility and encounters greater resistance. However, for our purposes, we may disregard these arguments for it can be argued that, in any case, the dismantling of the state does not necessarily weaken parties as agents of democracy. It could even strengthen them in this respect.

One point to which consideration must be given is that in both Britain and America the efforts at dismantling the state have gone hand in hand with strengthening state control over those activities which continue to be performed by governmental agencies. In Britain, this is reflected in the increased politicization of appointments to bodies like area health authorities or the BBC. In the United States there have been similar developments – the National Endowment for the Humanities, for example, is now dominated by appointees whose political views make them acceptable to the administration; in this case, many of them have close connections with the right-wing 'think tank', the Heritage Foundation. Nor, of course, are such developments incidental to the programme of dismantling the state. Among the ideas which lie behind this objective is that one of the causes of the expansion of the modern state is appointees and bureaucrats both tending to sympathize with the aims of those making demands on the state and also having a direct interest in extending their own spheres of influence. Only by having the 'right' people in place in these agencies can the programme of dismantling the state be effective. However, once this process is started, it is quite likely that incoming administrations with very different political views will want to continue it – but make sure that it is 'their people' who are in a position to advance their programmes. This politicization of a wide range of offices can only strengthen parties, because it is through parties, and organizations linked to parties, that the sorts of connections necessary for obtaining positions are most likely to be made.

Another issue concerns the response of parties which opposed the giving of contracts to private firms and the greater reliance on voluntary organizations in service provision. Suppose they find that a reversal to the *status-quo-ante* is impossible for technical reasons or electorally unpopular. What they are most likely to propose is some form of regulation and overview of these activities, to ensure both value for money and that these organizations are pursuing policies compatible with their own. But how is such oversight and regulation to be effected? If the conservative administrations have actually succeeded in changing popular attitudes to direct state control and provision, then other parties are more likely to turn to 'independent' or 'semi-independent' bodies to perform this function. And such bodies provide far more scope for parties to be indirectly involved in the placing of people on them than did a system which was centred more on government departments. In other words, the problems social democratic and other left-of-centre parties had in penetrating the state might actually be more easily overcome if state bureaucracies do not resume direct responsibility for some of these oversight functions.

A further consideration is that there is no reason to believe that, even if public expectations of what the state can and should do are reduced, this will lead to a less issue-oriented style of politics in which parties are merely elites seeking to obtain public office. Indeed, not only has party conflict in Britain and the United States in the 1980s been rather ideological in character, but there is no reason at all to believe that there is any connection between the *scope* of government activity and the nature of party conflict. States in which governments provide relatively few services can involve a high degree of conflict between parties over policy objectives. From the perspective of an industrialized state, where class conflict permeates many aspects of party competition, the issues that divided Democrats and Whigs in the 1830s and 1840s in the United States may seem rather obscure. But there were genuine disagreements between the parties over a range of issues at that time – conflicts that were more intense in many ways than those dividing Democrats and Republicans, say, in the 1950s. Consequently, the fashionable view in the 1950s and 1960s, that the 'end of ideology' was approaching, has not only been undermined by the experience of the last twenty years but also seems a poor guide as to how politics might develop should the policies of the conservative administrations be successful. Narrowing the scope of state activity may well have little effect in reducing divisions between parties or in producing greater competition over leadership styles rather than policy objectives.

CHANGES IN THE HUMAN ENVIRONMENT

How closely people live to each other and the sorts of housing units they live in has always affected how parties have operated. Close personal contact by party officials with voters, especially during election campaigns, has always been far easier in communities of terraced houses in cities than in low population density suburbs or, especially, in scattered farming communities along the side of a fjord. It might be argued that there are a number of changes in the locations in which people live that may make it more difficult for parties in the future to maintain the levels of contact with voters that they had in the past. There are two such developments which are relevant here: continuing suburbanization; and the growth of security measures in apartment buildings and in entire, specially planned, suburban communities, so that unannounced outsiders cannot gain entry. Both of these developments may well reduce inter-personal contact, and the organizational and participatory aspects of parties are among the activities likely to be affected. (In addition, 'neighbourhood watches' in all kinds of communities may serve to discourage political volunteers from canvassing for parties outside their own neighbourhoods.) To parody this argument, we might say that the citizen of the twenty-first century is more likely to be 'locked away' in a relatively self-contained home, and that in such an environment parties will rely far more on telecommunications and much less on personal contact in getting their messages to the citizen. How plausible is this scenario?

The simple answer to this, as with many of the aspects of parties we have examined, is that there is likely to be considerable variation because of relevant differences between countries. It must not be forgotten that, proportionately, the rural population continues to decline because of growing efficiency in agricultural production in western states. Rural populations have often been more difficult for parties to penetrate and rural elites have continued to exercise political influence. (In southern Italy, though, neither the DC nor the PCI found it difficult to mobilize agrarian voters.) While this will have only a slight impact in, say, Britain, in a state like France it will continue to affect party politics because of continuing mobility among the rural population and the decline of local social networks. It is no coincidence that the growth of party politics in the Fifth Republic has paralleled a decline in the number of people in France who derive their livelihood from the land. In several southern European states, such as Spain, it may be expected that the relative decline of the rural population will make political mobilization by parties easier.

The degree to which suburbanization is either possible, or will lead to lower population densities, depends very much on the amount of land into which urban populations can spread. This ranges from the Netherlands, where land is in such short supply that in purchasing an apartment buyers must prove to the state that their family units are of a sufficient size to warrant apartments of a particular size, to countries with no land shortage. Suburban sprawl, of the kind found in the United States, Canada or Australia, is not possible in Britain, let alone in the Netherlands.

Again, even within those countries where there has been rapid suburbanization since the 1940s, it is not correct to portray all suburbs as places where there is little contact between neighbours, virtually no community life and no sense of community identity. This was a popular image of the American suburbs in the late 1950s, but it is not true of all kinds of suburban developments. For example, the rapidly expanding retirement communities to be found in New Jersey, Florida and Arizona, among other places, have a highly developed (perhaps an overly developed) ethos of community and participation. Getting people together in support of a political cause in these sorts of places is likely to prove far less difficult than in the 'boxes made of ticky-tacky' that Peter Seeger satirized in his famous song about suburban life in the early 1960s. Just as political scientists discovered that American suburbs did not become uniformly conservative or Republican, so we may well find in the future that there is considerable variation, both between and within countries, in the ability of parties to organize successfully in suburbs.

Furthermore, increased use of security devices to prevent entry to apartments or suburban developments will decrease the ability of parties to mobilize activists and voters in the short term, but in the longer term it is less clear that it will have this effect. Much depends on how seriously parties take the 'spirals of silence' argument much discussed in connection with German politics. For the Christian Democrats in West Germany in the early 1970s the problem of the 'spirals of silence' required the party to build up its local organizations in communities where Social Democrats could 'win the debate' by default, because there were no organized CDU supporters to challenge the SPD position. This was precisely the strategy they adopted and seemingly it was successful.[7] If parties accept the argument that no amount of communication through television can break dominating views or opinions within communities, then organizing potential sympathizers to undermine this hegemony is imperative. Their priority must then be to make contact with residents within these 'secure units' and get them to organize a party branch. Relying on organization based outside these communities will be largely ineffective. If, however, they believe that they can do little to change opinions through mobilizing activists, then these communities are likely to remain under-organized.

It is not surprising, then, that it becomes difficult to make generalizations as to how parties will be affected by likely changes in the human environment. It is unlikely, though, that there will be one model that is appropriate to most liberal democracies; as elsewhere, diversity among parties will probably persist.

STATE INTERVENTION IN PARTY AFFAIRS

We saw earlier in this book that state funding of parties, which did not exist before the late 1950s, was subsequently adopted in several liberal democracies. It might be thought that the further extension of this would have two adverse results for parties in the future. To the extent that state funding provides a disincentive for parties to acquire a large dues-paying membership, it might weaken parties as arenas of democracy; again, if states become large sources of funds, it might eventually produce demands for regulation of certain aspects of party activities. That is, as in the United States earlier this century, the state might restrict the ability of parties to act as cohesive units. The first of these arguments has some merit, but, as we shall see, the second does not.

The central point about state funding of parties is that the effects it has on the recipients very much depends on the form that funding takes. When income from the state is tied to the number of dues-paying members a party has, or to its having already raised a certain amount of money from small contributors, there is no reason to believe that it will weaken the incentive for parties to recruit members. To the contrary, members are more necessary than ever – either because their presence in the party brings money directly from the state, or because they are an important resource in raising money in the form of small contributions. Of course, traditionally social democratic parties have been among the parties with the largest memberships and we might expect that they would be among the most enthusiastic supporters of 'linked' state aid in the future. However, there are several reasons for believing that not all of these parties will respond in this way. One consideration is that parties, like the British Labour party, which have an indirect structure with an affiliated trade union movement that contributes a large share of party income, will be under pressure not to support 'linked' funding. It poses a threat to the influence of the unions within the party and few party leaders would wish to provoke a rift in the party on this issue. Then again, in many countries funding tied in some way to membership levels might be difficult to police, and it is far from obvious that socialist parties would be at an advantage in recruiting 'phantom' members. The comparative advantage in membership size that socialist parties once enjoyed is no longer so evident and other parties may have better resources with which to sign up such members. Moreover, if, as in the United States, state aid was tied to gifts made to parties, and not to the number of members or to revenue raised from sales of party newspapers and so on, it is also uncertain that all socialist parties would have an advantage over their rivals. In Ireland, for example, we might expect that the networks through which Fianna Fail operates would place it in a much better position for this form of fund-raising than the Irish Labour party. In view of these uncertainties about the consequences of 'linked' state aid, it is far from clear that there will be any pressure for the adoption of a form of funding that is least harmful to parties as arenas of democracy.

When state funding is not linked to membership or membership activity, then it certainly can weaken the parties internally. They have less need for dues-paying members because the money they generate is less important for the parties. In turn this provides less incentive for party leaders to pay as much attention as they would to the preferences of members. For the 'exercising of control' element of democracy this has two adverse results. One is that it reduces the constraints on parties to compete with each other in terms of objectives and policies, rather than over the personalities of leaders or party 'images'. It also weakens parties as bodies in which people can participate and can exercise control over certain aspects of public life. In Norway and West Germany, for example, there is some evidence that non-linked state funding is having this effect on parties. We have seen that the West German Greens, heavily dependent on state funding, have the lowest membership density of any party in the country, and in Norway state aid seems to have weakened local parties. This point has been emphasized by Urwin who argues that:

> [An] indication of centralization and the erosion of the local base can perhaps be deduced from the scattered information on party expenditure, which suggests that the bulk of party income is consumed by administrative costs and salaries: only a small proportion is spent upon fostering broad activities such as conferences and campaigning.[8]

Given that there is likely to be pressure for greater state aid in the future, this result of public subsidies does pose problems for the extension of democracy.

There is, however, no reason to believe that any expansion of state funding will lead to state regulation of parties, thereby opening the way for the dismantling of parties in a fashion similar to that seen eighty years ago in the United States. As we noted earlier, this was the result of a peculiar historical experience and there is no justification for concluding that it will have any counterpart elsewhere. In the United States itself, though, the period since the early 1920s has witnessed the gradual erosion of the remaining pockets of state party strength. Virtually all the states that continued to use party conventions for nominating candidates for some offices have now abandoned the practice, including New York and Connecticut. Indeed, the most recent significant change in nominating practice at the state level, in Louisiana, has brought about a further weakening of party. Going beyond the practice of the 'free love' primaries, in which voters could vote in the primary of a different party for different offices, the contemporary Louisiana practice has virtually obliterated parties as devices in the nomination process. Candidates in Louisiana now run in a single primary and there is a subsequent 'run-off' (at the general election) between the two leading candidates should no candidate secure more than fifty per cent of the total vote in the primary. Thus, it is quite possible that 'the general election' could consist of a contest between two candidates with the same party affiliation. While it breaks with previous practices in the United States, this does not so much represent a change of direction in party politics in that country, but rather the further 'working through' of the reforms of three generations ago.

FURTHER ADVANCES IN CAMPAIGN TECHNOLOGY

In our earlier discussion, in chapter 5, we argued that the new campaign technologies of the last twenty to thirty years have posed a threat to participation in parties. Because of television, campaigns may become more centralized and computer analysis of voting patterns in electoral districts may make more routine the tasks left for campaign activists. In addition, television tends to focus campaigning more on personalities and 'images', thereby distorting the notion of electoral choice. However, we have emphasized that several other factors have influenced the precise impact the new technologies have had in particular countries, and the American experience remains atypical. But what of possible future changes in these technologies?

One argument might be that the continuing revolution in information technology will lead to depoliticization and to the marginalization of parties. On this view, devices like cable television, 'dishes' for receiving television broadcasts transmitted by satellite, and so on, will make it more difficult for national political leaders to communicate with citizens. The latter will have more opportunities than they do now for listening to foreign broadcasts and to stations providing programmes only for entertainment. Again, when every home has several computers, and television–telephone links, there will be precious little left for party activists to do. Door-to-door canvassing and 'taking soundings' in the district will no longer be necessary – parties could virtually do without their activists, especially if these developments are accompanied by extensive, 'non-linked', state funding. Yet, there are at least two reasons for believing that the dominance of party elites will not be as complete as this.

If people really do become as removed from face-to-face political activity as this view posits, then the argument about 'spirals of silence' becomes a serious one. Being able to make contact with citizens, through telecommunications, may well be inadequate in communities where one political view predominates. Indeed, if, as some have speculated, computers will make it possible for far more work to be done at home, then 'breaking into' communities from which a party finds itself 'excluded' becomes vital in the quest for votes.

There is also an argument about British parties that Bulpitt developed several years ago which is relevant here. He argued that activities like fund-raising, and the standard chores associated with election campaigning, got in the way of politics. The British party elites were able to avoid much discussion about objectives and policies because so much of the time and energy of members was channelled into these mundane tasks.[9] Now, it is certainly arguable that this point was far more pertinent with respect to the Conservative than to the Labour party, even in the mid-1970s, but for our purpose the interesting aspect of the argument is that it throws a rather different light on what might happen to parties if a party workforce was no longer required to perform routine tasks. Rather than caucus–cadre parties re-emerging, we might instead see parties facing more internal debate and conflict. Those interested in policy would no longer be sidetracked by having to organize the next fund-raising event. From this perspective, while some party elites might find themselves more free from the constraints of party members, in other parties demands by members for participation in the formation of party policy could well increase. This tendency would be reinforced by a development we discussed earlier – the rise of social groups wanting more participatory structures in the institutions with which they are involved.

What this suggests is that the transformation in information technology could well accentuate the differences between parties in liberal democracies. There would be no single dominant model – but more likely major parties could vary from caucus–cadre parties of self-perpetuating elites centred on parliaments, to highly participatory, membership-oriented structures. Unlike contemporary South Africa, where the caucus–cadre structure of the Progressive Federal Party both reflects its lack of resources and contributes to its inability to challenge the Nationalists, there may well be a number of parties in the future that are able to survive with very little organization or membership participation.[10] These could exist alongside parties which are far more participatory and which give greater control to members than most parties do today.

INTEREST GROUPS AS ALTERNATIVES TO PARTIES

Yet another threat to parties has been said to come from corporatist tendencies in a number of liberal democracies. Neo-(or liberal) corporatism has been described as:

a process of interest intermediation which involves the negotiation of policy between state agencies and interest organizations arising from the division of labour in society, where the policy agreements are implemented through the collaboration of the interest organizations and their willingness and ability to secure the compliance of their members.[11]

Corporatism *could* be a future threat to parties if demands from below came to be channelled exclusively through these interest organizations, so that parties were no longer articulators of interests and were peripheralized in the political system. There might be two aspects to peripheralization: parties would have less input to the process of policy negotiation, because the state agencies concerned developed their own *modus operandi*; and parties would exist primarily, therefore, to elect representatives to parliaments. Unlike most pluralist models of the state, the links parties have with both the state and with citizens might be weakened under such arrangements.

Corporatist tendencies have been identified in several European countries, and most especially in Austria and the Scandinavian countries, and weaker tendencies have been detected in several other regimes including West Germany and Belgium. While in the early years of the debate about corporatism a number of extravagant claims were made about the generalizability of the evidence from these countries, more recently those who advocate a 'corporatist approach' in political science are more modest in their claims. Corporatism is now viewed less as an alternative to capitalism or socialism, and is seen much more as the result of a specific historic experience in certain countries. (A charge, incidentally, that has led one critic to argue that corporatist theorists 'move the goalposts back after their opponents score three goals'.) Yet, when we examine the evidence in the most obviously corporatist regimes, the effects on the parties are rather complex.

Of Norway Urwin reports that organizations in the corporatist network had achieved extensive penetration of the political system by the mid-1970s and that the memberships embraced more than seventy per cent of adults. The effect of this on the parties was to make citizens regard interest organizations as the best vehicle for protecting their interests:

What was most worrying, perhaps, was a facet revealed in a 1969 survey, where 46% said that professional organizations were the best guardians of their interests: while 27% regarded politicians as the most effective defenders of their interests, only 11% saw the parties in this light.[12]

However, the proliferation of interest organizations and their entrenchment throughout the political system has not led to the atrophy of Norwegian parties. To the contrary the major parties have accommodated themselves to the new situation and many leaders 'have at least a foot in the corporatist camp'. This kind of amalgamation with the groups is both electorally popular and makes the policy process easier. But most especially Urwin argues that the parties remain responsible for political decisions so they still dominate the political system. In other words, in this case corporatism may have changed the parties but it has not undermined them.

Similarly, in Sweden non-socialist critics of corporatism have focused on the weakening influence of *opposition* parties in national decision-making during the years of Social Democratic dominance, rather on the weakening of the party influence *per se*. During the four decades of Social Democratic governments, corporatist tendencies did not weaken that party's influence in decision-making, although left-wing critics of corporatism did argue that it helped accentuate the weakness of the party and the working class in relation to organizations promoting capitalist interests.[13]

Again, in the case of Austria, the state which is often regarded as the prime exemplar of corporatist tendencies, there is no evidence that corporatism displaces parties. Here every kind of economic interest is statutorily organized into a nationwide 'chamber', so that everyone is tied into the chamber system and, in many cases, through membership of several different chambers. However, rather than chambers being outside the sphere of influence of parties, there is an extra-ordinary inter-penetration of parties and organized interests. This has been well summarized by Marin:

> Political parties are incorporated into interest associations, associations into political parties. Parties are (more or less) composed of associational segments . . . and leading positions are filled according to their strength in respective constituencies; associations are differentiated by political factions and their leadership is constituted according to their electoral strength within the chambers or [the trade union confederation] . . . In this way compulsory or unitary associations internalize political competition, parties internalize corporatist interest intermediation . . .[14]

Nor are parties neutralized in their relations with interest organizations. As Katzenstein notes, the parties are assertive in these arrangements, and this has led to a passive bureaucracy and 'the partisan neutralization of state power'.[15] Because the parties have differing views about the public sector of the economy, state power remains weak; moreover these differences are reflected in the ideological content of much debate between the parties. What emerges, therefore, is not a picture of parties being replaced by other bodies but rather of their mutual colonization and of parties continuing to have an impact on the state.

While in pluralist states parties and interest groups are both articulators of interests, under corporatism this function is performed mainly by the groups. But, this does not lead so much to the replacement of parties by other actors in the political system but to a new set of arrangements in which parties can remain a powerful influence in the policy process. But corporatism does pose two *potential* threats to parties as agents of democracy. As in Norway, people may come to regard interest associations as far more important than parties in defending their interests, and this may help to depress participation in parties. But it also threatens the ability of parties to control the state – a party committed to radical policy change in certain areas may find that established, direct relationships between state and interest groups are difficult to modify. Once again, we may suspect that the extension of liberal corporatism may produce varying results in terms of its effect on parties – there is unlikely to be a single dominant model.

THE RISE OF SINGLE-ISSUE GROUPS

Yet another area in which initially it might be claimed that the activities of parties are being taken over by alternative organizations is in connection with the promotion of single issues. Of course, 'cause' groups are not a new phenomenon – indeed, in the debates about the extension of the franchise in mid-nine-teenth-century Britain, the principal fears expressed about mass democracy did not concern parties but extra-parliamentary groups. In the period after 1832 the elite parliamentary parties had tended to disintegrate while external organizations, like the Chartists and the Anti-Corn Law League, had been at the centre of politics in the 1840s. Similarly, in the United States organizations like the Anti-Saloon League were a significant force in late nineteenth century politics. Nevertheless, it has been argued that there has been a significant proliferation in single-issue politics since about the 1950s, and some have argued that there has been a displacement of parties in the development of political issues. What, then, is the evidence for this?

We must first be careful not to place too much emphasis on the experience of the United States. The rise of single-issue groups there took place against a background of rapidly weakening party organizations in a system where parties were already weak. In part, there was a vacuum in the institutional framework which these groups filled. However, in America, as in other advanced industrial states, there are more general developments influencing the proliferation of single-issue groups. One factor is that the patterns of political cleavage found in industrial society have been modified as new social groups have emerged in the growth of what is sometimes, and misleadingly, termed post-industrial societies. As we have seen, this has given rise to concerns and issues which fall outside the traditional lines of division between the types of parties characteristic of industrial society. Environmental issues are an obvious example, as are moral issues, such as abortion and divorce. For the parties the 'handling' of such issues raises fears about the possible erosion of electoral support and often they have been prepared to let single-issue groups develop the issue until it becomes clear how their own party interests will be affected by particular stances. Again, the revolution in mass communications has enabled relatively small groups to gain nation-wide attention from activities which are deemed especially newsworthy for public affairs programmes on television. Not only do these constitute resources not previously available, but the very uncertainty of public response to direct-action tactics once again inclines parties to let groups take the lead in this. Moreover, to the extent that they are hierarchical, and to the extent that the more senior members will be the ones most inclined to resist change in the political agenda, junior members may find it difficult for the party to respond and hence they will 'exit' to group activity. In some cases, as seems most common in Norway, for example, this will involve them remaining in the party at the same time as they are active in groups. But this necessarily reduces the time and resources they can devote to the party. In other cases they abandon the party. In Germany dissatisfied SPD members, who in the 1970s discovered that having captured parts of the party bureaucracy they still had little influence over the Schmidt government, left the party and were instrumental in the founding of the Greens, which initially was not a party. What is interesting about this example, is that the organization has some of the characteristics of a 'cause' group, while at the same time after 1980 it became a party which ran candidates in elections.

A further factor affecting 'cause groups' has been the declining role of parties as social organizations. One of the reasons for the success of mass political parties was that often they could offer the best recreational facilities available. At the end of the nineteenth century parties were as much social as political institutions. Since then, and especially since the Second World War, there have been changes in the opportunities for socializing as well as changing social values which have extended the range of 'acceptable' activities. Parties have been among the major losers. Consequently, the unique blend of social and political activities parties could offer has disappeared. The person who is politically active because of a concern for issues has less need for the social aspects of a party, and any choice between participation in a group and through a party can be made on the basis of a judgement about their relative effectiveness.

Yet while these changes can be said, in a sense, to weaken parties, it would be inaccurate to suggest that issue groups are displacing, or will displace, parties. One of the main problems such groups face is keeping an issue 'alive' in a period when public attention is directed to other issues. It was precisely this which led to the Campaign for Nuclear Disarmament in Britain becoming such a small and peripheral body in the period 1964–79. Parties, on the other hand, survive as organizations because of the need to fight periodic elections. They can help to keep an issue in public view, even when it has little support, through debate and public campaigning. Consequently, it can be argued that single-issue groups need parties – at least they do when the issue is one that cannot be simply resolved by legislation or executive action. The problem, then, for single-issue groups is how close a relationship with parties they should maintain – which can range from the informal links between, say, CND and the Labour party to the more symbiotic relationships found in a movement like the West German Greens. For the parties the problem is precisely the same. Too close an identification with particular groups may cost the party votes, while the groups' 'political workforce' may be a valuable electoral asset. None of these arrangements, though, involve developments which are likely to dissolve parties as promoters of political issues.

However, if single-issue groups are unlikely to replace parties, might they still not be weakening them? Such groups do reduce the time (and perhaps other resources) that party members (and potential party members) can devote to party activity. Of course, if it is the case that much electoral organization will require less labour in the future, then this may have little effect on party membership or on the ability of parties to perform their campaign tasks. The greater difficulty might be that parties are reduced to an *irregular* channel for developing and promoting issues, rather than being used as complementary channels alongside single-issue groups. Not only would this reduce the role of parties as participatory devices but it may well increase the opportunities for party elites to resist efforts to increase membership control. Indeed, it is far from fanciful to imagine party leaders encouraging the formation of groups as a means of preserving their own control; shunting activists off into other organizations would be the equivalent of the strategy identified by Bulpitt: 'Those peculiar people who joined the party to discuss politics could be shunted off to party auxiliary organizations or socialized into accepting the prevailing culture of *apolitisme*.'[16]

The most difficult issue to assess in relation to single-issue groups is whether the comparative advantage in operating through this organizational form will continue to work in their favour. Television, in particular, has provided opportunities for them to gain widespread attention for their causes – much greater opportunities than that available through the print medium alone. But there is a potential problem of 'crowding' – of too many causes competing for attention, time and money – and this is something that can be exploited by parties. The old, familiar argument that parties perform a useful function in aggregating interests and preferences, thus, returns. It should be noted too that crowding can be a real and not just a hypothetical problem – a point which becomes evident if we consider the parallel case of charitable organizations.

In many American cities in the early part of this century competition in fund-raising events between different charities became so intense, because there were so many charities, that two difficulties became evident. One was that, accosted on the street every day for some cause or another, many people might develop a resistance to giving that would harm all charities. But the uncertainty of not knowing against whom they might have to compete on any given day made financial planning precarious for many local charities. The solution was consolidation, and the result was the idea of the Community Chest (subsequently immortalized on 'Monopoly' boards all over the world); fund-raising would be centralized with one annual fund-raising drive and the proceeds would be distributed on an agreed basis between the participating charities. Later the various Community Chests became affiliates of the organization now known as the United Way. It is precisely this kind of co-ordinating role – one which does not result in the constituent organizations losing their separate identity – for which most parties are well-placed in relation to single-issue groups.

CONCLUDING REMARKS

Having outlined some of the more important factors likely to affect parties as agents of democracy in the future, we must now assess the overall prospects for parties in furthering democratization. Unlike the conventional wisdom of the period up to the late 1960s, which tended to overemphasize the possible achievements of parties, and unlike the dominant views of the succeeding period which tended to underestimate them, we must admit that the issue is a complex one. There are reasons for believing that some parties could come to play a much greater role in extending citizen control and, possibly, in creating a more publicly oriented citizenry than have parties hitherto. Yet there are also factors working in the opposite direction, marginalizing parties in a number of respects and making it more difficult for them to advance any of the elements of democracy. It might be tempting, but it would be wrong, to suggest that the consequence will be a cancelling out of the different forces involved, so that the next one hundred years of party politics will much resemble the first one hundred or so years. It would be wrong for the obvious reason that the two sets of factors are likely to have differential effects on the various liberal democratic regimes and on the various parties within particular states. What we are most likely to see is continuing heterogeneity in party development, with programmatic, participatory and internally democratic parties, like the West German Greens, co-existing with non-participatory parties based mainly on legislative elites. Unlike the views put forward by Duverger in the 1950s and Epstein in the 1960s, we might expect that there will be no tendency for one kind of party structure to predominate.

But what does this conclusion suggest more generally for the advancement of democracy? It is, surely, that democrats are foolish to ignore the roles parties might play in democratization; but they are equally short-sighted if they believe that much greater democracy could be attained by parties alone. Even in societies like Austria, where party penetration is extensive, there are many aspects of people's lives over which there is no possibility of exercising control through parties, simply because parties are not active in these arenas. Nor would democracy necessarily be advanced by having social life entirely organized around parties. For example, extensive party involvement in industrial democracy might well make it more difficult for consultation procedures to work smoothly and might well result in shop-floor participation giving way to delegation to party representatives. Parties are most likely to be effective as democratizing agents when there are other arenas to which democratic procedures are also being extended but in which parties are not involved directly. Ultimately, then, we must be sure to place the relative failure of parties in the twentieth century in the context of the failure of democracy in other arenas. Parties developed in the nineteenth century in a social universe of hierarchical structures which have remained largely intact since then. If parties have not contributed much, say, to the development of a more publicly oriented electorate, it is largely because there have been few other structures contributing to this. While parties may be necessary for democratization they are not a sufficient condition for its realization. In the twenty-first century, then, the real problem facing democrats is to provide integrated proposals for reform that will allow a wide range of institutions to promote the different elements of that complex political ideal – democracy.

NOTES

1 PARTIES AND DEMOCRATIC THEORY

1 M. Ostrogorski, *Democracy and the Organization of Political Parties* (Quadrangle Books, Chicago, 1964), first published 1902; Robert Michels, *Political Parties* (Free Press, New York, 1962), first published in English 1915.
2 Joseph Schumpeter, *Capitalism, Socialism and Democracy* (George Allen and Unwin, London, 1943).
3 E. E. Schattschneider, *Party Government* (Holt, Rinehart and Winston, New York, 1942).
4 Robert A. Dahl and Charles E. Lindblom, *Politics, Economics and Welfare* (Harper and Brothers, New York, 1953).
5 See especially Robert A. Dahl, *A Preface to Democratic Theory* (University of Chicago Press, Chicago, 1956), and *Who Governs?* (Yale University Press, New Haven and London, 1961).
6 A. H. Birch, *Representative and Responsible Government* (George Allen and Unwin, London, 1964).
7 David Easton, *The Political System* (Alfred E. Knopf, New York, 1953); on the sociology of Talcott Parsons, see especially Talcott Parsons, *The Social System* (Free Press, Glencoe, Ill., 1951).
8 Robert A. Dahl, 'The Behavioral Approach in Political Science: Epitaph for a Monument to a Successful Protest', *American Political Science Review*, 55 (1961), pp. 763–72.
9 In Britain the sceptical and less positivist tradition in political science restricted the impact of behaviouralism, while the insularity of political science in France similarly protected it.
10 Kenneth J. Arrow, *Social Choice and Individual Values* (John Wiley, New York, 1951).
11 Iain McLean, 'Some Recent Work in Public Choice', *British Journal of Political Science*, 16 (1986), p. 378.
12 William H. Riker, *Liberalism Against Populism* (W. H. Freeman, San Francisco, 1982).

13 Klaus von Beyme, *Political Parties in Western Democracies* (Gower, Aldershot, 1985).

14 Maurice Duverger, *Political Parties*, 2nd English edn (Methuen, London, 1959).

15 Carole Pateman, *Participation and Democratic Theory* (Cambridge University Press, Cambridge, 1970).

16 For a denial of the relevance of the state as an 'arena' of democracy, see John Burnheim, *Is Democracy Possible?* (Polity Press, Cambridge, 1985), chap. 1.

17 Dennis F. Thompson, *The Democratic Citizen* (Cambridge University Press, Cambridge, 1970), p. 41.

18 An example was Marian Irish and James Prothro, *The Politics of American Democracy*, 5th edn (Prentice-Hall, Englewood Cliffs, NJ, 1971).

19 John Rawls, *A Theory of Justice* (Oxford University Press, Oxford, 1972).

20 Brian Barry, 'Is Democracy Special?', in Peter Laslett and James Fishkin (eds), *Philosophy, Politics and Society*, 5th series (Basil Blackwell, Oxford, 1979), pp. 156–7.

21 Riker, *Liberalism Against Populism*.

22 An example of a voting cycle would be the following: A's preferences (in descending order of preference) are x, y, z; B's preferences are y, z, x; C's preferences are z, x, y. A majority of voters (A, C) prefer x to y, but another majority (B, C) prefer z to x, while yet another majority (A, B) prefer y to z.

23 A preference is sincere when, irrespective of any decision-making mechanism, a person actually prefers, say, x to y. A preference is strategic when the person votes (or otherwise expresses a preference) for y instead of x, even though he or she sincerely prefers x to y, because voting in this way will make it more likely that either he or she will eventually get x or that he or she will be able to stop another alternative, say z, which he or she really does not want to have enacted.

24 For Sartori's ideas, see especially Giovanni Sartori, *Democratic Theory* (Wayne State University Press, Detroit, 1962) and *Parties and Party Systems* (Cambridge University Press, Cambridge, 1976).

25 This argument is developed most explicitly in Robert A. Dahl, *Modern Political Analysis* (Prentice-Hall, Englewood Cliffs, NJ, 1963), p. 8.

26 For Macpherson's ideas on democracy see especially C. B. Macpherson, *The Real World of Democracy* (Clarendon Press, Oxford, 1966) and *Democratic Theory: Essays in Retrieval* (Clarendon Press, Oxford, 1973).

27 Kenneth Janda, *Political Parties: A Cross-National Survey* (Free Press, New York, 1980), p. 5. Italics in original.

28 Von Beyme, *Political Parties in Western Democracies*, p. 11.

29 Ibid., p. 12.

30 Alastair MacIntyre, 'Is a Science of Comparative Politics Possible?', in Peter Laslett, W. G. Runciman and Quentin Skinner, *Philosophy, Politics and Society*, 4th Series (Basil Blackwell, Oxford, 1972), p. 14.

31 Some of the similarities between South African parties and those in liberal democracies are discussed in Richard Hodder-Williams, 'South Africa: Democratic Centralism versus Elite-based Parties', in Alan Ware (ed.), *Political Parties: Electoral Change and Structural Response* (Basil Blackwell, Oxford, 1987). The relevance of states where democratic control extended to only some groups in understanding democratization was recognized by Dahl. He used the term 'dual polyarchy' to describe these regimes, but he did not develop the point that the real value of these regimes was that they provide further evidence about the organization of democracy among those 'included' in the regime. They are certainly *not* nascent liberal democracies. Robert A. Dahl, *Polyarchy: Participation and Opposition* (Yale University Press, New Haven and London, 1971).

32 Nils Sternquist, 'Sweden: Stability or Deadlock?', in Robert A. Dahl (ed.), *Political Oppositions in Western Democracies* (Yale University Press, New Haven and London, 1966). pp. 119–20.

33 On the emergence of a party-oriented electorate in England, see Gary W. Cox, 'The Development of a Party-Orientated Electorate in England, 1832–1918', *British Journal of Political Science*, 16 (1986), pp. 187–216.

34 Ostrogorski, *Democracy and the Organization of Political Parties*.

35 It should be noted, though, that while Germany is often regarded as a regime which has always had well-resourced parties, this was not true of all parties until the regime established in 1949. Indeed, with the exception of the Catholics, the Social Democrats, and the Communists, the parties in the Weimar republic had access to very few resources, and this contributed to the regime's instability.

36 For Dahl, see notes 4, 5 and 25 above. For Truman, see David B. Truman, *The Governmental Process* (Alfred E. Knopf, New York, 1951).

37 Albert Weale, 'Social Choice Versus Populism? An Interpretation of Riker's Political Theory', *British Journal of Political Science*, 14 (1984), p. 373.

38 The electoral law which, perhaps, came closest to providing a guarantee of a majority party in a legislature was one introduced in Romania in 1926. This gave a party which won over 40 per cent of the popular vote a premium of half the parliamentary seats plus a proportion of the remaining seats corresponding to its percentage of the electoral vote.

39 Samuel Brittan, 'The Economic Contradictions of Democracy', *British Journal of Political Science*, 5 (1975), pp. 129–59.

2 DEMOCRACY IN A ONE-PARTY SYSTEM

1 See, for example, Peter Singer, *Democracy and Disobedience* (Clarendon Press, Oxford, 1973).
2 The classic study of 'exit' and 'voice' as mechanisms is Albert O. Hirschman, *Exit, Voice and Loyalty* (Harvard University Press, Cambridge, Mass., 1970).
3 David Hine, 'Italy: Parties and Party Government under Pressure', in Alan Ware (ed.), *Political Parties: Electoral Change and Structural Response* (Basil Blackwell, Oxford, 1987), p. 88.
4 C. B. Macpherson, *The Real World of Democracy* (Clarendon Press, Oxford, 1966).
5 Ibid., pp. 20–1.
6 Paul Nursey-Bray, 'Consensus and Community: The Theory of African One-party Democracy', in Graeme Duncan (ed.), *Democratic Theory and Practice* (Cambridge University Press, Cambridge, 1983), pp. 96–7.
7 Nursey-Bray, 'Consensus and Community', p. 106.
8 Sartori, *Parties and Party Systems*, pp. 50–1.
9 Nursey-Bray, 'Consensus and Community', p. 107.
10 Jack Lively, *Democracy* (Basil Blackwell, Oxford, 1975).
11 Ibid., p. 45.
12 Sartori, *Parties and Party Systems*, pp. 70–3.
13 Ibid., p. 72.
14 Alan Ware, *The Logic of Party Democracy* (Macmillan, London, 1979).
15 Lively, *Democracy*, p. 45, n. 20.
16 The requirement that party officials not be formally involved in intra-party elections, because it provides a bias in favour of incumbents, has been enacted in the laws of a number of states in the US. There party organizations are prohibited from formally endorsing particular candidates in primary elections. In the era of one-party dominance at the state level earlier this century, this was one of a number of constraints to prevent primary elections being manipulated entirely by party elites.
17 Andrew J. Nathan, *Chinese Democracy* (Alfred E. Knopf, New York, 1985), p. 229.
18 Nursey-Bray, 'Consensus and Community', p. 107.
19 Ibid., pp. 106–7.
20 On Yugoslavia see April Carter, *Democratic Reform in Yugoslavia* (Pinter, London, 1982); M. G. Zaninovich, 'Yugoslav Party Evolution: Moving Beyond Institutionalization' in Samuel P. Huntington and Clement H. Moore, *Authoritarian Politics in Modern Societies* (Basic Books, New York, 1970), and Peter Ferdinand, *Communist Regimes in Comparative Perspective: The Soviet, Chinese and Yugoslav Models* (Wheatsheaf, Brighton, forthcoming).

21 Jerzy Wiatr, 'The Hegemonic Party System in Poland', in Erik Allardt and Stein Rokkan (eds), *Mass Politics: Studies in Political Sociology* (Free Press, New York, 1970).
22 Ferdinand, *Communist Regimes*.
23 See ibid. for a discussion of the data contained in *Klasno-socijalna struktura saveza komunista jugoslavije* (Komunist, Belgrade, 1984).
24 See Carter, *Democratic Reform in Yugoslavia*, pp. 121–2; and D. Rusinow, *The Yugoslav Experiment* (Hurst, London, 1977), p. 201.
25 P. Morača *Istorija saveza komunista jugoslavije* (Rad, Belgrade, 1976). I am grateful to Peter Ferdinand for drawing my attention to this work and for translating the relevant passages.

3 THE IMPACT OF PARTY COMPETITION

1 *New York Times*, 25 November 1986.
2 H. R. Edwards, *Competition and Monopoly in the British Soap Industry* (Clarendon Press, Oxford, 1962).
3 Giovanni Sartori, *Parties and Party Systems* (Cambridge University Press, Cambridge, 1976), pp. 217–21.
4 Ibid., p. 219.
5 Ibid., p. 219.
6 Ibid., p. 220.
7 Ibid., p. 220.
8 James Mill, 'Essay on Government', in Jack Lively and John Rees (eds), *Utilitarian Logic and Politics* (Clarendon Press, Oxford, 1978), p. 73.
9 A. H. Birch, *Representation* (Macmillan, London, 1972), p. 98.
10 Dennis C. Mueller, *Public Choice* (Cambridge, Cambridge University Press, 1979), p. 1.
11 M. Ostrogorski, *Democracy and the Organization of Political Parties* (Quadrangle Books, Chicago, 1978), p. 293.
12 Committee on Political Parties of the American Political Science Association, 'Towards a More Responsible Two-Party System', *American Political Science Review*, 44 (1950), supplement, pp. 22–3.
13 Joseph A. Schlesinger, *Ambition and Politics* (Rand-McNally, Chicago, 1966); Michael L. Mezey, 'Ambition Theory and the Office of Congressman', *Journal of Politics* 32 (1970), pp. 563–79; Kenneth Prewitt, 'Political Ambitions, Volunteerism, and Electoral Accountability', *American Political Science Review*, 64 (1970), pp. 5–17; Kenneth Prewitt and William Nowlin, 'Political Ambitions and the Behavior of Incumbent Politicians', *Western Political Quarterly*, 22 (1969), pp. 298–308.
14 Sartori, *Parties and Party Systems*, p. 40.
15 Charles R. Adrian, 'A Typology of Nonpartisan Elections', *Western Political Quarterly*, 12 (1959), 449–58.

16   Jeffrey L. Pressman, 'Preconditions of Mayoral Leadership', *American Political Science Review*, 66 (1972), pp. 511–24.

17   A. Clarke Hagensick, 'Influences of Partisanship and Incumbency on a Nonpartisan Election System', *Western Political Quarterly*, 17 (1964), pp. 117–24.

18   Chester B. Rogers and Harold D. Arman, 'Nonpartisanship and Election to City Office', *Social Science Quarterly*, 51 (1971), pp. 941–5.

19   Ibid.

20   Susan Welch and Eric H. Carlson, 'The Impact of Party on Voting in a Nonpartisan Legislature', *American Political Science Review*, 68 (1973), pp. 865–6.

21   William H. Riker, *The Theory of Political Coalitions* (Yale University Press, New Haven, 1962).

22   Giovanni Sartori, 'European Political Parties: The Case of Polarized Pluralism', in Joseph LaPalombara and Myron Weiner (eds), *Political Parties and Political Development* (Princeton University Press, Princeton, NJ, 1966) p. 151.

23   Iain McLean, 'A Non-zero Sum Game of Football', *British Journal of Political Science*, 10 (1980), pp. 253–9.

24   Alan Ware, *Logic of Party Democracy*, (Macmillan, London, 1979) chap. 3.

25   Among the most important essays on this subject are those contained in Seymour Martin Lipset and Stein Rokkan (eds), *Party Systems and Voter Alignments: Cross-national Perspectives* (Collier–Macmillan, New York, 1967).

26   Sartori, *Parties and Party Systems*, p. 313.

27   Samuel J. Eldersveld, *Political Parties: A Behavioral Analysis* (Rand McNally, Chicago, 1964); James Q. Wilson, *The Amateur Democrat* (University of Chicago Press, Chicago, 1962).

28   Lipset and Rokkan, *Party Systems and Voter Alignments*.

29   E. E. Schattschneider, *The Semisovereign People*, reissued edn (Dryden Press, Hinsdale, Ill., 1975), p. 73. Italics in original.

30   Peter Bachrach and Morton S. Baratz, 'Two Faces of Power', *American Political Science Review*, 56 (1962), pp. 947–52; Matthew A. Crenson, *The Un-Politics of Air Pollution* (Johns Hopkins University Press, Baltimore and London, 1971).

31   Walter Dean Burnham, *The Current Crisis in American Politics* (Oxford University Press, New York, 1982) and his *Critical Elections and the Mainsprings of American Politics* (W. W. Norton, New York, 1970).

32   Martin Shefter, 'Party and Patronage: Germany, England and Italy', *Politics and Society*, 7 (1977), pp. 403–51; 'Party, Bureaucracy, and Political Change in the United States', in Louis Maisel and Joseph Cooper (eds), *The Development of Political Parties* (Sage, Beverly Hills and London, 1979); 'Regional Receptivity to Reform: The Legacy of the Progressive Era', *Political Science Quarterly*, 98 (1983), pp. 459–83.

33 Theda Skocpol, 'Bringing the State Back In: Strategies of Analysis in Current Research', in Peter B. Evans, Dietrich Rueschemeyer and Theda Skocpol (eds), *Bringing the State Back In* (Cambridge University Press, Cambridge, 1985), pp. 24–5. In relation to British parties one of the leading exponents of an 'institutionalist' view is Jim Bulpitt; see especially his *Territory and Power in the United Kingdom* (Manchester University Press, Manchester, 1983), and 'The Discipline of the New Democracy: Mrs Thatcher's Domestic Statecraft', *Political Studies*, 34 (1986), pp. 19–39.

34 Ware, *The Logic of Party Democracy*.

35 The classic studies of this era were Angus Campbell et al., *The American Voter* (John Wiley, New York, 1960); and Angus Campbell et al. *Elections and the Political Order* (John Wiley, New York, 1960).

36 Richard Rose and Harve Mossawir, 'Voting and Elections: A Functional Analysis', *Political Studies*, 15 (1967), p. 186.

37 V. O. Key, *The Responsible Electorate* (Belknap Press, Cambridge, Mass., 1966).

38 This similarity between the act of voting and the act of purchasing has been developed in the so-called 'consumer model' of voting by Hilde T. Himmelweit, et al., *How Voters Decide* (Academic Press, London, 1981). In this study the authors apply their approach to Britain for the period 1959–74.

39 Norman H. Nie, Sidney Verba and John R. Petrocik, *The Changing American Voter* (Harvard University Press, Cambridge, Mass., 1976).

40 On the rise of the cult of the leader in Jamaica in the 1960s and 1970s, see J. Edward Greene, 'Jamaica: The Persistence of Party Democracy', in Ware (ed.), *Political Parties*.

41 On this campaign, see Mary Ellen Leary, *Phantom Politics* (Public Affairs Press, Washington, DC, 1977).

42 For the analysis of ambiguity in political campaigning, see Benjamin I. Page, *Choices and Echoes in Presidential Elections* (University of Chicago Press, Chicago, 1978).

43 Martin Pugh, *The Tories and the People 1880–1935* (Basil Blackwell, Oxford, 1985).

44 On the American experience, see especially Burnham, *The Current Crisis in American Politics*.

45 Doris A. Graber, *Mass Media and American Politics* (CQ Press, Washington, DC, 1980), p. 186.

46 Derek W. Urwin, 'Norway: Parties Between Mass Membership and Issue-Oriented Professionalism?', in Alan Ware (ed.), *Political Parties: Electoral Change and Structural Response* (Basil Blackwell, Oxford, 1987), p. 198.

47 Graber, *Mass Media and American Politics*, p. 185.

48 Samuel Brittan, 'The Economic Contradictions of Democracy', *British Journal of Political Science*, 5 (1975), p. 147.

4 PUBLIC AND PRIVATE DIMENSIONS OF PARTIES

1 Anthony Barker (ed.), *Quangos in Britain* (Macmillan, London, 1982), p. 220.
2 See, for example, Lester Salamon, 'Rethinking Public Management: Third Party Government and the Changing Forms of Public Action', *Public Policy*, 29 (1981), pp. 255–75; and Lester Salamon, *The Federal Budget and the Non-Profit Sector* (Urban Institute, Washington, DC, 1982).
3 *New York Times*, 29 July 1986.
4 Estelle James, 'How Non-profits grow: A Model', *Journal of Policy Analysis and Management*, 2 (1983), pp. 350–65.
5 David B. Truman, *The Governmental Process* (Alfred E. Knopf, New York, 1951).
6 Jeffrey Obler, 'Private Giving in the Welfare State', *British Journal of Political Science*, 11 (1981), pp. 17–48.
7 Derek W. Urwin, 'Norway: Parties Between Mass Membership and Consumer-Oriented Professionalism', in Alan Ware (ed.), *Political Parties: Electoral Change and Structural Response* (Basil Blackwell, Oxford, 1987), p. 184.
8 Austin Ranney, *Curing the Mischiefs of Faction* (University of California Press, Berkeley, 1975), p. 78.
9 Ibid., p. 81.
10 Alan Ware, *The Breakdown of Democratic Party Organization 1940–1980* (Clarendon Press, Oxford, 1985), pp. 115–16.
11 The autonomy left by the state to party organizations has been emphasized by Epstein: 'despite pages of statutory provision for party nomination and party structure, states commonly leave a large amount of party organizational work to be conducted under rules the parties themselves adopt. For example, a recent study of leadership of state party organization found that state election laws provided only 5 per cent of the controlling provisions with respect to powers of party chairpersons'. Leon D. Epstein, *Political Parties in the American Mold*, (University of Wisconsin Press, Madison, 1986), pp. 173–4.
12 As far as I am aware, I was the first person to suggest the parallels between political parties and public utilities in *The Logic of Party Democracy*, chap. 9. However, I sketched out only a few aspects of the argument and, quite independently, a far more complete analysis was developed subsequently by Epstein in relation to American parties. See Epstein, *Political Parties in the American Mold*, chap. 6.
13 David Paul Crook, *American Democracy in English Politics, 1815–1850* (Clarendon Press, Oxford, 1965), pp. 133–4.
14 Ranney, *Curing the Mischiefs of Faction*, p. 93.
15 *New York Times*, 11 December 1986.
16 Epstein, *Political Parties in the American Mold*, p. 177.

17 *New York Times*, 29 July 1986 and 29 August 1986.
18 Ware, *Breakdown of Democratic Party Organization*, pp. 160–72.
19 Klaus von Beyme, *Political Parties in Western Democracies* (Gower, Aldershot, 1985), p. 206. In fact, von Beyme does not identify Norway as one of the countries that has state subsidies.
20 Ibid., p. 209.
21 Ibid., p. 203.
22 J. A. A. Stockwin, 'Japan: The Leader–Follower Relationship in Parties', in Ware, *Political Parties*, p. 107.
23 *Report of the Committee on Financial Aid to Political Parties* (Cmnd. 6601, 1976).
24 A more recent version of Simon's ideas are to be found in Herbert A. Simon, *Administrative Behavior*, 3rd edn (Free Press, New York, 1976).
25 William A. Niskanen, *Bureaucracy and Representative Government* (Aldine, Chicago, 1971). Criticism of the assumptions Niskanen made about the objectives of bureaucrats are made by Patrick Dunleavy, 'Bureaucrats, Budgets and the Growth of the State: Reconstructing an Instrumental Model', *British Journal of Political Science*, 15 (1985), pp. 299–328.
26 Anthony Downs, *An Economic Theory of Democracy* (Harper and Brothers, New York, 1957); William H. Riker, *The Theory of Political Coalitions* (Yale University Press, New Haven and London, 1962); Joseph A. Schlesinger, *Ambition and Politics* (Rand McNally, Chicago, 1966).
27 Joseph A. Schlesinger, 'The Primary Goals of Political Parties: A Clarification of Positive Theory', *American Political Science Review*, 69 (1975), pp. 840–9; for a critique of Schlesinger, see Ware, *The Logic of Party Democracy*, chap. 4.
28 William E. Wright, 'Comparative Party Models: Rational–Efficient and Party Democracy', in William E. Wright (ed.), *A Comparative Study of Party Organization* (Charles E. Merrill, Columbus, Ohio, 1971).
29 E. E. Schattschneider, *Party Government* (Holt, Rinehart and Winston, New York, 1942); see also his *The Struggle for Party Government* (University of Maryland Press, College Park, Md., 1948).
30 Anthony King, 'Political Parties in Western Democracies', *Polity*, 2 (1969), p. 118.
31 Leon D. Epstein, *Political Parties in Western Democracies* (Pall Mall, London, 1967).
32 Steven J. Brams, *Paradoxes in Politics* (Free Press, New York, 1976), chap. 4, and his *Game Theory in Politics* (Free Press, New York, 1975), chap. 4.
33 Von Beyme, *Political Parties in Western Democracies*, p. 261. For Barry, see Brian Barry, *Political Argument* (Routledge and Kegan Paul, London, 1965), chaps 14 and 15.

34   The concept of polarized pluralism which was developed fully in *Parties and Party Systems* was first outlined in Giovanni Sartori, 'European Political Parties: The Case of Polarized Pluralism', in J. LaPalombara and M. Weiner (eds), *Political Parties and Political Development* (Princeton University Press, Princeton, NJ, 1966).
35   Von Beyme, *Political Parties in Western Democracies*, pp. 261–3.

5   PARTICIPATION IN POLITICAL PARTIES

1   Geraint Parry, 'The Idea of Political Participation', in Parry (ed.), *Participation in Politics* (Manchester University Press, Manchester, 1972), p. 1.
2   Larry J. Sabato, *The Rise of Political Consultants* (Basic Books, New York, 1981).
3   However, as Gash points out, central electioneering funds did exist, even in the 1830s. Norman Gash, *Politics in the Age of Peel* (Longman, London, 1953), p. 435. But Hanham's point that in mid-Victorian Britain 'general elections were not general' still holds. H. J. Hanham, *Elections and Party Management* (Longman, London, 1959), p. 191.
4   Of course, the best-known example of this was in the fictitious Eatanswill constituency: ' "The night afore the last day o' the last election here, the opposite party bribed the barmaid at the Town Arms to hocus the brandy and water of fourteen unpolled electors as was a stoppin' in the house" ', Charles Dickens, *The Posthumous Papers of the Pickwick Club* (Penguin Books, Harmondsworth, 1972), p. 246. More important, though, was that political organization itself was in the hands of those paid for their services. Hanham points out that, even after 1885, most political organization in the constituencies was conducted by those who were paid to do it. Hanham, *Elections and Party Management*, p. 233.
5   Maurice Duverger, *Political Parties* 2nd English Edn (Methuen, London, 1959).
6   One consequence of this was that many of the newly enfranchised voters already had a clear and stable preference between parties. See Adam Przeworski, 'Institutionalisation of Voting Patterns, or Is Mobilization the Source of Decay?', *American Political Science Review*, 64 (1975), pp. 49–67.
7   The idea of a building society was 'transplanted' to the US in the 1830s, where later they became known as Savings and Loan Associations.
8   See Derek W. Urwin, 'Towards the Nationalization of British Politics? The Party System 1885–1940', in Otto Busch (ed.), *Wählerbewegung in der Europäischen Geschichte* (Colloquium Verlag, Berlin, 1980), p. 251, table 3.
9   Sometimes, however, the first Labour candidates in rural areas campaigned in ways which suggested that the prospects of success

were not thought to be high and that little pressure was being felt by other parties. In rural Scotland in the 1920s Labour often had to field candidates from their lowland strongholds rather than local people. In one of the Aberdeenshire seats at a general election in the early 1920s such a candidate was fielded. He made only one visit to the constituency, and had been told that he should speak in the square on market day at one of the towns. He duly addressed the assembled local farmers, only to be told by one of them at the end of his speech that the town he had been speaking in was not in the constituency he had hopes of representing at Westminster.

10 Duverger, *Political Parties*.

11 See Richard Hodder-Williams, 'South Africa: Democratic Elitism versus Elite-Based Parties?' in Alan Ware (ed.), *Political Parties: Electoral Change and Structural Response* (Basil Blackwell, Oxford, 1987).

12 Klaus von Beyme, *Political Parties in Western Democracies* (Gower, Aldershot, 1985), p. 163.

13 Bryon Criddle, 'France: Parties in a Presidential System', in Ware, *Political Parties*, p. 151.

14 In the case of Ireland, Carty has demonstrated that it is political structures, and especially the electoral laws, which have been the key to the survival of a patronage style of politics with individual legislators maintaining personal machines of about a hundred people. R. K. Carty, 'Brokerage and Partisanship: Politicians, Parties and Elections in Ireland', *Canadian Journal of Political Science*, 14 (1981), pp. 53–81.

15 Steffen Schmidt, 'Patrons, Brokers and Clients: Party Linkages in the Colombian System', in Kay Lawson (ed.), *Political Parties and Linkage* (Yale University Press, New Haven and London, 1980), p. 284.

16 J. Edward Greene, 'Jamaica: The Persistence of Party Democracy', in Ware (ed.), *Political Parties*.

17 It is important to distinguish between access to governmental power and access to government *per se*. There have been instances (such as the German party in inter-war Romania) where a party has nearly always joined a government coalition, but has not been crucial to the coalition's success and has thereby neither exercised much power nor enjoyed the spoils of office.

18 Kay Lawson, 'Political Parties and Linkage', in Lawson (ed.), *Political Parties and Linkage*, p. 17.

19 J. A. A. Stockwin, 'Japan: The Leader–Follower Relationship in Parties', in Ware (ed.), *Political Parties*. In this regard there are some similarities between modern Japanese electoral politics and that found in Britain in the 1830s and 1840s. For a discussion of Britain, see Gash, *Politics in the Age of Peel*, chap. 5.

20 Olof Ruin, 'Participatory Democracy and Corporativism: The Case of Sweden', *Scandinavian Political Studies*, 9 (1974), p. 174.

21 Martin Shefter, 'Regional Receptivity to Reform: The Legacy of the Progressive Era', *Political Science Quarterly*, 98 (1983), pp. 459–83.

22 Charles V. Hamilton, 'The Patron–Recipient Relationship and Minority Politics in New York', *Political Science Quarterly*, 94 (1979), pp. 211–27.

23 David Hine, 'Leaders and Followers: Democracy and Manageability in the Social Democratic Parties of Western Europe', in William E. Paterson and Alastair H. Thomas (eds), *The Future of Social Democracy* (Oxford University Press, Oxford, 1986).

24 For example, this seems to be the case in Norway.

25 Sabato, *The Rise of Political Consultants*, p. 31.

26 Duverger, *Political Parties*; Leon D. Epstein, *Political Parties in Western Democracies* (Pall Mall, London, 1967).

27 For the German experience see William E. Paterson 'West Germany: Between Party Apparatus and Basis Democracy', in Alan Ware (ed.), *Political Parties: Electoral Change and Structural Response* (Basil Blackwell, Oxford, 1987) p. 163. The theoretical development of the idea of 'spirals of silence' which underlies this is Elizabeth Noelle-Neumann, *The Spiral of Silence* (University of Chicago Press, Chicago, 1984).

28 Jeffrey Obler, 'Intraparty Democracy and the Selection of Parliamentary Candidates: The Belgian Case', *British Journal of Political Science*, 4 (1974), p. 164.

29 Michael Gallagher, 'Candidate Selection in Ireland: The Impact of Localism and the Electoral System', *British Journal of Political Science* 10 (1980), p. 501.

30 Alan Ware, *Logic of Party Democracy* (Macmillan, London, 1979), chap. 5.

31 See Ware, *The Breakdown of Democratic Party Organization*, chap. 4.

32 Austin Ranney, *Curing the Mischiefs of Faction* (University of California Press, Berkeley, 1975) pp. 150–69.

33 Dwaine Marvick, 'Political Linkage of Rival Party Activists in the United States: Los Angeles, 1969–1974', in Lawson, *Political Parties and Linkage*, p. 126.

34 Jeffrey L. Pressman and Dennis G. Sullivan, 'Convention Reform and Conventional Wisdom: An Empirical Assessment of Democratic Party Reforms', *Political Science Quarterly*, 89 (1974), pp. 539–62. For the earlier studies which established the conventional wisdom see James Q. Wilson, *The Amateur Democrat* (University of Chicago Press, Chicago, 1962) and Aaron B. Wildavsky, 'The Goldwater Phenomenon: Purists, Politicians and the Two-Party System', *Review of Politics*, 27 (1965), pp. 386–413.

35 Ronald B. Rapoport, Alan I. Abramowitz and John McGlennon (eds), *The Life of the Parties* (University of Kentucky Press, Lexington, 1986).

36   Von Beyme, *Political Parties in Western Democracies*, p. 183.
37   Thomas M. Guterbock, *Machine Politics in Transition* (University of Chicago Press, Chicago, 1980), pp. 173–4.
38   Byron Criddle, 'France: Parties in a Presidential System', in Ware (ed.) *Political Parties*, pp. 155–60.
39   Ware, *The Logic of Party Democracy*, p. 105.
40   Fred Hirsch, *Social Limits to Growth* (Routledge and Kegan Paul, London, 1977).
41   For the distinction between these types of rewards, see Peter B. Clark and James Q. Wilson, 'Incentive Systems: A Theory of Organization', *Administrative Science Quarterly*, 6 (1961), pp. 129–66.
42   Von Beyme, *Political Parties in Western Democracies*, p. 235.
43   Ibid., p. 235.

6   CONTROL OVER POLITICAL PARTIES

1   Robert Michels, *Political Parties* (Free Press, New York, 1962).
2   Klaus von Beyme, *Political Parties in Western Democracies* (Gower, Aldershot, 1985), p. 1.
3   On the development of Michels' work in later years, see David Beetham, 'From Socialism' to Fascism: The Relation between Theory and Practice in the Work of Robert Michels. II: The Fascist Ideologue', *Political Studies*, 25 (1977), pp. 161–81.
4   Gordon Hands, 'Roberto Michels and the Study of Political Parties', *British Journal of Political Science*, 1 (1971), p. 155.
5   Ibid., p. 171.
6   Paul Barnes, *Building Societies: The Myth of Mutuality* (Pluto Press, London, 1984). More generally on building societies, see Martin Boddy, *The Building Societies* (Macmillan, London, 1980).
7   Mancur Olson, *The Logic of Collective Action* (Harvard University Press, Cambridge, Mass., 1965).
8   Richard Rose, *The Problem of Party Government* (Penguin Press, Harmondsworth, 1976), p. 390.
9   Alan Ware, *The Breakdown of Democratic Party Organization 1940–1980* (Clarendon Press, Oxford, 1985) p. 101.
10   R. K. Carty, 'Brokerage and Partisanship'. Politicians, Parties and Elections in Ireland', *Canadian Journal of Political Science*, 14 (1981), p. 54.
11   Von Beyme, *Political Parties in Western Democracies*, p. 230.
12   For an analysis of the idea of symbolic rewards, see Robert E. Goodin, 'Symbolic Rewards: Being Bought Off Cheaply', *Political Studies*, 25 (1977), pp. 383–96.
13   On dealignment in the US, see Walter Dean Burnham, *The Current Crisis in American Politics* (W. W. Norton, New York, 1970). For a most interesting application of arguments about dealignment to Scandinavia, see Gøsta Esping-Andersen, *Politics Against Markets* (Princeton University Press, Princeton, NJ, 1985), chap. 4.

14 Von Beyme, *Political Parties in Western Democracies*, p. 297.
15 William E. Wright, 'Comparative Party Models: Rational–Efficient and Party Democracy', in Wright (ed.), *A Comparative Study of Party Organization* (Merrill, Columbus, Ohio, 1971) p. 20.
16 Indeed imprecision about what exactly 'winning' is vitiates much analysis that relies on this concept in defining parties. Schlesinger, for example, seeks to distinguish parties from both interest groups and commercial enterprises, and begins by saying that he refers only to 'parties which are able over time to win elections'. Joseph A. Schlesinger, 'On the Theory of Party Organization', *Journal of Politics*, 46 (1984), p. 374.
17 For the US, see Leo M. Snowiss, 'Congressional Recruitment and Representation', *American Political Science Review*, 60 (1966), pp. 627–39.
18 Kenneth Prewitt, 'Political Ambitions, Volunteerism, and Electoral Accountability', *American Political Science Review*, 64 (1970), pp. 5–17, and Kenneth Prewitt and William Nowlin, 'Political Ambitions and the Behavior of Incumbent Politicians', *Western Political Quarterly*, 22 (1969), pp. 298–308.
19 Michael Gallagher, 'Candidate Selection in Ireland: The Impact of Localism and the Electoral System', *British Journal of Political Science*, 10 (1980), pp. 500–1.
20 Ware, *The Logic of Party Democracy*, chaps 5 and 6.
21 Von Beyme, *Political Parties in Western Democracies*, p. 220; David Hine, 'Italy: Parties and Party Government under Pressure', in Ware (ed.) *Political Parties*.
22 Von Beyme, *Political Parties in Western Democracies*, p. 220.
23 David Hine, 'Leaders and Followers: Democracy and Manageability in the Social Democratic Parties of Western Europe', in W. E. Paterson and A. H. Thomas (eds), *The Future of Social Democracy*, (Oxford University Press, Oxford, 1986), p. 271, in which he cites the data of J. Chandler, D. S. Morris and M. J. Barker, 'The Ascent of Middle Class Politics: The Middle Class Membership of the Labour Party', paper presented to the Annual Conference of the Political Studies Association, 1982.
24 Hine, 'Leaders and Followers', p. 272.
25 The classic study propounding this view of a small working-class base in the SPD is S. Neumann, *Die deutschen Parteien: Wesen und Wandel nach dem Kriege* (Junker and Dummhaupt, Berlin, 1932); a more recent discussion of the view is found in Adam Przeworski, *Capitalism and Social Democracy* (Cambridge University Press, Cambridge, 1985).
26 Dennis Kavanagh, *Political Science and Political Behaviour* (George Allen and Unwin, London, 1983), p. 139.
27 William E. Paterson, 'The Chancellor and his Party: Political Leadership in the Federal Republic', in William E. Paterson and Gordon Smith (eds), *The West German Model: Perspectives on a Stable State* (Frank Cass, London, 1981), p. 12.

28 Kenneth F. Dyson, *Party, State and Bureaucracy* (Sage, Beverly Hills and London, 1977), pp. 30–1.

29 Hine, 'Leaders and Followers', p. 282.

30 Joseph J. Houska, *Influencing Mass Political Behavior* (Institute of International Studies, University of California, Berkeley, 1985), p. 31.

31 Kenneth F. Dyson, *Party, State and Bureaucracy in Western Germany* (Sage, Beverly Hills and London, 1977), p. 23.

32 See Greene, 'Jamaica: The Persistence of Party Democracy', in Ware (ed.) *Political Parties*.

33 Hine, 'Leaders and Followers', p. 285.

34 Joseph Rothschild, *East Central Europe Between the Two World Wars* (University of Washington Press, Seattle and London, 1974), p. 295.

35 Derek W. Urwin, 'Norway: Parties Between Mass Membership and Issue-Oriented Professionalism', in Ware (ed.), *Political Parties*, p. 194.

36 Don Murray and Věra Murray, 'The Parti Québécois: From Opposition to Power', in Hugh G. Thorburn (ed.), *Party Politics in Canada*, 4th edn (Prentice-Hall, Scarborough, Ont., 1979), pp. 248–9.

37 Murray and Murray, 'The Parti Québécois', p. 251.

38 Much of the material in this next section first appeared in an essay, 'Political Parties', in David Held and Christopher Pollitt (eds), *New Forms of Democracy* (Sage, Beverly Hills and London, 1986).

7 CONTROL EXERCISED BY POLITICAL PARTIES

1 For Wilson's ideas, see Austin Ranney, *The Doctrine of Responsible Party Government* (University of Illinois Press, Urbana, Ill., 1962), chap. 3.

2 Committee on Political Parties, 'Toward a More Responsible Two-Party System', *American Political Science Review*, 44 (1950), supplement.

3 Richard Rose, *The Problem of Party Government* (Penguin Books, Harmondsworth, 1976), pp. 372–4.

4 Ibid., pp. 438–9.

5 Kenneth F. Dyson, *Party, State and Bureaucracy in Western Germany* (Sage, Beverly Hills and London, 1977), pp. 1–2.

6 S. E. Finer, 'Patronage and the Public Service', *Public Administration*, 30 (1952), p. 336.

7 Ibid., p. 356.

8 Ibid., p. 355.

9 Roger G. Brown, 'Party and Bureaucracy: From Kennedy to Reagan', *Political Science Quarterly*, 97 (1982), pp. 279–80.

10 Hugh Heclo, 'Issue Networks and the Executive Establishment', in Anthony King (ed.), *The New American Political System* (American Enterprise Institute, Washington, DC, 1978), p. 106.

11 Gordon Smith, *Politics in Western Europe*, 4th edn (Heinemann, London, 1983), p. 65.
12 There is a considerable literature on 'iron triangles', and Heclo's notion of 'issue networks' was conceived as an alternative to this model; 'Issue Networks and the Executive Establishment'.
13 William E. Wright, 'Comparative Party Models: Rational–Efficient and Party Democracy', in Wright (ed.) *A Comparative Study of Party Organization* (Merrill, Columbus, Ohio, 1971), pp. 20–1.
14 Dyson, *Party, State and Bureaucracy*, p. 22.
15 Ibid., p. 29.
16 William E. Paterson, 'The Chancellor and his Party: Political Leadership in the Federal Republic', in W. E. Paterson and Gordon Smith (eds), *The West German Model: Perspectives on a Stable State* (Frank Cass, London, 1981), p. 12.
17 Anthony King, 'Modes of Executive–Legislative Relations: Great Britain, France, and West Germany', *Legislative Studies Quarterly*, 1 (1976), pp. 11–36.
18 Robert Leonardi, 'Political Power Linkages in Italy: The Nature of the Christian Democratic Party Organization', in Kay Lawson, *Political Parties and Linkage* (Yale University Press, New Haven and London, 1980), p. 264.
19 Joseph J. Houska, *Influencing Mass Political Behavior* (Institute of International Studies, University of California, Berkeley, 1985), p. 13.
20 Ibid., p. 16 provides data on this.
21 Adriano Pappalardo, 'The Conditions for Consociational Democracy: A Logical and Empirical Critique', *European Journal of Political Research*, 9 (1981), p. 370.
22 Ibid., p. 370.
23 David Hine, 'Leaders and Followers: Democracy and Manageability in the Social Democratic Parties of Western Europe', in William E. Paterson and Alastair H. Thomas (eds), *The Future of Social Democracy* (Oxford University Press, Oxford, 1986), p. 273, who cites S. B. Wolinetz, 'La leadership e il potere nel Partito Socialista olandese', *Città e Regione*, 9 (1983), pp. 135–8.
24 Richard Hodder-Williams. 'South Africa: Democratic Elitism versus Elite-Based Parties?' in Alan Ware (ed.), *Political Parties: Electoral Change and Structural Response* (Basil Blackwell, Oxford, 1987), p. 37.
25 David Hine, 'Italy: Parties and Party Government under Pressure', in Ware (ed.), *Political Parties*, p. 74.
26 Percy Allum and Renato Mannheimer, 'Italy', in Ivor Crewe and David Denver (eds), *Electoral Volatility in Western Europe* (Croom Helm, London, 1985).
27 William E. Paterson, 'West Germany: Between Party Apparatus and Basis Democracy', in Ware (ed.), *Political Parties*, p. 163.
28 Byron Criddle, 'France: Parties in a Presidential System', in Ware (ed.), *Political Parties*, p. 157.

29 Alan Ware, *The Breakdown of Democratic Party Organization, 1940–1980* (Clarendon Press, Oxford, 1985).
30 See, for example, James Warner Björkman, 'India: Party, Personality, Dynasty', in Ware (ed.), *Political Parties*.
31 Francis G. Castles and R. D. McKinlay, 'Public Welfare Provision, Scandinavia and the Sheer Futility of the Sociological Approach to Politics', *British Journal of Political Science*, 9 (1979), pp. 157–71. For a critique of this article, see Barbara Roweth, Frank Gould and Desmond S. King, 'The Growth of Public Welfare Provision: Does Politics Matter?', *British Journal of Political Science*, 10 (1980), pp. 525–30.
32 One of the influential early studies was R. Dawson and J. Robinson, 'Inter-Party Competition, Economic Variables and Welfare Policies in the United States', *Journal of Politics*, 25 (1963), pp. 265–89.
33 Robert C. Fried, 'Communism, Urbanism and the Two Italies', *Journal of Politics*, 33 (1971), p. 1038.
34 Ibid., p. 1045.
35 Anthony Downs, *An Economic Theory of Democracy* (Harper and Brothers, New York, 1957).
36 Alan Ware, *The Breakdown of Democratic Party Organization*, pp. 43–5.
37 Norman Schofield and Michael Laver, 'Bargaining Theory and Portfolio Payoffs in European Coalition Governments, 1945–83', *British Journal of Political Science*, 15 (1985), p. 162.
38 Norman Schofield and Michael Laver, 'Bargaining Theory and Portfolio Payoffs in European Coalition Governments, 1945–83', *British Journal of Political Science*, 15 (1985), p. 163.
39 E. E. Schattschneider, *The Semisovereign People*, reissued edn (Dryden Press, Hinsdale, Ill., 1975) p. 66.
40 Richard Rose, *Do Parties Make a Difference?*, 2nd edn (Macmillan, London, 1984).
41 See, for example, Edward T. Jennings, Jr, 'Competition, Constituencies and Welfare Policies', *American Political Science Review*, 73 (1979) pp. 414–29, and Douglas A. Hibbs, Jr, 'Political Parties and Macro-Economic Policy', *American Political Science Review*, 71 (1977), pp. 1467–87. On the difference parties make in Britain, see especially L. J. Sharpe and K. Newton, *Does Politics Matter? The Determinants of Public Policy* (Oxford University Press, New York, 1984).
42 Richard Rose, *Do Parties Make a Difference?* 2nd edn (Macmillan, London, 1984), p. xxx.
43 Richard Rose and Guy Peters, *Can Governments Go Bankrupt?* (Basic Books, New York, 1978), p. 55, cited in Dennis Kavanagh, *Political Science and Political Behaviour* (George Allen and Unwin, London, 1983), p. 163.
44 Hine, 'Italy', p. 75.
45 Von Beyme, *Political Parties in Western Democracies*, pp. 351–2

provides a convincing account of the difference whole systems of parties can make.

46 Ibid., p. 353.

8 THE FUTURE OF PARTIES AS AGENTS OF DEMOCRACY

1 Samuel J. Eldersveld, *Political Parties: A Behavioral Analysis* (Rand McNally, Chicago, 1964).

2 A. Lijphart, *The Politics of Accommodation* (University of California Press, Berkeley, 1968).

3 David McKay, *American Politics and Society* (Martin Robertson, Oxford, 1983), p. 23, table 2.9.

4 Percy Allum and Renato Mannheimer, 'Italy', in Ivor Crewe and David Denver (eds), *Electoral Volatility in Western Europe* (Croom Helm, London, 1985).

5 Ronald Inglehart, *The Silent Revolution* (Princeton University Press, Princeton, NJ, 1977), p. 313.

6 Ibid., p. 314.

7 William E. Paterson, 'West Germany: Between Party Apparatus and Basis Democracy', in Alan Ware (ed.), *Political Parties: Electoral Change and Structural Response* (Basil Blackwell, Oxford, 1987), p. 163.

8 Derek W. Urwin, 'Norway: Parties Between Mass Membership and Issue-Oriented Professionalism?', in Ware (ed.) *Political Parties*, p. 195.

9 Jim Bulpitt, 'English Local Politics: The Collapse of the *Ancien Regime?*', paper presented at the Annual Conference of the Political Studies Association, 1976.

10 Richard Hodder-Williams, 'South Africa: Democratic Elitism versus Elite-Based Parties?', in Ware (ed.), *Political Parties*, pp. 46–8.

11 Wyn Grant (ed.), *The Political Economy of Corporatism* (Macmillan, London, 1985), pp. 3–4.

12 Urwin, 'Norway', p. 187.

13 Olof Ruin, 'Participatory Democracy and Corporativism: The Case of Sweden', *Scandinavian Political Studies*, 9 (1974), p. 175.

14 Bernd Marin, 'Austria – The Paradigm Case of Liberal Corporatism?', in Wyn Grant (ed.), *The Political Economy of Corporatism* (Macmillan, London, 1985), p. 101.

15 Peter Katzenstein, 'Small Nations in an Open International Economy: The Converging Balance of State and Society in Switzerland and Austria', in Peter Evans, Dietrich Rueschemeyer and Theda Skocpol, *Bringing the State Back In* (Cambridge University Press, Cambridge, 1985), p. 237.

16 Jim Bulpitt, 'English Local Politics: The Collapse of the *Ancien Regime?*', paper presented at the Annual Conference of the Political Studies Association, 1976.

BIBLIOGRAPHY

BOOKS

Allardt, Erik and Rokkan, Stein (eds), *Mass Politics: Studies in Political Sociology* (Free Press, New York, 1970)

Arrow, Kenneth, *Social Choice and Individual Values* (John Wiley, New York, 1951)

Barker, Anthony (ed.), *Quangos in Britain* (Macmillan, London, 1982)

Barnes, Paul, *Building Societies: The Myth of Mutuality* (Pluto Press, London, 1984)

Barry, Brian, *Political Argument* (Routledge and Kegan Paul, London, 1965)

Beyme, Klaus von, *Political Parties in Western Democracies* (Gower, Aldershot, 1985)

Birch, A. H., *Representative and Responsible Government* (George Allen and Unwin, 1964)

Birch, A. H. *Representation* (Macmillan, London, 1972)

Boddy, Martin, *The Building Societies* (Macmillan, London, 1980)

Brams, Steven J., *Game Theory in Politics* (Free Press, New York, 1975)

Brams, Steven J., *Paradoxes in Politics* (Free Press, New York, 1975)

Bulpitt, Jim, *Territory and Power in the United Kingdom* (Manchester University Press, Manchester, 1983)

Burnham, Walter Dean, *Critical Elections and the Mainsprings of American Politics* (W. W. Norton, New York, 1970)

Burnham, Walter Dean, *The Current Crisis in American Politics* (Oxford University Press, New York, 1982)

Burnheim, John, *Is Democracy Possible?* (Polity Press, Cambridge, 1985)

Busch, Otto (ed.), *Wählerbewegung in der Europäischen Geschichte* (Colloquium Verlag, Berlin, 1980).

Campbell, Angus, *et al.*, *The American Voter* (John Wiley, New York, 1960)

262   BIBLIOGRAPHY

Campbell, Angus, *et al.*, *Elections and the Political Order* (John Wiley, New York, 1960)

Carter, April, *Democratic Reform in Yugoslavia* (Pinter, London, 1982)

Crenson, Matthew A., *The Un-politics of Air Pollution* (Johns Hopkins University Press, Baltimore and London, 1971)

Crewe, Ivor, and Denver, David (eds), *Electoral Volatility in Western Europe* (Croom Helm, London, 1985)

Crook, David Paul, *American Democracy in English Politics, 1815–1850* (Clarendon Press, Oxford, 1965)

Dahl, Robert A., *A Preface to Democratic Theory* (University of Chicago Press, Chicago, 1956)

Dahl, Robert A., *Who Governs?* (Yale University Press, New Haven and London, 1961)

Dahl, Robert A., *Modern Political Analysis* (Prentice-Hall, Englewood Cliffs, NJ, 1963)

Dahl, Robert A., (ed.), *Political Oppositions in Western Democracies* (Yale University Press, New Haven and London, 1966)

Dahl, Robert A., *Polyarchy: Participation and Opposition* (Yale University Press, New Haven and London, 1971)

Dahl, Robert A. and Lindblom, Charles E., *Politics, Economics and Welfare* (Harper and Brothers, New York, 1953)

Dickens, Charles, *The Posthumous Papers of the Pickwick Club* (Penguin Books, Harmondsworth, 1972)

Downs, Anthony, *An Economic Theory of Democracy* (Harper and Brothers, New York, 1957)

Duncan, Graeme (ed.), *Democratic Theory and Practice* (Cambridge University Press, Cambridge, 1983)

Duverger, Maurice, *Political Parties*, 2nd English edn (Methuen, London, 1959)

Dyson, Kenneth F., *Party, State and Bureaucracy in Western Germany* (Sage, Beverly Hills and London, 1977)

Easton, David, *The Political System* (Alfred E. Knopf, New York, 1953)

Edwards, H. R., *Competition and Monopoly in the British Soap Industry* (Clarendon Press, Oxford, 1962)

Eldersveld, Samuel J., *Political Parties: A Behavioral Analysis* (Rand McNally, Chicago, 1964)

Epstein, Leon D., *Political Parties in Western Democracies* (Pall Mall, London, 1967)

Epstein, Leon D., *Political Parties in the American Mold* (University of Wisconsin Press, Madison, 1986)

Esping-Andersen, Gøsta, *Politics Against Markets* (Princeton University Press, Princeton, NJ, 1985)

Evans, Peter B., Rueschmeyer, Dietrich and Skocpol, Theda (eds), *Bringing the State Back In* (Cambridge University Press, Cambridge, 1985)

Ferdinand, Peter, *Communist Regimes in Comparative Perspective: The Soviet, Chinese and Yugoslav Models* (Wheatsheaf, Brighton, forthcoming)

Gash, Norman, *Politics in the Age of Peel* (Longman, London, 1953)

Graber, Doris A., *Mass Media and American Politics* (Congressional Quarterly Press, Washington, DC, 1980)

Grant, Wyn (ed.), *The Political Economy of Corporatism* (Macmillan, London, 1985)

Guterbock, Thomas M., *Machine Politics in Transition* (University of Chicago Press, Chicago, 1980)

Hanham, H. J., *Elections and Party Management* (Longman, London, 1959)

Held, David, and Pollitt, Christopher, (eds), *New Forms of Democracy* (Sage, Beverly Hills and London, 1986)

Himmelweit, Hilde, et al., *How Voters Decide* (Academic Press, London, 1981)

Hirsch, Fred, *Social Limits to Growth* (Routledge and Kegan Paul, London, 1977)

Hirschman, Albert O., *Exit, Voice and Loyalty* (Harvard University Press, Cambridge, Mass., 1970)

Houska, Joseph J., *Influencing Mass Political Behavior* (Institute of International Studies, University of California, Berkeley, 1985)

Huntington, Samuel P. and Moore, Clement H., *Authoritarian Politics in Modern Societies* (Basic Books, New York, 1970)

Inglehart, Ronald, *The Silent Revolution* (Princeton University Press, Princeton, NJ, 1977)

Irish, Marion, and Prothro, James, *The Politics of American Democracy* 5th edition (Prentice-Hall, Englewood Cliffs, NJ, 1971)

Janda, Kenneth, *Political Parties: A Cross-National Survey* (Free Press, New York, 1980)

Kavanagh, Dennis, *Political Science and Political Behaviour* (George Allen and Unwin, London, 1983)

Key, V. O., *The Responsible Electorate* (Belknap Press, Cambridge, Mass., 1966).

King, Anthony, (ed.), *The New American Political System* (American Enterprise Institute, Washington, DC, 1978)

Klasno-socijalna struktura saveza komunista jugoslavije (Komunist, Belgrade, 1984)

LaPalombara, Joseph, and Weiner, Myron, (eds), *Political Parties and Political Development* (Princeton University Press, Princeton, NJ, 1966)

Laslett, Peter and Fishkin, James (eds), *Philosophy, Politics and Society* 5th Series (Basil Blackwell, Oxford, 1979)

Laslett, Peter, Runciman, W. G. and Skinner, Quentin (eds), *Philosophy, Politics and Society*, 4th series (Basil Blackwell, Oxford, 1972)

Lawson, Kay (ed), *Political Parties and Linkage* (Yale University Press, New Haven and London, 1980)

Leary, Mary Ellen, *Phantom Politics* (Public Affairs Press, Washington, DC, 1977)

Lijphart, A., *The Politics of Accommodation* (University of California Press, Berkeley, 1968)

Lipset, Seymour Martin, and Rokkan, Stein (eds), *Party Systems and Voter Alignments: Cross-national Perspectives* (Collier–Macmillan, New York, 1967)

Lively, Jack, *Democracy* (Basil Blackwell, Oxford, 1975)

Lively, Jack and Rees, John (eds), *Utilitarian Logic and Politics* (Clarendon Press, Oxford, 1978)

McKay, David, *American Politics and Society* (Martin Robertson, Oxford, 1983)

Macpherson, C. B., *The Real World of Democracy* (Clarendon Press, Oxford, 1966)

Macpherson, C. B., *Democratic Theory: Essays in Retrieval* (Clarendon Press, Oxford, 1973)

Maisel, Louis, and Cooper, Joseph (eds), *The Development of Political Parties* (Sage, Beverly Hills and London, 1979)

Michels, Robert, *Political Parties* (Free Press, New York, 1962)

Morača, P., et al., *Istorija saveza komunista jugoslavije* (Rad, Belgrade, 1976)

Mueller, Dennis C., *Public Choice* (Cambridge University Press, Cambridge, 1979)

Nathan, Andrew J., *Chinese Democracy* (Alfred E. Knopf, New York, 1985)

Neumann, S., *Die deutschen Parteien: Wesen und Wandel nach dem Kriege* (Junker und Dummhaupt, Berlin, 1932)

Nie, Norman H., Verba, Sidney and Petrocik, John R., *The Changing American Voter* (Harvard University Press, Cambridge, Mass., 1976)

Niskanen, William H., *Bureaucracy and Representative Government* (Aldine, Chicago, 1971)

Noelle-Neumann, Elizabeth, *The Spiral of Silence* (University of Chicago Press, Chicago, 1984)

Olson, Mancur, *The Logic of Collective Action* (Harvard University Press, Cambridge, Mass., 1965)

Ostrogorski, M., *Democracy and the Organization of Political Parties* (Quadrangle Books, Chicago, 1964)

Page, Benjamin I., *Choices and Echoes in Presidential Elections* (University of Chicago Press, Chicago, 1978)

Parry, Geraint (ed.), *Participation in Politics* (Manchester University Press, Manchester, 1972)

Parsons, Talcott, *The Social System* (Free Press, Glencoe, Ill., 1951)

Pateman, Carole, *Participation and Democratic Theory* (Cambridge University Press, Cambridge, 1970)

Paterson, William E., and Smith, Gordon (eds), *The West German Model: Perspectives on a Stable State* (Frank Cass, London, 1981)

Paterson, William E., and Thomas, Alastair H. (eds), *The Future of Social Democracy* (Oxford University Press, Oxford, 1986)

Przeworski, Adam, *Capitalism and Social Democracy* (Cambridge University Press, Cambridge, 1985)

Pugh, Martin, *The Tories and the People 1880–1935* (Basil Blackwell, Oxford, 1985)

Ranney, Austin, *The Doctrine of Responsible Party Government* (University of Illinois Press, Urbana, Ill., 1962)

Ranney, Austin, *Curing the Mischiefs of Faction* (University of California Press, Berkeley, 1975)

Rapoport, Ronald B., Abramowitz, Alan I. and McGlennon, John (eds), *The Life of the Parties* (University of Kentucky Press, Lexington, 1986)

Rawls, John, *A Theory of Justice* (Oxford University Press, Oxford, 1972)

Report of the Committee on Financial Aid to Political Parties (Cmnd. 6601, 1976)

Riker, William H., *The Theory of Political Coalitions* (Yale University Press, New Haven and London, 1962)

Riker, William H., *Liberalism Against Populism* (W. H. Freeman, San Francisco, 1982)

Rose, Richard, *The Problem of Party Government* (Penguin Books, Harmondsworth, 1976)

Rose, Richard, *Do Parties Make a Difference?* 2nd edn (Macmillan, London, 1984)

Rose, Richard, and Peters, Guy, *Can Governments Go Bankrupt?* (Basic Books, New York, 1978)

Rothschild, Joseph, *East Central Europe between the Two World Wars* (University of Washington Press, Seattle and London, 1974)

Rusinow, D., *The Yugoslav Experiment* (Hurst, London, 1977)

Sabato, Larry J., *The Rise of Political Consultants* (Basic Books, New York, 1981)

Salamon, Lester, *The Federal Budget and the Non-Profit Sector* (Urban Institute, Washington, DC, 1982)

Sartori, Giovanni, *Democratic Theory* (Wayne State Universtiy Press, Detroit, 1962)

Sartori, Giovanni, *Parties and Party Systems* (Cambridge University Press, Cambridge, 1976)

Schattschneider, E. E., *Party Government* (Holt, Rinehart and Winston, New York, 1942)

Schattschneider, E. E., *The Struggle for Party Government* (University of Maryland Press, College Park, Md., 1948)

Schattschneider, E. E., *The Semisovereign People* Reissued edition (Dryden Press, Hinsdale, Ill., 1975).

Schlesinger, Joseph A., *Ambition in Politics* (Rand McNally, Chicago, 1966)

Schumpeter, Joseph, *Capitalism, Socialism and Democracy* (George Allen and Unwin, London, 1943)

Sharpe, L. J. and Newton, K., *Does Politics Matter? The Determinants of Public Policy* (Oxford University Press, New York, 1984)

Simon, Hebert A., *Administrative Behavior* (Free Press, New York, 1976)

Singer, Peter, *Democracy and Disobedience* (Clarendon Press, Oxford, 1973)

Smith, Gordon, *Politics in Western Europe* 4th edn (Heinemann, London, 1983)

Thompson, Dennis F., *The Democratic Citizen* (Cambridge University Press, Cambridge, 1970)

Thorburn, Hugh G., (ed.), *Party Politics in Canada* 4th edition (Prentice-Hall, Scarborough, Ont., 1979)

Truman, David B., *The Governmental Process* (Alfred E. Knopf, New York,, 1951)

Ware, Alan, *The Logic of Party Democracy* (Macmillan, London, 1979)

Ware, Alan, *The Breakdown of Democratic Party Organization, 1940–1980* (Clarendon Press, Oxford, 1985)

Ware, Alan, (ed.), *Political Parties: Electoral Change and Structural Response* (Basil Blackwell, Oxford, 1987)

Wilson, James Q., *The Amateur Democrat* (University of Chicago Press, Chicago, 1962)

Wright, William E., (ed.), *A Comparative Study of Party Organization* (Merrill, Columbus, Ohio, 1971)

ARTICLES AND ESSAYS

Adrian, Charles R., 'A Typology of Nonpartisan Elections', *Western Political Quarterly*, 12 (1959), pp. 449–58

Allum, Percy, and Mannheimer, Renato, 'Italy', in I. Crewe and D. Denver (eds), *Electoral Volatility in Western Europe*

American Political Science Association, Committee on Political Parties of, 'Toward a More Responsible Two-Party System', *American Political Science Review*, 44 (1950), supplement

Bachrach, Peter, and Baratz, Morton S., 'Two Faces of Power', *American Science Review*, 56 (1962), pp. 947–52

Barry, Brian, 'Is Democracy Special?', in P. Laslett and J. Fishkin, *Philosophy, Politics and Society*

Beetham, David, 'From Socialism to Fascism: The Relation between Theory and Practice in the Work of Robert Michels. II: The Fascist Ideologue', *Political Studies*, 25 (1977), pp. 161–81

Björkman, James Warner, 'India: Party, Personality and Dynasty, in Alan Ware (ed.), *Political Parties*

Brittan, Samuel, 'The Economic Contradictions of Democracy', *British Journal of Political Science*, 5 (1975), pp. 129–59

Brown, Roger G., 'Party and Bureaucracy: From Kennedy to Reagan', *Political Science Quarterly*, 97 (1982), pp. 279–94

Bulpitt, Jim, 'English Local Politics: The Collapse of the *Ancien Regime?*', paper presented at the Annual Conference of the Political Studies Association, 1976.

Bulpitt, Jim, 'The Discipline of the New Democracy: Mrs Thatcher's Domestic Statecraft', *Political Studies*, 34 (1986), pp. 19–39

Carty, R. K., 'Brokerage and Partisanship: Politicians, Parties and Elections in Ireland', *Canadian Journal of Political Science*, 14 (1981), pp. 53–81

Castles, Francis G. and McKinlay, R. D., 'Public Welfare Provision, Scandinavia and the Futility of the Sociological Approach to Politics', *British Journal of Political Science*, 9 (1979), pp. 157–71

Chandler, J., Morris, D. S., and Barker, M. J., 'The Ascent of Middle-Class Politics: The Middle Class Membership of the Labour Party', paper presented at the Annual Conference of the Political Studies Association, 1982

Clark, Peter B. and Wilson, James Q., 'Incentive Systems: a Theory of Organization, *Administration Science Quarterly*, 6 (1961), pp. 129–66

Cox, Gary, W., 'The Development of a Party-Orientated Electorate in England, 1832–1918', *British Journal of Political Science*, 16 (1986), pp. 187–216

Criddle, Byron, 'France: Parties in a Presidential System', in Alan Ware (ed.), *Political Parties*

Dahl, Robert A., 'The Behavioral Approach in Political Science: Epitaph for a Monument to a Successful Protest', *American Political Science Review*, 55 (1961), pp. 563–72

Dawson, R. and Robinson, J., 'Inter-party Competition, Economic Variables and Welfare Policies in the United States', *Journal of Politics*, 25 (1963), pp. 265–89

Dunleavy, Patrick, 'Bureaucrats, Budgets and the Growth of the State: Reconstructing an Instrumental Model', *British Journal of Political Science*, 15 (1985), pp. 299–328

Finer, S. E., 'Patronage and the Public Service', *Public Administration*, 30 (1952), pp. 329–60

Fried, Robert C., 'Communism, Urbanism and the two Italies', *Journal of Politics*, 33 (1971), pp. 1008–51

Gallagher, Michael, 'Candidate Selection in Ireland: The Impact of Localism and the Electoral System', *British Journal of Political Science*, 10 (1980), pp. 489–503

Goodin, Robert E., 'Symbolic Rewards: Being Bought Off Cheaply', *Political Studies*, 25 (1977), pp. 383–96

Greene, J. Edward, 'Jamaica: The Persistence of Party Democracy', in Alan Ware (ed.), *Political Parties*

Hagensick, A. Clarke, 'Influence of Partisanship and Incumbency on a Nonpartisan Election System', *Western Political Quarterly*, 17 (1964), pp. 117–24

Hamilton, Charles V., 'The Patron–Recipient Relationship and Minority Politics in New York', *Political Science Quarterly*, 94 (1979), pp. 211–27

Hands, Gordon, 'Roberto Michels and the Study of Political Parties', *British Journal of Political Science*, 1 (1971), pp. 155–72

Heclo, Hugh, 'Issue Networks and the Executive Establishment', in Anthony King (ed.), *The New American Political System*

Hibbs, Douglas A., Jr, 'Political Parties and Macro-Economic Policy', *American Political Science Review*, 71 (1977), pp. 1467–87

Hine, David, 'Leaders and Followers: Democracy and Manageability in the Social Democratic Parties of Western Europe', in William E. Paterson and Alastair H. Thomas, *The Future of Social Democracy*

Hine, David, 'Italy: Parties and Party Government under Pressure', in Alan Ware (ed.), *Political Parties*

Hodder-Williams, Richard, 'South Africa: Democratic Elitism versus Elite-Based Parties?', in Alan Ware (ed.), *Political Parties*

James, Estelle, 'How Non-profits Grow: A Model', *Journal of Policy Analysis and Management*, 2 (1983), pp. 350–65

Jennings, Edward T., Jr, 'Competition, Constituencies and Welfare Policies', *American Political Science Review*, 73 (1979), pp. 414–29

Katzenstein, Peter, 'Small Nations in an Open Industrial Economy: The Converging Balance of State and Society in Switzerland and Austria', in P. Evans, D. Rueschemeyer and T. Skocpol, *Bringing the State Back In*

King, Anthony, 'Political Parties in Western Democracies', *Polity*, 2 (1969), pp. 111–41

King, Anthony, 'Modes of Executive–Legislative Relations: Great Britain, France, and West Germany', *Legislative Studies Quarterly*, 1 (1976), pp. 11–36

Lawson, Kay, 'Political Parties and Linkage', in K. Lawson (ed.), *Political Parties and Linkage*

Leonardi, Robert, 'Political Power Linkages in Italy: The Nature of the Christian Democratic Party Organization', in K. Lawson (ed.), *Political Parties and Linkage*

MacIntyre, Alasdair, 'Is a Science of Comparative Politics Possible?', in P. Laslett, W. G. Runciman and Q. Skinner (eds), *Philosophy, Politics and Society*

McLean, Iain, 'A Non-zero-sum Game of Football', *British Journal of Political Science*, 10 (1980), pp. 253–9

McLean, Iain, 'Some Recent Work in Public Choice', *British Journal of Political Science*, 16 (1986), pp. 377–94

Marin, Bernd, 'Austria – The Paradigm Case of Liberal Corporatism?', in W. Grant (ed.), *The Political Economy of Corporatism*

Marvick, Dwaine, 'Political Linkage of Rival Party Activists in the United States: Los Angeles, 1969–1974', in K. Lawson (ed.), *Political Parties and Linkage*

Mezey, Michael L., 'Ambition Theory and the Office of Congressman', *Journal of Politics*, 32 (1970), pp. 563–79

Mill, James, 'Essay on Government', in J. Lively and J. Rees, *Utilitarian Logic and Politics*

Murray, Don and Murray, Věra, 'The Parti Québécois: From Opposition to Power', in H. G. Thorburn, *Party Politics in Canada*

Nursey-Bray, Paul, 'Consensus and Community: The Theory of African One-party Democracy', in G. Duncan (ed.), *Democratic Theory and Practice*

Obler, Jeffrey, 'Intra-party Democracy and the Selection of Parliamentary Candidates: The Belgian Case', *British Journal of Political Science*, 4 (1974), pp. 163–85

Obler, Jeffrey, 'Private Giving in the Welfare State', *British Journal of Political Science*, 11 (1981), pp. 17–48

Pappalardo, Adriano, 'The Conditions for Consociational Democracy: A Logical and Empirical Analysis', *European Journal of Political Research*, 9 (1981), pp. 365–90.

Parry, Geraint, 'The Idea of Political Participation', in G. Parry (ed.), *Participation in Politics*

Paterson, William E., 'The Chancellor and his Party: Political Leadership in the Federal Republic', in W. E. Paterson and G. Smith (eds), *The West German Model*

Paterson, William E., 'West Germany: Between Party Apparatus and Basis Democracy', in Alan Ware (ed.), *Political Parties*

Pressman, Jeffrey L., 'Preconditions of Mayoral Leadership', *American Political Science Review*, 66 (1972), pp. 511–24

Pressman, Jeffrey L. and Sullivan, Dennis G., 'Convention Reform and Conventional Wisdom: An Empirical Assessment of Democratic Party Reforms', *Political Science Quarterly*, 89 (1974), pp. 539–62

Prewitt, Kenneth and Nowlin, William, 'Political Ambitions and the Behavior of Incumbent Politicians', *Western Political Quarterly*, 22 (1969), pp. 298–308

Prewitt, Kenneth, 'Political Ambitions, Volunteerism and Electoral Accountability', *American Political Science Review*, 64 (1970), pp. 5–17

Przeworski, Adam, 'Institutionalisation of Voting Patterns, or is Mobilization the Source of Decay?', *American Political Science Review*, 64 (1975), pp. 49–67

Rogers, Chester B. and Arman, Harold D., 'Nonpartisanship and Election to City Office', *Social Science Quarterly*, 51 (1971), pp. 941–5

Rose, Richard and Mossawir, Harve, 'Voting and Elections: A Functional Analysis', *Political Studies*, 15 (1967), pp. 173–201

Roweth, Barbara, Gould, Frank, and King, Desmond S., 'The Growth of Public Welfare Provision: Does Politics Matter?', *British Journal of Political Science*, 10 (1980), pp. 525–30

Ruin, Olof, 'Participatory Democracy and Corporativism: The Case of Sweden', *Scandinavian Political Studies*, 9 (1974), pp. 171–84

Salamon, Lester, 'Rethinking Public Management: Third Party Government and the Changing Forms of Public Action, *Public Policy*, 29 (1981), pp. 255–75

Sartori, Giovanni, 'European Political Parties: The Case of Polarized Pluralism', in J. LaPalombara and M. Weiner (eds), *Political Parties and Political Development*

Schlesinger, Joseph A., 'The Primary Goals of Political Parties: A Clarification of Positive Theory', *American Political Science Review*, 69 (1975), pp. 840–9

Schlesinger, Joseph A., 'On the Theory of Party Organization', *Journal of Politics*, 46 (1984), pp. 369–400

Schmidt, Steffen, 'Patrons, Brokers, and Clients: Party Linkages in the Colombian System', in K. Lawson (ed.), *Political Parties and Linkage*

Schofield, Norman and Laver, Michael, 'Bargaining Theory and Portfolio Payoffs in European Coalition Governments, 1945–83', *British Journal of Political Science*, 15 (1985), pp. 143–64

Shefter, Martin, 'Party and Patronage: Germany, England and Italy', *Politics and Society*, 7 (1977), pp. 403–51

Shefter, Martin, 'Party, Bureaucracy and Political Change in the United States', in L. Maisel and J. Cooper (eds), *The Development of Political Parties*

Shefter, Martin, 'Regional Receptivity to Reform: The Legacy of the Progressive Era', *Political Science Quarterly*, 98 (1983), pp. 459–83

Skocpol, Theda, 'Bringing the State Back In: Strategies of Analysis in Current Research', in P. Evans, D. Rueschemeyer and T. Skocpol (eds.), *Bringing the State Back In*

Snowiss, Leo M., 'Congressional Recruitment and Representation', *American Political Science Review*, 60 (1966), pp. 627–39

Sternquist, Nils, 'Sweden: Stability or Deadlock?', in R. A. Dahl (ed.), *Political Oppositions in Western Democracies*

Stockwin, J. A. A., 'Japan: The Leader–Follower Relationship in Parties', in Alan Ware (ed.), *Political Parties*

Urwin, Derek W., 'Towards the Nationalization of British Politics? The Party System 1885–1940', in O. Busch (ed.), *Wählerbewegung in der Europäischen Geschichte*

Urwin, Derek W., 'Norway: Parties Between Mass Membership and Issue-Oriented Professionalism?', in Alan Ware (ed.) *Political Parties*

Ware, Alan, 'Political Parties', in D. Held and C. Pollitt (eds), *New Forms of Democracy*

Weale, Albert, 'Social Choice Versus Populism? An Interpretation of Riker's Political Theory', *British Journal of Political Science*, 14 (1984), pp. 369–85

Welsh, Susan and Carlson, Eric H., 'The Impact of Party on Voting in a Nonpartisan Legislature', *American Political Science Review*, 68 (1973), pp. 854–67

Wiatr, Jerzy, 'The Hegemonic Party System in Poland', in E. Allardt and S. Rokkan (eds), *Mass Politics*

Wildavsky, Aaron B., 'The Goldwater Phenomenon: Purists, Politicians and the Two-Party System', *Review of Politics*, 27 (1965), pp. 386–413

Wolinetz, S. B., 'La leadership e il potere nel Partito Socialista olandese', *Città e Regione*, 9 (1983), pp. 135–8

Wright, William E., 'Comparative Party Models: Rational-Efficient and Party Democracy', in W. E. Wright (ed.), *A Comparative Study of Party Organization*

Zaninovich, M. G., 'Yugoslav Party Evolution: Moving Beyond Institutionalization', in S. P. Huntington and C. H. Moore, *Authoritarian Politics in Modern Societies*

INDEX